A Lesbian History of Britain

A Lesbian History of Britain

Love and Sex between Women since 1500

Rebecca Jennings

Greenwood World Publishing
Oxford / Westport, Connecticut
2007

First published in 2007 by Greenwood World Publishing

1 2 3 4 5 6 7 8 9 10

Greenwood World Publishing
Wilkinson House
Jordan Hill
Oxford OX2 8EJ
An imprint of Greenwood Publishing Group, Inc
www.greenwood.com

British Library Cataloguing-in-Publication Data: a catalogue record for this book is available from the British Library

Library of Congress Cataloging-in-Publication Data

Jennings, Rebecca.
  A lesbian history of Britain / Rebecca Jennings.
      p. cm.
  Includes bibliographical references and index.
  ISBN-13: 978-1-84645-007-5 (alk. paper)
    1. Lesbianism – Great Britain – History. I. Title.
  HQ75.6.G7J46 2007
  306.76'63094 – dc22

                                                              2007023727

Designed by Fraser Muggeridge studio
Picture researched by Zooid
Typeset by TexTech
Printed and bound by South China Printing Company

For Vicky

Contents

Acknowledgements

I would like to thank my editor, Simon Mason, both for commissioning this book in the first place and for his boundless enthusiasm, patience and advice throughout.

I am very grateful to Laura Doan and Alison Oram, for their encouragement and advice and for the major contribution they have made, through their own work, to our understanding of British lesbian history. This book would not have been possible without the effort and dedication of a growing number of lesbian historians, whose work has enriched our knowledge of the past.

I would also like to thank Penny Summerfield and the School of Arts, Histories and Cultures at the University of Manchester; Harry Cocks; and Angela Woollacott and my new colleagues at Macquarie University, Sydney, for their support.

Introduction

In 1742, Sarah Churchill, Dowager Duchess of Marlborough, published a detailed and intimate account of her close friendship with the late Queen Anne (1702–1714). The two women had been childhood friends, playing together as young ladies-in-waiting and referring to each other as equals by the aliases 'Mrs Morley' and 'Mrs Freeman'. In 1692, Anne resisted the orders of her sister, Queen Mary, to drop Sarah for political reasons, and their friendship was further strengthened. Anne assured Sarah of her 'most sincere and tender passion', and Sarah enjoyed considerable political influence when Anne became queen in 1702.[1] However, their relationship was gradually undermined by political differences, and Anne, growing increasingly resentful at Sarah's attempts to influence policy, began a new friendship with Sarah's lower-ranking relative, Abigail Hill Masham. When she discovered that Abigail was spending two hours each day in private with the queen, Sarah reacted with anger. Her secretary, Arthur Maynwaring, is likely to have been the author of a number of ballads and pamphlets that circulated the court in 1708, speculating on the 'sweet Service' provided to Anne by Abigail, which allegedly included 'some dark Deeds at Night'.[2] Sarah showed the ballad to the queen personally and later wrote to Anne, accusing her of 'having discover'd so great a passion for such a woman'.[3] Both Sarah's role in circulating these accusations of same-sex eroticism and her certainty that her own relationship with Anne would not be interpreted by others in the same way tell us much about the complex ways in which love and desire between women were viewed and discussed in this period. However, while Anne's friendships with Sarah and Abigail have been widely commented on by historians in the context of political struggles between the Whig and Tory parties in this period, the precise nature of the personal relationship between these women has received considerably less attention.

Lesbian history has frequently been associated with silence, invisibility and denial. In a pioneering essay on lesbian history published in 1979, US historian Blanche Wiesen Cook referred to the 'historical denial of lesbianism' and the lack of historical evidence relating to desire between women.[4] In the 1980s, research into lesbian history was published in books with titles such as *Hidden from History* and *Not a Passing Phase*.[5] In the early 1990s, the activist group, the Lesbian Avengers, staged a demonstration in front of the statue of Queen Victoria outside Buckingham Palace, in protest at that monarch's supposed role in denying the existence of lesbianism (although the legend is almost certainly apocryphal). These historians and activists highlighted the ways in which the experience of women – to an even greater extent, women who desired women – has been undervalued and unrecorded in British culture. This has meant that historians seeking evidence of women's lives and desires in the past often have few sources on which to draw. While historians working on the late nineteenth and twentieth centuries have benefited from increased cultural debate about sexuality in this period and have been able to supplement written sources with oral history interviews, the task of identifying evidence of same-sex desire prior to the modern period is more difficult. Changing attitudes to women's social role, offering women in the modern period expanding opportunities for economic and social independence, have also had an impact on evidence of lesbian experience and communities. Despite these difficulties, a growing number of studies of lesbian history have appeared in recent decades, uncovering evidence of desire and affection between women from sources ranging from sixteenth-century poetry and travel accounts to nineteenth-century diaries and twentieth-century lesbian wedding photographs.

Much of this research has been motivated by a belief that an under-standing of the past can help shape our sense of what it means to be a lesbian in the present. Introducing a volume of lesbian history in 1989, the Lesbian History Group claimed:

> A knowledge of lesbian history is essential to everyone because we will never have more than a sketchy and distorted view of the past until history tells the experience of *all people*, including lesbians ... For lesbians themselves, the need for lesbian history is self-evident. Every social group needs access to its own history. Knowledge of our past gives us cultural roots and a heritage with models and experiences to learn from and emulate, or to choose not to follow.[6]

This sense of history as offering lesbians a collective heritage meant that lesbian histories began to appear alongside the emerging lesbian communities of the 1960s. When the first British lesbian magazine, *Arena Three*, began publication in 1964, it included a regular series of historical essays by Lorna Gulston, in addition to occasional contributions by other readers. These articles explored the history of lesbian murderesses from the eighteenth century and the 1940s; passing women, from the only female Egyptian pharaoh, Hatshepsut, to the early-twentieth-century Colonel Barker; and famous lesbians such as Queen Christina of Sweden. In the 1970s and 1980s, lesbians involved in the political movements of feminism and gay liberation also regarded an understanding of lesbian history as important in developing a sense of lesbian community. Like women's historians, they made a political commitment to uncovering a hidden history of gay experience, which had not been addressed by mainstream historians. The Lesbian History Group was formed in 1984 and a Lesbian Archives Collective was founded in London the same year, relocating to its present home in Glasgow in 1995. In February 2005, Schools OUT, originally founded in the 1970s to promote lesbian and gay equality in education, initiated a Lesbian, Gay, Bisexual and Trans History Month. Throughout this period, lesbian historians have been working both within universities and as independent researchers, studying desire between women in the past. The role of political ideas and movements in motivating much of this recent interest in lesbian history has meant that approaches to lesbian history have been heavily influenced by developments in sexual politics, particularly lesbian and gay politics.

Approaches to Lesbian History

The history of homosexuality has, for much of the twentieth century, been dominated by two contrasting viewpoints: the essentialist and the constructionist approaches. The essentialist approach has been based on an assumption that lesbians have existed in every historical period and location in a form recognisable to us today and that this history simply needs to be uncovered and reclaimed. Constructionist approaches, however, argue that sexual practices and identities – the ways in which sexual desire is expressed and given meaning – are defined by wider culture and therefore vary in different periods and locations. The dominance of either approach has shifted in relation to the specific political and social needs of the time and also, to some extent, in response to wider trends within the discipline of history. From the late 1950s to the 1970s, an emerging lesbian and gay historiography was written largely by 'out' lesbians and gay men with a particular political aim. The

ideology of the 'homophile' movement in the United States and Britain
in the 1950s and 1960s characterised gay history of this period. Liberal
reformers in an era before the partial legalisation of male homosexual
acts (1967 in the United Kingdom), the members of the Homosexual
Law Reform Society and Campaign for Homosexual Equality based
their campaigns for legal reform on the argument that there was little
difference between homosexual and heterosexual people. Historiography
reflected this argument, employing an essentialist, transhistorical notion
of the gay subject and focusing on biographies of famous homosexuals
in an attempt to demonstrate the valuable contributions made
by homosexuals to society. Developments in gay politics in the late 1960s
and early 1970s, centring on the Stonewall Riots of 1969 in the United
States, and the subsequent formation of the Gay Liberation Front (GLF)
resulted in a change in emphasis towards a more affirmative model of gay
politics. The GLF conceived of gay people as an oppressed minority, and
histories written in this era explored the oppressive power relationship
between homosexuals and heterosexuals. The political focus on the
importance of community-building was also reflected in historical
research, with studies being undertaken into early lesbian and gay
subcultures and communities. As was the case with the biographical
model, which preceded it, this affirmative gay history was based upon
an essentialist notion of the gay subject.

This approach has come under considerable attack in the latter half
of the century but essentialists are still fighting back, as the 1997 publication of Rictor Norton's book, *The Myth of the Modern Homosexual*,
demonstrates.[7] From the late 1970s onward, however, constructionist
historians have challenged the notion of a transhistorical homosexual,
arguing instead that sexual identity is a cultural construct and that the
modern idea of the homosexual cannot be taken as the blueprint for
homosexuality in the past. This approach grew out of a number
of different strands of thought, from the disciplines of psychology,
sociology and feminist theory. Within the field of sociology, a number
of theorists, including the extremely influential French philosopher,
Michel Foucault, argued that the modern notion of sexuality
is a construct which has only been around for the last hundred
or so years.[8] His approach encouraged historians to deconstruct the
concept of sexuality, examining in particular the processes by which ideas
about the normal and the deviant have been defined.[9] The debate
between essentialist and constructionist approaches dominated lesbian

and gay history throughout the 1970s and 1980s and remains unresolved. The constructionist approach has proved more attractive to academic historians, but the essentialist approach continues to appeal to popular historians and to gay activists whose primary aim is to establish the authenticity of homosexual identities and experiences.

How Important Is Sex?

In the context of these broader debates, lesbian historians have also been preoccupied with a number of specific issues, including the question of how to define 'lesbianism'. The debate has centred upon the significance of sexual activity in defining a lesbian relationship in the past.[10] Many lesbian historians have based their work on a definition of lesbians suggested by Blanche Wiesen Cook:

> Women who love women, who choose women to nurture and support and to create a living environment in which to work creatively and independently are lesbians.[11]

Cook's definition emphasised the importance of emotional support and affection between women but downplayed the issue of desire and sexual practice in lesbian relationships. This approach was most popular with lesbian feminist historians in the 1980s and 1990s and was developed in response to the difficulty of conclusively establishing a sexual component to relationships before the twentieth century. Drawing on Adrienne Rich's concept of a 'lesbian continuum' on which all relationships between women have a place, these historians sought out historical evidence of close friendships between women, regardless of the sexual component, and made an important contribution in establishing the frequency and 'normalcy' of romantic friendships in the past.[12] However, this approach has increasingly been criticised for failing to take into account the issue of same-sex desire in lesbian relationships and for underestimating the social disapproval and marginal status experienced by women who desired other women. Proposing a narrower definition of lesbianism, historians taking this approach have concentrated their research on the post-1910 period when they feel lesbianism unquestionably meant genital contact, such as the self-identified lesbian subcultures which emerged in Paris and Berlin in the interwar years, and the bar cultures of the 1950s. Studies such as Madeline Davis and Elizabeth Kennedy's research into the US lesbian bar community in 1950s and 1960s Buffalo, have focused on the ways in which lesbians created their own space and culture by refusing to compromise with a hostile environment.[13]

A further dimension has been added to this debate by the most recent approach to the history of sexuality: queer history. Queer theory emerged in the early 1990s out of the twin strands of a political movement and academic theory. The first meeting of Queer Nation, the group which initiated queer politics, was held in New York in April, 1990, and a number of queer groups, including AIDS Coalition to Unleash Power (ACTUP) and OutRage! in Britain, were formed during the decade. The political movement articulated a new inclusive approach to lesbian and gay politics, seeing itself as 'opposed to gay assimilationists and straight oppressors while inclusive of people who have been marginalised by anyone in power'.[14] This emphasis on a sense of marginality from mainstream heterosexuality has enabled queer groups to appeal to all people who experience themselves as sexually deviant, from gay men and lesbians to transvestites, transsexuals and indeed even 'straight' people who consider themselves different from the norm. The political stance is defiant and dependent on a belief that 'queers' can be and do whatever they want, without seeking approval from mainstream society. One of the most important academic contributions to queer theory has been that of Judith Butler, through her work on the concept of performativity.[15] Butler has argued that political and social power is located in discourse or language, not in the individual subject: an individual is not born a 'queer' but acquires this identity by being named 'queer' by the wider culture and by 'performing' the identity themselves.

In queer history, the political concept of defining 'queer' sexuality in direct opposition to normative, or socially accepted, sexuality has been translated into a move away from the positive, affirmative model of lesbian and gay history, which sought to reclaim a heroic past of community-building and resistance to oppression. Instead, queer histories analyse systems of knowledge about sexuality, exploring different ways in which sexuality has been thought about and described in different periods. Historians working within this approach consider the connections between ideas about normative and deviant sexuality, arguing that the category of the normal is always defined in opposition to 'queers'. This theory has been useful to lesbian historians in a number

of ways, enabling them to overcome the difficulties posed by a lack
of explicit sources about lesbians by examining sources which
demonstrate the ways in which mainstream society understood desire
between women and the impact of these ideas on attitudes to 'normative'
sexuality.[16] The queer approach has also highlighted the importance
of exploring same-sex desire in the context of wider attitudes towards
gender and sexuality, and as a result lesbian historians have increasingly
considered the connections between lesbian experience and contemporary ideas about sexuality and the social role of women.

An Overview

The queer approach has been influential in demonstrating the ways
in which attitudes to sexuality have changed over time. Recent research
has shown that both the meanings attributed to same-sex desire and the
language used to describe it were specific to different historical periods.
Prior to the mid-twentieth century, the term 'lesbian' was not used
to indicate a woman who sexually desired other women: instead, words
such as 'Sapphist' or 'tribade' might be employed in the eighteenth
century or 'invert' in the late nineteenth and early twentieth centuries.
Attitudes towards same-sex desire between women also changed over the
period. In the sixteenth and seventeenth centuries, desire and even sexual
contact between women was not necessarily a cause of social concern
and, in the late eighteenth and nineteenth centuries, women enjoyed
considerable license in the expression of love and affection for each other.
Such behaviour did not necessarily indicate to contemporaries, or to the
women themselves, an exclusive sexual interest in women or a rejection
of heterosexuality, marriage and motherhood. Other connections can,
however, be made across the period: masculinity and the appropriation
of a masculine image and persona offered women from the sixteenth
to the twentieth centuries a means of expressing and acting upon
same-sex desires. Evidence of wedding ceremonies between women and
'female husbands' exists from both the eighteenth century and the 1970s,
suggesting that same-sex marriage continued to offer women social and
economic advantages and protection.

   This book will explore evidence of love and sex between women from
the sixteenth to the twentieth century. Considering five centuries
of lesbian history in Britain will allow some of these connections and

differences to be traced across the period. However, while recent research has added greatly to our understanding of desire between women in the early part of this period, the availability of evidence means that we still have a much more detailed knowledge of the modern period and this is reflected in the structure of this book. Chapter 1 will explore attitudes to same-sex desire in the sixteenth, seventeenth and eighteenth centuries, analysing evidence of female same-sex eroticism in travel accounts, medical works and literature. In Chapter 2, female husbands and passing women in the seventeenth and eighteenth centuries will be examined. A surprising number of cases have come to light of women who passed as men in the eighteenth century and earlier, a number of whom entered fraudulent marriages with women. This chapter will consider how these women were viewed by their contemporaries and what motivations the women may have had for passing as men. Much of the research into lesbian history in the eighteenth and nineteenth centuries has focused on 'romantic friendships' or passionate emotional attachments between women, and Chapter 3 will consider this debate. The domi-nance of ideas of female sexuality as essentially passive in the nineteenth century meant that it was widely regarded as acceptable for middle- and upper-class women to form close relationships with other women, often alongside marriage. Historians have debated whether such relationships might have included a sexual element and whether they should be included within histories of lesbianism, a question which was given a new dimension with the discovery of Anne Lister's diaries, chronicling this early-nineteenth-century gentlewoman's sexual encoun-ters and relationships with other women.

Chapters 4 and 5 focus on the emergence of new ideas about gender and sexuality which began to be articulated in the nineteenth century. The rise of feminism and an increase in educational and employment opportunities for middle- and upper-class women in the late nineteenth century resulted in a number of women conducting successful and high-profile careers in education and the professions. Many of these women decided to remain unmarried and retain the independence of a single woman, developing instead emotionally supportive and sometimes life-long relationships with another woman. Chapter 4 will compare the experience of some of these women with contemporary literary and cartoon representations of the 'New Woman'. The emergence of a science of sexuality in the late nineteenth century led to the creation of new categories of sexual identity, and Chapter 5 will explore the ideas of some of the key sexologists and trace the development of the female 'invert' and the notion of the lesbian as a 'man trapped inside a woman's body'. Chapter 6 will consider how these ideas developed in the early twentieth century in the context of the First World War. Wartime has frequently been associated with a relaxation in sexual morality, and this chapter will consider how anxieties about promiscuity and lesbianism were expressed during the First World War. Focusing on women ambulance drivers and the newly formed women's police patrols, the connections between lesbianism and uniforms, and the opportunities provided by same-sex environments for lesbian sexual activity will be explored.

The years between the First and Second World Wars have often been regarded as a turning point in lesbian history, and historians have argued that the 1920s and 1930s saw the emergence of the modern notion of lesbian identity. Chapter 7 will explore the impact of the 1921 parliamentary debate on lesbianism and the scandal surrounding the 1928 banning of Radclyffe Hall's *The Well of Loneliness*, asking whether these debates increased public awareness of lesbianism. Lesbians have been frequenting bars and nightclubs throughout most of the twentieth century, and Chapter 8 will explore the development of the lesbian scene around Britain. Focusing in detail on venues in London, Manchester and Brighton, the chapter will examine the changing behavioural codes and fashions of lesbian bar communities and their significance in developing new forms of lesbian identity. In 1964, the first British lesbian magazine, *Arena Three*, was published, offering lesbians the opportunity to write in with their views on female homosexuality and seeking to relieve the isolation of its readers. Chapter 9 will examine the history of *Arena Three* and the social organisations Minorities Research Group, Kenric and Sappho, which emerged in the 1960s and 1970s. The final chapter, Chapter 10, will explore the different political movements and campaigns in which lesbians have been involved in the last three decades of the twentieth century, examining the Gay Liberation Front in the 1970s, the campaigns around AIDS and Section 28 in the 1980s and the development of a queer politics in the 1990s. Lesbians also engaged with feminist politics in this period, and the involvement of lesbians in the Women's Liberation Movement, the rise of lesbian feminism and lesbian separatism and the debates surrounding the 'sex wars' will be explored.

Chapter 1

Invisibility or Cultural Renaissance? Same-Sex Desire, 1500–1800

Female same-sex desire in the early-modern period has been presented by many historians as invisible, insignificant and potentially almost non-existent. This is partly the result of limited legal sanctions against female homoerotic acts in this period. In England, the 1533 Act of Parliament, which made buggery or sodomy a crime punishable by death, referred to sodomy between men, a man and a woman or a person and an animal, but not between two women. Sexual acts between women were equally absent from legal dictionaries, textbooks and theological texts in the sixteenth and seventeenth centuries. In Scotland, Kirk Sessions records show just one case of female sodomy, in 1625. Two Eglishame parishioners Elspeth Faulds and Margaret Armour were charged by the Glasgow Presbytery and sentenced to part on pain of excommunication from the church.[1] This lack of explicit legal sanctions has led historians of sexuality, who have tended to rely heavily on legal sources as evidence of homosexuality between men and in other periods, to conclude that female same-sex desire was largely invisible in early-modern British culture.

However, recent research has challenged this view and demonstrated that representations of female same-sex desire were relatively widespread in early-modern cultural media. Female homoeroticism was a common theme in the plays of William Shakespeare, Ben Jonson and others, in medical texts and travel accounts, in visual art and in a wide range of popular and serious literature. Valerie Traub has claimed that the proliferation of references to female–female desire was so marked that it is possible to argue that a renaissance of lesbianism occurred in early-modern Britain. She suggests that this was prompted by a number of developments which occurred in the sixteenth century, including the circulation of classical texts in English, the rise of the theatre, the development of non-religious visual arts and new literary genres such as travel writing and pornography, the emergence of the science of anatomy and the development of printing technologies.[2] Female same-sex desire was presented in these texts either as culturally insignificant or as a potential threat to society, depending on the circumstances of the specific relationship and on the way in which the women's bodies were interpreted by contemporaries. Towards the end of the eighteenth century, however, anxieties about the female body and sexuality meant that female same-sex desire was increasingly likely to be satirised or regarded as potentially deviant.

Attitudes to female homoeroticism in this period were shaped by understandings of sexuality more broadly. Both religious and medical thinking in the early-modern period represented women as inherently lustful. The biblical example of Eve was taken to demonstrate women's weakness and susceptibility to temptation, while women's bodies were thought to be intrinsically vulnerable to passion and resistant to reason. Chastity, therefore, was seen as woman's ultimate virtue. As the Humanist educator, Juan Luis Vives observed in 1523: 'chastity is the principal virtue of a woman, and counterpeiseth with all the rest. If she have that, no man will look for any other; and if she lack that, no man will regard other.'[3] However, chastity had a very specific meaning in this period. In the context of a culture in which marriage was the dominant framework for thinking about sexuality, phallic penetration was the only type of sexual activity which threatened a woman's chastity. An intact hymen was considered the ultimate guarantee of a woman's virtue, allowing women to engage in a wide range of non-penetrative erotic activity without loss of chastity.

In the context of marriage, female sexuality was understood in largely positive terms. Moderate sex within marriage was thought to cement the bond between husband and wife and was considered so important that the word 'marriage' could be used as a synonym for sexual activity. This belief was linked with the medical view that moderate sexual activity was beneficial for the health. Early-modern thinking about the body was based on the Galenic theory of the humours, which argued that the human body was composed of a combination of four humours. The humours – blood, choler, melancholy and phlegm – were each either hot or cold, moist or dry. Women were typically cold and moist, while men were hot and dry. Good health was achieved by attaining the appropriate balance of the humours within the body and moderate sexual activity could assist in this process. Orgasm, it was believed, purged the body by expelling evil humours together with the emission of seed. Medical writers often advised women suffering from greensickness or suffocation of the womb to marry, in the belief that orgasm would purge their bodies of the evil humours. If marriage was not an immediate option, midwives were encouraged to manually manipulate a woman's genitals in order to achieve the same effect. Nicholas Fontanus, author of *The Woman's Doctour*, cited Galen's example of how 'the abundance of the spermatick humour was diminished by the hand of a skilfull Midwife, and a convenient ointment, which passage will also furnish us with this argument, that the use of Venery [sexual activity] is exceeding wholesome, if the woman will confine her selfe to the laws of moderation, so that she feele no wearisomnesse, nor weaknesse in her body, after those pleasing conflicts'.[4] Moderate sexual activity was not just important for an individual's physical health, but the quality of intercourse was vital in the production of children. The belief that both men and women needed to emit seed in order to achieve conception meant that considerable attention was paid to women's sexual pleasure. Medical texts and conduct books advised husbands on the importance of attending to their wives' erotic desires, advocating a wide range of erotic activity to arouse the woman, prior to phallic penetration.

This concern with sex within the context of marriage meant that erotic behaviour which threatened marriage, either by cuckolding a husband or producing a child out of wedlock, was the focus of anxieties about illicit sexual behaviour in this period. Other erotic activities, including a wide range of sexual contacts between women, do not appear to have been regarded as necessarily a cause for social concern, allowing considerable opportunity both for the representation of erotic activity between women in literature and wider culture and for women to express and act upon desire for each other. A number of early-modern texts focused on the 'safe' and non-reproductive nature of erotic activity between women. Pierre de Bourdeille, seigneur de Brantome, chronicler of the late-sixteenth-century French court, discussed erotic activity between women in detail in his *Lives of Fair and Gallant Ladies*. He asked himself: 'if two ladies are amorous one of another, as one can find, for such pairs are often seen sleeping together, in the fashion called in imitation of the learned Lesbian Sappho, *donna con donna*, can they be said to commit adultery and by their joint act make their husbands cuckolds?'[5] After a detailed discussion of a number of such incidents, he concluded that 'unmarried girls and widows may be excused for liking such frivolous, vain pleasures, and preferring to give themselves to each other thus and so get rid of their heat than to resort to men and be put in the family way and dishonoured by them, or have to get rid of their

fruit'.[6] Erotic activity between married women was equally unthreatening: 'the men are not cuckolded by it' and indeed many husbands
'were right glad their wives did follow after this sort of affection rather
than that of men, deeming them to be thus less wild'.[7] In Brantome's
view, women could therefore engage in erotic encounters with other
women without endangering their chastity.

This understanding of chastity was reflected in the sleeping arrange-
ments and habits of women in early-modern Britain. Bedchambers
in early-modern households were often communal and multi-purpose
and beds could also be located in any possible space throughout the
house, including hallways, parlours and kitchens. As a result, beds and
bedchambers were not private spaces, instead allowing a high degree
of transparency in the sexual behaviour of the household. The common
practice of sharing beds across the social ranks meant that both girls
and adult women shared beds with their kinswomen, female friends
and servants. Margaret Hunt has argued of labouring single women
in the eighteenth century that this practice could frequently result
in erotic exchanges between women:

> Many female servants would have experienced the sleeping
> arrangements of half a dozen households before they turned thirty,
> and that during a period when they were lonely, often deprived
> of affection, and, at least part of the time, at a high libidinal pitch.
> The potential this system offered for risk-free, same-sex erotic
> activity was very great.[8]

This is a view supported by Valerie Traub in relation to the sixteenth and
seventeenth centuries, who claims: 'With sharing beds a usual practice
in households across the social spectrum, bodily intimacy conserved heat,
fostered companionship, and enabled erotic contact.'[9] In this context,
an invitation to a woman to share the bed of her kinswoman or mistress
was regarded as a sign both of favour and, in some cases, of a close
emotional bond.

Literary references to female bed companions demonstrate the belief
that the practice of women sharing beds was 'safe' and helped to preserve
chastity. In Book Four of The Faerie Queen (1590–1609), Edmund
Spenser portrayed an encounter between the lady Amoret and the
Amazon Britomart, disguised as a man. The two engage in intimate,
erotic talk, but the bounds of chastity prevent any further erotic

exchange between a woman and a supposed man. However, when Britomart removes her disguise and reveals herself to be a woman, Amoret is able to issue an 'innocent' invitation for Britomart to join her in bed:

And eke fayre Amoret now freed from feare,
More franke affection did to her afford,
And to her bed, which she was wont forbeare,
Now freely drew, and found right safe assurance theare.
Where all that night they of their loues did treat,
And hard adventures twixt themselues alone,
That each the other gan with passion great,
And griefull pittie priuately bemoane.[10]

Freed from the fear that Britomart was a man, Amoret was able to show her 'franke affection', 'treat[ing]' of their love and engaging in 'hard adventures twixt themselues alone'. Other texts also suggest that this belief that it was 'safe' for women to share beds coincided with an awareness and acceptance of the possibility of erotic activity between female companions. In Sir Philip Sidney's *New Arcadia* (1590), the sisters Pamela and Philoclea

impoverished their clothes to enrich their bed which for that night might well scorn the shrine of Venus: and there, cherishing one another with dear though chaste embracements, with sweet though cold kisses, it might seem that love was come to play him there without dart, or that, weary of his own fires, he was there to refresh himself between their sweetbreathing lips.[11]

Richard Brome's play, *The Antipodes* (1640), also refers to homoerotic activity between bed companions in a humorous depiction of sexual naivety. Appealing to a friend for help, Martha Joyless confesses that her marriage has not been consummated and that she is unclear about exactly how children are made:

For were I now to dye, I cannot guesse
What a man do's in child-getting. I remember
A wanton mayd once lay with me, and kiss'd
And clip't, and clapt me strangely, and then wish'd

That I had beene a man to have got her with child
What must I then ha' done, or (good now tell me)
What has your husband done to you?[12]

Indicating that her only sexual experience to date had occurred
in adolescence with a 'wanton mayd', Martha Joyless proceeds to ask
her female friend if she will take Martha or, failing that, Martha's
husband into her bed to educate them.

Cultural Representations of Same-Sex Desire

As in depictions of female bed companions, cultural representations
of female same-sex desire more broadly tended to reinforce the message
that this behaviour was insignificant and unthreatening at the same
time as describing it. This was achieved in a number of different ways.
At the heart of the belief in the largely non-threatening nature of female
homoerotic activity was the notion that such behaviour was titillating
but ultimately unsatisfying, regarded by women as simply a prelude
to men. John Cleland's *Memoirs of a Woman of Pleasure* (1749),
a pornographic romance set in the world of prostitution, presented
sexual activity between women in this way. On arriving at a brothel,
the young and inexperienced heroine, Fanny Hill, is initiated into
the pleasures of sex by the older 'hackneyed' prostitute, Phoebe.
The experience, described by Fanny in salacious detail, whets Fanny's
appetite:

> Encouraged by [Fanny's innocent returning of her kisses], her hands
> became extremely free, and wandered over my whole body, with
> touches, squeezes, pressures, that rather warmed and surprised
> me with their novelty, than they either shocked or alarmed me...
> But not contented with these outer-posts, she now attempts the
> main-spot, and began to twitch, to insinuate, and at length to force
> an introduction of a finger into the quick itself, in such a manner,
> that had she not proceeded by insensible gradations, that enflamed
> me beyond the power of modesty to oppose its resistance to their
> progress, I should have jumped out of bed, and cried out for help
> against such strange assaults.[13]

However, despite being 'transported, confused, out of myself' with 'tears of pleasure [which] gushed from my eyes', Fanny remained ultimately unsatisfied by the experience. Having been introduced to the pleasures of the body, Fanny 'now pined for more solid food, and promised tacitly to myself that I would not be put off much longer with this foolery from woman to woman'. This representation of a woman gaining sexual pleasure from another woman at the same time as desiring a man was common in early-modern literary texts, which often depicted desire flowing freely between heterosexual and homosexual modes.

The depiction of female same-sex desire as a prelude or apprentice-ship for heterosexual intercourse enabled many early-modern writers to present relationships between women as having occurred in the past. Renaissance plays, in particular, often located intense attachments between female characters in a period of pastoral innocence which predated the events of the play itself.[14] The characters Hermia and Helena in Shakespeare's *A Midsummer Night's Dream* are presented as having shared an intense, emotional intimacy before their involvement in the complex heterosexual entanglements of the play tore them apart. Helena reminds Hermia:

> We, Hermia, like two artificial gods,
> Have, with our needles created both one flower,
> Both on one sampler, sitting on one cushion,
> Both warbling of one song, both in one key,
> As if our hands, our sides, voices, and minds
> Had been incorporate. So we grew together,
> Like to a double cherry, seeming parted,
> But yet an union in partition;
> Two lovely berries molded on one stem;
> So, with two seeming bodies, but one heart;
> Two of the first, like coats in heraldry,
> Due but to one and crowned with one crest.[15]

Invoking the heraldic practice of uniting the coats of arms of spouses in matrimony and referring to the primrose beds where they 'were wont to lie' and where Hermia now meets her male lover, Lysander, Helena invites the audience to compare her love for Hermia with Hermia's present relationship with a man. However, Helena and Hermia's love is placed firmly in the past through one woman's betrayal of another: while

Helena asks 'And will you rent our ancient love asunder...?' Hermia denies the importance of their relationship in favour of her love for Lysander.[16] Their love is not allowed to threaten the central heterosexual romance of the play. The homoerotic love of another female character in the play, the fairy queen Titania, is presented as posing a potentially greater threat to marriage. The argument between Titania and her husband, Oberon, which is at the root of much of the conflict in the play, has been caused by the abduction of an 'Indian boy'. The boy is the son of an intimate female friend of Titania's, and, on the woman's death, Titania had decided to steal the boy from his father and bring him up herself in memory of his mother. In doing so, she has defied the wishes of her own husband, Oberon, as well as denying the patriarchal rights of the boy's father. Although the intimate friendship between Titania and the boy's mother is a source of conflict in Titania and Oberon's marriage, its threat is again limited by locating it in the past and overseas, 'in the spiced Indian air'.[17]

The strategy of presenting desire and erotic activity between women as exotic was repeatedly used to distance any threat posed by female homoeroticism from Britain. In an era of exploration and early colonialism, travel writing was emerging as a popular new genre of literature. Sixteenth- and seventeenth-century accounts by travellers to the New World, Africa and the East commented on cultural practices which differed from those in Europe and often used the language of gender and sexuality to demonstrate cultural difference. At the same time, however, they reinforced assumptions about the inherent lustfulness of women, interpreting the partial nudity of women in some African nations as evidence of their licentiousness and the Muslim practice of purdah as a sign of the desirability of women's bodies. Although accounts of sexual activity between women were relatively rare, certain locations, such as Turkey, were repeatedly singled out in accounts of female same-sex eroticism. The Sultan's Seraglio, or harem, in Constantinople was mentioned in a number of narratives as a location for female homoeroticism. In an account published in 1587, Robert Withers described the precautions taken in the layout of the women's sleeping quarters, to prevent sexual contact between women:

> Now, in the Womens lodgings, they live just as the Nunnes doe
> in their great Monasteries; for, these Virgins have very large Roomes
> to live in, and their Bed-chambers will hold almost a hundred

of them a piece: they sleepe upon Sofaes, which are built long wise
on both sides of the Roome, so that there is a large space in the
midst for to walke in. Their Beds are very course and hard, and
by every ten Virgins there lies an old woman: and all the night long
there are many lights burning, so that one may see very plainely
throughout the whole Roome; which doth both keepe the young
Wenches from wantonnesses, and serve upon any occasion which
may happen in the night.[18]

Further precautions were taken during the daytime to prevent any illicit
activity:

Now it is not lawfull for any one to bring ought in unto them, with
which they may commit the deeds of beastly uncleannesse; so that
if they have a will to eate Cucumbers, Gourds, or such like meates,
they are sent in unto them sliced, to deprive them of the meanes
of playing the wantons; for, they being all young, lustie, and
lascivious Wenches, and wanting the societie of Men (which would
better instruct them) are doubtlesse of themselves inclined to that
which is naught, and will be possest with unchast thoughts.[19]

The need to guard against sexual activity between women in the harem
was discussed in other accounts, while, in his *A New Relation of the
Present Grand Seignor's Seraglio*, French baron Jean-Baptiste Tavernier
claimed 'it is not only in the Seraglio, that that abominable Vice reigns,
but it is predominant also in the City of Constantinople, and in all the
Provinces of the Empire'.[20] Descriptions of the hannam or Turkish bath
also inspired comments on same-sex passion. The exposure of young
girls' bodies to older women in the baths was identified as a concern
by travel writers, who thought the sight of such beauty might incite other
women to lascivious behaviour. Nicholas de Nicholay noted in his *The
Navigations, Peregrinations, and Voyages, Made into Turkie* (translated
into English 1585):

[They] do familiarly wash one another, wherby it cometh to passe
that amongst the women of Levan, ther is very great amity
proceding only through the frequentation & resort to the bathes:
yea & sometimes become so fervently in love the one of the other
as if it were with men, in such sort that perceiving some maiden

or woman of excellent beauty they wil not ceasse until they have
found means to bath with them, & to handle & grope them every
where at their pleasures, so ful they are of luxuriousnes & feminine
wantonness: Even as in times past wer the Tribades, of the number
whereof was Sapho the Lesbian.[21]

A number of accounts of the hannam included the story of an older
woman who, encountering a beautiful young girl at the baths in this way,
fell in love with her. Having failed in her advances to the young woman,
she disguised herself as a male high official and approached the girl's
father to request her hand in marriage. On the wedding night, she
abandoned the disguise and revealed herself to the girl in a final attempt
to persuade her. However, she was handed over to the authorities, who
put her in a barrel and drowned her.[22] The assertion that female
homoerotic activity was a foreign practice – confined if not to the East,
then at least to other parts of Europe such as France and Italy – was
widely repeated in early-modern literature. The idea was sufficiently
influential that, in the libel trial brought by Scottish schoolmistresses Jane
Pirie and Marianne Woods, to defend themselves against allegations of
sexual activity with each other, the judge declared: 'the crime of one
woman giving another the clitoris' was 'impossible in this country
to commit'. Instead, suspicion was cast on the Anglo-Indian girl who had
made the accusations.[23]

Other accounts located female–female desire in segregated all-female
communities, or associated them with dubious religions. In James
Shirley's play, *The Bird in a Cage* (1632–1633), the princess Eugenia has
been confined to a tower with her ladies by an over-protective father.
To pass the time, the ladies decide to stage a play depicting Jupiter's
seduction of Danae. However, in playing the part of Jupiter, Eugenia's
lady, Donella, begins to experience her own erotic desires for Eugenia
as Danae. Interrupted during the seduction scene by a bell, Donella
complains in disappointment: 'Beshrew the Belman, and [if] you had
not wak'd as you did Madam, I should ha' forgot my selfe and play'd
Jupiter indeed with you, my imaginations were strong upon me; and
you lay so sweetly – how now?'[24] In Margaret Cavendish, Duchess
of Newcastle's *The Convent of Pleasure* (1668), too, the action occurs
in an all-female community. The heroine, Lady Happy, has recently
inherited her father's estate, and, in order to avoid potential suitors, she
confines herself along with a select band of female companions within

a community dedicated to female pleasure. She is wooed by a foreign princess and, after the pair has indulged in the 'innocent' feminine pleasures of embracing and kissing, the couple's 'marriage' is celebrated with dancing around a maypole. It is only in the final scene that Lady Happy and the audience discover the true identity of the princess: a foreign prince who has disguised himself as a woman to infiltrate the community.[25]

Anti-Catholicism and hostility to the political, economic and emotional autonomy experienced by nuns meant that convents were often represented as a site of transgressive sexuality. In his *Actes of the Englishe Votaryes*, the radical Puritan John Bale railed against nuns and others who, through their 'prodgyouse lustes of uncleanesse ... leavying the naturall use of women ... have brent in their owne lustes one to an other ... man wyth man ... monke with monke, nonne with nonne, fryre with fryre & prest with prest'.[26] Nunneries are frequently mentioned in the plays of Shakespeare, where they function as a metaphor for bawdy or as an indication of female wilfulness. One of the most widely debated texts linking anti-clericalism with female same-sex eroticism was Denis Diderot's *La Religieuse* (translated as *The Nun* in 1797).[27] Located in a Catholic convent, the novel centres on the attempt by the Mother Superior to seduce the young Sister Susan. Emma Donoghue has argued that the novel is typical of many early texts depicting sex between women in that the central issue is actually one of knowledge, rather than the physical act. 'What she is really seducing her into', Donoghue claims, 'is knowledge; nothing physical the Superior can do constitutes a sin for Susan as long as Susan's mind stays pure. Only if the Superior can get the young nun to admit to sexual (and specifically lesbian) knowledge, to feel the same shame, will she be able to accomplish the seduction and lure her into the convent's lesbian network'.[28] Despite a scene in which the Mother Superior swoons orgasmically over Susan, kissing her bosom and squeezing her body, and another in which she enters Susan's room at night and lies on top of her, gasping, before getting under the covers with her, naked, Susan continues to claim ignorance of what is happening. It is only when she overhears the Mother Superior's confession that she finally understands the possibility of sexual acts between women: the loss of her innocence is the cause of her destruction and, fleeing the convent to escape the Mother Superior, she is, instead, raped and abandoned by a priest. Catholicism was not the only suspect religion to be associated with female same-sex desire in this period.

In Henry Fielding's *The Female Husband* (1746), a highly fictionalised account of the female cross-dresser, Mary Hamilton, the heroine is first seduced into same-sex passion by a Methodist, Anne Johnson. Mrs Johnson's religion and sexuality are presented as intrinsically linked: she is 'no novice in impurity, which, as she confess'd, she had learnt and often practiced at Bristol with her methodistical sisters'.[29]

Same-Sex Desire and the Female Body

Attitudes to erotic activity between women in the early-modern period were closely linked to ideas about the physical body. The 'one-sex' model of human anatomy, proposed by the Roman physician Galen remained the dominant understanding of the sexes until the sixteenth or seventeenth century. Within this model, the female genital organs were understood as identical but inverted versions of the male genitals. While the heat of a man's body prompted his penis to hang outside his body, a woman's vagina (or inverted penis) remained inside. This belief was the basis for a number of stories of miraculous sex changes which circulated in the sixteenth and seventeenth centuries. Nathaniel Wanley's *Wonders of the Little World* (1678), a compendium of oddities which was popular for children until the nineteenth century, included a chapter on 'such Persons as have changed their Sex'. The belief that the female body was an imperfect version of the male and that nature was always striving for perfection meant that stories of spontaneous sex change related primarily to women changing into men: in Wanley's collection, twenty-three out of the twenty-four cases of magical sex change cited were female to male. The stories explained the sex change as a prolapsed vagina, caused in some cases by the breaking of the hymen on the wedding night, which allowed the member to drop, or in others, as a result of excessive stimulation, as in the case of a sixteenth-century French girl who was 'wantoning in bed with a Maid that lay with her' when 'the signs of a man brake out of her'.[30]

Classical texts also provided examples of such incidents, many of which would have been widely available in the original and translation in the early-modern period. The Latin poet Ovid included the story of Iphis and Ianthe in Book 9 of his *Metamorphoses*. In order to satisfy her husband's wish for a son and avoid her daughter being killed, Iphis' mother, Telethusa, disguises her baby's sex and brings her up as a boy. When Iphis reaches the age of thirteen, she is engaged to be married

to the beautiful Ianthe, the daughter of a neighbour. Iphis and Ianthe
fall in love, but as the wedding day draws closer, Iphis despairs that she,
'A maid [who] with madness does a maid desire', has been cursed with
an unnatural and impossible love. Repenting of her deception, Telethusa
prays to the goddess Io for a miracle and is granted one: on the eve of the
wedding, Iphis miraculously becomes a man:

> The whiteness of her skin forsook her face;
> Her looks embolden'd, with an awful grace;
> Her features and her strength together grew,
> And her long hair to curling locks withdrew.
> Her sparkling eyes with manly vigour shone,
> Big was her voice, audacious was her tone.

Translating the text for the benefit of early-modern English readers,
Samuel Garth, John Dryden and others added a further reference
to the emergence of the penis: 'The latent parts, at length reveal'd
began/To shoot, and spread, and burnish into Man.'[31]

However, during the seventeenth century, physicians and anatomists
increasingly began to question the possibility of miraculous sex changes,
arguing instead that such incidents were actually cases of hermaphroditism or unusual genital anatomy. The early-eighteenth-century text
A Treatise of Hermaphrodites, attributed to Giles Jacob, claimed that
a woman who found herself to be a female hermaphrodite could use
her vagina for intercourse with a man or her member for penetrating
a woman.[32] Hermaphroditism was closely associated with female same-
sex desire, so that women involved in cases of homoerotic desire were
frequently assumed to be hermaphrodites. Legal proceedings relied
on physical examinations by midwives and physicians to establish the
nature of the individual's genitalia and then courts sought to impose
a consistent gender identity on the person. Following *Aristotle's Book
of Problems*, this decision was often determined by the individual's role
in sexual intercourse and 'in which member it is fittest for the act
of copulation'.[33] However, the concept of hermaphroditism was not
clearly defined in this period and the figure of the female hermaphrodite
was frequently confused with the tribade in sixteenth-, seventeenth-
and eighteenth-century medical texts. In an early-eighteenth-century
work on sex in marriage, translated as *The Mysteries of Conjugal Love
Reveal'd*, French surgeon Nicholas Venette described five types

of hermaphrodite. Three were essentially 'real Men', one was a 'perfect Hermaphrodite' with confused genitalia and the last were 'Women who have the Clitoris bigger and longer than others', whom the Greeks call Tribades.[34]

The concept of the tribade had been familiar in ancient and medieval texts as a woman with masculine attributes who desired other women. David Halperin claims:

> The female same-sex sexual practice that imperial Greek and Roman writers alike singled out for comment was 'tribadism', the sexual penetration of women (and men) by other women, by means of either a dildo or a fantastically large clitoris. The tribade makes memorable appearances, though not always under that name ... she is represented as a shaven-headed butch, adept at wrestling, able to subjugate men and to satisfy women.[35]

However, classical discussions of the tribade were largely confined to scholarly Latin literature in the medieval period and only resurfaced in the fifteenth and sixteenth centuries in vernacular translations of newly available Greek, Roman and Arabic texts. Under the influence of new anatomical discoveries and travel accounts of exotic female sexuality, the figure of the tribade was reshaped in early-modern medical texts as a monstrous symbol of uncontrollable female desire, who used her enlarged clitoris to engage in sexual acts with other women.

The most significant development in medical thinking about the female body and sexuality in this period which prompted the renewed focus on the tribade was the 'rediscovery' of the clitoris in the mid-sixteenth century. It seems reasonable to assume that many women were already aware of the erotic potential of this part of their bodies before it became a focus of medical interest in the mid-sixteenth century. The clitoris as a distinct anatomical organ, rather than a more generalised location of female sexual pleasure, had also been known to late Greek medical writers, but this knowledge had been lost in the medieval period due to inaccurate translations and medical writers had either confused it with the labia minora or seen it as an abnormal growth in some women. However, new access to Greek texts in the mid-sixteenth century, combined with the development of anatomical research by European physicians, led to the rediscovery of the clitoris as both an organ and a site of female sexual pleasure. The first clear definition of the clitoris in these terms was provided by Realdo Colombo in his *De re anatomica* (1559). He claimed:

> It is the principal seat of women's enjoyment in intercourse, so that if you not only rub it with your penis, but even touch it with your little finger, the pleasure causes their seed to flow forth in all directions, swifter than the wind, even if they don't want it to.[36]

The clitoris came to be understood as the female 'yard' or the equivalent of the penis in men: becoming erect when aroused and emitting seed during orgasm, it was central to female sexual pleasure and therefore to conception. However, while much of the medical discussion of the clitoris centred on its importance in heterosexual intercourse, the realisation that women could also gain sexual pleasure from the touch of a 'little finger' on their clitoris gave rise to concerns about the possibilities it offered for female homoeroticism. Anxieties about the potential 'abuse' of the clitoris to rub the genitals or penetrate another woman became increasingly apparent in seventeenth-century medical texts, centring on the issue of the size of the clitoris. Helkiah Crooke claimed in his *Microcosmographia* (1615) that:

> [S]ometimes [the clitoris] groweth to such a length that it hangeth without the cleft like a mans member, especially when it is fretted with the touch of the cloaths, and so strutteth and groweth to a rigiditie as doth the yarde [penis] of a man. And this part it is which those wicked women doe abuse called *Tribades* (often mentioned by many authors, and in some states worthily punished) to their mutual and unnatural lusts.[37]

The connection between tribadism and an enlarged clitoris was increasingly made in early- and mid-seventeenth-century medical texts, prompting a growing concern that erotic activity between women was not confined to exotic locations but was also possible between women in Britain. These fears were apparent in increasingly dramatic accounts of unnaturally extended clitorises. In his 1668 anatomical textbook, Thomas Bartholin discussed the size of the clitoris in some detail:

> Its Size is commonly small; it lies hid for the most part under the Nymphs in its beginning, and afterward it sticks out a little. For in Lasses that begin to be amorous, the Clitoris does first discover

it self. It is in several persons greater or lesser: in some it hangs out like a mans Yard, namely when young Wenches do frequently and continually handle and rub the same, as Examples testifie. But that it should grow as big as a Gooses neck, as Platerus relates of one, is altogether praeternatural and monstrous. Tulpius hath a like Story of one that had it as long as half a mans finger, and as thick as a Boys Prick, which made her willing to have to do with Women in a Carnal way. But the more this part encreases, the more does it hinder a man in his business. For in the time of Copulation it swells like a mans Yard, and being erected, provokes to Lust.[38]

Concerns about monstrously enlarged clitorises were exacerbated by a lack of clarity in medical thinking over the link between the enlargement of the clitoris and the desire for same-sex eroticism. A range of explanations were offered as to how the clitoris might become enlarged, including the friction of a woman's clothes on her genitals while walking and excessive masturbation. However, no clear explanation was offered as to the order of causation: whether a woman's enlarged clitoris prompted her to have sex with other women or whether the abuse of the clitoris caused it to enlarge. An early-eighteenth-century anti-masturbation manual, *The Supplement to the Onania* (c.1710), attributed to the quack clergyman, Balthazar Beckers, included a reference to one case, which suggested that excessive lust was both the cause and consequence of clitoral abuse. Beckers cited a letter which he claimed to have been sent by a young lady, 'Mrs. E.N.' after she had read his earlier work, *The Onania* (1708). She explained:

I began, sir, the folly at 11 years of age, was taught by my mother's chambermaid, who lay with me from that time all along until now, which is full seven years, and so intimate were we in the sin, that we took the opportunities of committing it, and invented all the ways we were capable of to heighten the titillation, and gratify our sinful lusts the more. We, in short, pleasured one another, as well as ourselves, but whether by the hard usage of my parts by her, or myself, or both, or whether from anything in nature more in my make, than is customary to the sex, I don't know, but for above half a year past I have had a swelling that thrusts out from my body, as big, and almost as hard, and as long or longer than my thumb, which inclines me to excessive lustful desires, and

from it there issues a moisture or slipperiness to that degree that
I am almost continually wet, and sometimes have such a forcing,
as if something of a large substance was coming from me, which
greatly frightens both me and my maid.[39]

While this account suggests that abuse of the clitoris was responsible
for its enlargement, Robert James' mid-eighteenth-century *Medicinal
Dictionary* defined 'tribades' as women whose members had grown
to the point that they had experimented in intercourse with women.
When these acts became habitual and developed into a preference for sex
with women, rather than men, the women then became tribades.[40] This
confusion over what caused women to abuse their enlarged clitorises
with other women, combined with the revival of the term 'tribade' and
new anatomical knowledge about female genitalia, prompted growing
anxieties and social disapproval of female same-sex eroticism from the
late seventeenth century onwards.

Female Same-Sex Eroticism and Social Disapproval

Class distinctions became increasingly important in concerns about
same-sex desire: servants and working women were represented as
infecting gentry women from below, while a debauched aristocracy
seduced them from above. In Jane Barker's *A Patch-Work Screen for the
Ladies; or, Love and Virtue Recommended* (1723), the 'unaccountable
wife' refuses to be parted from a female servant despite the disgrace this
brings to her family and an attempt by the queen to intervene. Ignoring
the servant woman's adulterous relationship with her husband, the wife
takes on the servant's household chores and, on the death of the husband,
goes begging in the streets to support the woman and her illegitimate
offspring.[41]

Late seventeenth- and eighteenth-century political satires and
polemics employed accusations of female same-sex desire in an attempt
to discredit powerful or autonomous women. Anthony Hamilton's
anecdotal biography of his brother-in-law, Count Grammont, contained
a satirical account of a senior maid of honour at the court of Charles II.
Mistress Hobart is described as having an 'irregular Fancy' and 'a tender
Heart, whose Sensibility, some pretended, was in Favour of the Fair Sex'.
Hobart makes a number of unsuccessful approaches to other women,
which cause rumours to begin circulating at court. Nevertheless, she

is asked by the queen to take charge of a new maid of honour, Mistress Temple, and exploits her senior position to influence the girl and encourage an intimate friendship between them. However, she is frustrated in her attempts by a former rival, Lord Rochester, who informs the naïve Temple that Hobart is a hermaphrodite who has already impregnated her own maid: when Hobart next visits Temple, the girl screams in fear and only the intervention of the queen saves Hobart's place at court.[42] Mrs Anne Seymour Damer, a sculptor and the heiress of Horace Walpole's fortune, was the subject of a number of political satires in the eighteenth century. After her husband's death, she developed a close friendship with Miss Mary Berry and her home in Strawberry Hill became associated with a 'sapphic' set including the actresses Kitty Clive and Miss Elizabeth Farren. One satire, entitled *A Sapphick Epistle*, by 'Jack Cavendish', referred to a Mrs D_r and claimed:

> Strawberry-hill at once doth prove,
> Taste, elegance, and Sapphic love,
> In gentle Kitty _.[43]

Another referred to Miss Elizabeth Farren before her marriage to Lord Derby, observing: 'superior to the influence of MEN, she is supposed to feel more exquisite delight from the touch of the cheek of Mrs D_r than the fancy of any *novelties* which the wedding night can promise with such a partner as his lordship'.[44] In the late eighteenth century, Marie-Antoinette's alleged affairs with other women were repeatedly satirised. The erotic magazine, *Bon Ton Magazine* serialised a satire entitled 'The Spirit of the Ring: Containing Secret Anecdotes of Many Illustrious Personages of This and the Neighbouring Kingdoms' between September 1795 and February 1796. Linking Marie-Antoinette's sexuality with the theme of aristocratic corruption, the satire suggested that the French king was unable to satisfy Marie-Antoinette's insatiable desire, forcing her to pursue other options:

> None but the most beautiful women would answer her purposes; she tried therefore every artifice she was mistress of, to inveigle them into her snares ... and by these means too often succeeded in making them subservient to the gratification of her unnatural passions. Yet variety in this respect constituted Antoinette's

supreme pleasure – Hence no woman remained in her good graces for any length of time.[45]

Same-sex passion, insatiable desire and aristocratic corruption were presented as intrinsically linked in this and other erotic satires.

Katherine Binhammer has suggested that by the late eighteenth century, erotic and pornographic literature was representing female same-sex activity together with flagellation and the erotics of pain, as examples of a range of 'immoderate' sexual practices.[46] Although early-modern medical and religious texts had noted the importance of female sexual pleasure for conception and the significance of sexual activity as a bond within marriage, both genres emphasised the importance of moderation. Immoderate sexual activity was believed to actually hinder reproduction so conjugal advice literature advised couples to practice moderation. As immoderate sexual activity came to be seen as increasingly transgressive, pornographic periodicals such as *Bon Ton Magazine*, *Ramblers Magazine* and *Rangers Magazine* featured erotic acts between women and erotic flagellation as signs of excessive female desire. In 1792 *Bon Ton Magazine* included an account of a club of female flagellants who met at a house in Jermyn Street in London, every Thursday night:

> The respectable society, or club, of which we now treat, are never less than 12 in number. There are always six down, or stooping down, and six up. They cast lots for the choice of station, and after a lecture which is every evening read or spoken extempore, upon the effects of flagellation, as experienced from the earliest days to the present moment ... the six patients [passive participants] take their respective situations, and the six agents [active participants] placing bare those parts which are ... the most exquisite in point of sensation, begin the courses of practice ... Sometimes the wanton, vagrant fibres are directed to the more secret sources of painful bliss! ... and sometimes, as the passions of the fair directress rise, they penetrate even the sacred cave of Cupid.[47]

Although the writer 'does not presume to say, that is to say for a certainty, what ceremonies succeed those meetings, or whether the stimulus exceeds the boundaries of conjugal fidelity', the account hints strongly at an element of homoerotic activity.[48] Unlike previous accounts of female same-sex desire, which presented erotic activity between women as a prelude to heterosexual sex, this and other late-eighteenth-century accounts represent homoeroticism as a sign of sexual excess practised by experienced women seeking new sensations. The Jermyn Street women are all described as older matrons 'who, grown weary of wedlock in its accustomed form, and possibly impatient of that cold neglect and indifference which, after a certain term, become attendant upon Hymen, determined to excite, by adventitious applications, those extasies [sic] which in the earlier period of marriage they had experienced'.[49]

Chapter 2

Cross-Dressing and Female Husbands, 1600–1800

Gender inversion and cross-dressing provided one significant medium for the expression and representation of female same-sex desire in the early-modern period. In a period in which clothing and the outward performance of gender roles were accepted, largely unquestioningly, as indicators of biological sex, the adoption of masculine clothing carried with it the ability to assume male social roles and privileges. Concerns about the socially disruptive potential of female cross-dressing erupted in occasional cultural panics about the issue throughout the early-modern period. In the 1620s, a pamphlet war flared up as women's supposedly masculine clothing fashions were interpreted as a sign of broader social disintegration. The pamphlet *Hic Mulier* (or masculine women) claimed that 'since the days of Adam women were never so Masculine' and accused women:

> … you have taken the monstrousness of your deformity in apparel, exchanging the modest attire of the comely Hood, Cowl, Coif, handsome Dress or Kerchief, to the cloudy Ruffianly broad-brimmed Hat and wanton Feather; the modest upper parts of a concealing straight gown, to the loose, lascivious civil embracement of a French doublet being all unbuttoned to entice, all of one shape to hide deformity, and extreme short waisted to give a most easy way to every luxurious action; the glory of a fair large hair, to the shame of most ruffianly short locks; the side, thick gathered, and close guarding Safeguards to the short, weak, thin, loose, and every hand-entertaining short bases; for Needles, Swords; for Prayerbooks, bawdy legs; for modest gestures, giant like behaviours; and for women's modesty, all Mimic and apish incivility.

Haec Vir (or effeminate man), published the same year in response to *Hic Mulier*, agreed that women were becoming increasingly masculine, but blamed the effeminacy of men for the development: cross-dressing was evidence of a fundamental breakdown in distinctions between the sexes. Concerns about the possibilities offered by female cross-dressing for lewd activity with men, expressed during this controversy, ultimately prompted James I to instruct the clergy to preach against the practice. In the early eighteenth century, a similar controversy broke out over the practice of women's cross-dressing in masquerades. In 1719 the *Freethinker* warned that the practice of women wearing masculine costumes to masquerades was blurring the distinction between the sexes and could result in women being accidentally seduced by other women.[1]

Theatrical Cross-Dressing

Despite these concerns, cross-dressing remained a significant feature of English cultural life in this period. Male cross-dressing had been a central aspect of theatrical practice until the seventeenth century, with the tradition of boys playing women's parts on the stage. However, towards the end of the seventeenth century, this practice began to decline, as a result of changing fashions and growing concerns about gender ambiguity in men. It was replaced by a new fashion, which continued throughout the eighteenth century, for women playing men's, or 'breeches', parts on the stage. Women's appearance on the stage, both in female and male parts, was motivated to an extent by the expectation that conventionally attractive women on stage would sell tickets in an era of intense economic competition between theatres. However, the process may have been more complex than this, with the sex appeal of cross-dressed actresses extending across gender and sexual boundaries to both male and female spectators.[2] Margaret Woffington, one of the most well-known cross-dressed actresses of the eighteenth century, was described as appealing equally to men and women in her theatrical appearances:

> When first in Petticoats you trod the Stage,
> Our Sex with Love you fir'd, your own with Rage!
> In Breeches next, so well you play'd the Cheat,
> The pretty Fellow, and the Rake compleat –
> Each sex, were then, with different Passions mov'd,
> The Men grew envious, and the Women loved.[3]

Actresses in breeches parts were very popular with female as well as male spectators. Richard Steele's play, *The Tender Husband* (1705), which featured a female cross-dresser wooing another woman, was so popular with female audiences that it was performed on Ladies' Nights, when women could request a particular play, on average every two years throughout the first half of the eighteenth century.[4]

Cross-dressing was also a common theme in early-modern plays and literature, enabling same-sex desire between women to be suggested and represented. In Shakespeare's *Twelfth Night*, Viola disguises herself as a young man, Cesario, and gains employment with the Duke Orsino. Acting as a surrogate for the Duke in his wooing of the lady Olivia, Cesario (Viola) speaks some of the key love lyrics of the play to another woman. Asked by Olivia how he – Cesario – would love her, Cesario replies that (s)he would:

Make me a willow cabin at your gate,
And call upon my soul within the house;
Write loyal cantons of contemned love
And sing them loud even in the dead of night;
Halloo your name to the reverberate hills,
And make the babbling gossip of the air
Cry out 'Olivia!' O, you should not rest
Between the elements of air and earth
But you should pity me![5]

Olivia responds, 'You might do much,' and falls in love with Cesario, only transferring her affections at the end of the play to Viola's twin brother, Sebastian. The homoerotic tension of these scenes between Olivia and the cross-dressed Viola is further heightened by puns referring to hermaphroditism. In one scene, Viola refers to herself in male costume as a 'poor monster', using the popular term for a hermaphrodite and, on being forced into a duel with Sir Andrew, Cesario jokes, 'A little thing would make me tell them how much I lack of a man.'[6]

In other texts the cross-dressing was reversed, with male characters disguising themselves as women in order to gain access to a woman. Eliza Haywood's *La Belle Assemblee* (1754), a translation of Madeleine-Angelique de Gomez's novel, *Les Journees amusantes* (1744), included one such incident. The novel depicts six friends, spending a week

in a country house, who while away the time by telling stories.
The stories all focus on different aspects of sexual anxiety or taboo,
including incest between a brother and a sister, intergenerational
romance and lesbian love. In the lesbian story, the heroine Camilla
describes falling in love with the beautiful Alphonsina and experiencing
considerable distress over her love for another woman. She tells her
friend and cousin Florinda:

> The Image of that charming Lady has never left me one single
> moment.
>   All that she said, each kind Embrace, every Action was in Sleep
> repeated.
>   One while I thought myself bless'd in the assurance of her eternal
> Friendship.
>   Another time, my Imagination, ingenuous [sic] in tormenting
> me, represented her unkind, and forgetful of all the soft Professions
> we had made each other.
>   Was there ever anything like this, Florinda? Could you
> believe it possible, that one Woman should love another to this
> extravagant, this distracted degree?[7]

The disruptive potential of this same-sex passion is resolved in a final
twist, in which it emerges that Alphonsina is actually a man, Alphonso.
However, the force of this heterosexual conclusion is undermined when
it emerges that Alphonso adopted his disguise because he believed
he would be more successful in wooing Camilla as a woman. Camilla,
it appears, has a reputation for 'Insensibility' and indifference towards
men, while, as she herself admits, she is 'nicely delicate in my Affections
to the Women'.[8]

Female Cross-Dressers in Chapbooks and Ballads

Female cross-dressing was not confined to literature in the early-modern
period: newspapers and chapbooks provide evidence of a number
of instances of real women who adopted male clothing or sought to pass
as men. Historians have suggested a number of reasons why women
might have disguised themselves as men in this period. Rictor Norton has
argued that women did so 'in order to exercise the privileges and freedom

usually reserved for men – freedom of movement, freedom to engage in business, freedom to travel unmolested, freedom to express oneself in a frank manner, freedom to be assertive and outgoing'.[9] Lillian Faderman agrees, claiming cross-dressed women as early feminists:

> Transvestites were, in a sense, among the first feminists. Mute as they were, without a formulated ideology to express their convictions, they saw the role of women to be dull and limiting. They craved to expand it – and the only way to alter that role in their day was to become a man … Transvestism must have been a temptation or, at the very least, a favorite fantasy for many an adventurous young woman who understood that as a female she could expect little latitude or freedom in her life.[10]

Despite the fact that cross-dressing, as a form of fraud, was potentially a serious offence, popular ballads and autobiographical accounts from the period celebrated such women as eccentric adventurers.

Many accounts were framed within a broader narrative of heterosexual love or marriage, suggesting that women embarked on their adventures in pursuit of a male lover. *The Life and Adventures of Mrs Christian Davies, the British Amazon* (1741) attributed to Daniel Defoe and claiming to have been taken down from Davies' own dictation, begins in this way. Christian is happily married to a servant, Richard Davies, until he is press-ganged into the army. Apparently inspired by a silver strap-on 'urinary instrument', which she found in the guest bed as a child, after a visit from a 'male' friend of her father's, Christian decides to go after her husband disguised as a man. Taking the 'urinary instrument' with her, she dresses in one of her husband's suits, leaves her children with her mother and sets out to follow the army to Flanders. However, the heterosexual motivation of the narrative soon begins to break down as, unable to find her husband, Christian passes the time by flirting with women. The first such encounter is described light-heartedly – 'in my Frolicks, to kill Time, I made my Addresses to a Burgher's Daughter, who was young and pretty' – and Davies parodies heterosexual courtship behaviour, indulging in sighs and lingering looks. She then tries to take an 'indecent freedom' with the girl but claims to be gratified by the girl's virtue when she is rebuffed. Nevertheless, Davies appears to become increasingly emotionally entangled with the Burgher's Daughter. When a man tries to rape the girl, Christian challenges him to a duel, demanding to know 'how he durst attempt the Honour of a Woman, who was, for aught he knew, my Wife; to whom he was sensible I had long made honourable Love'. The account tries to minimise the emotional significance of the relationship, claiming 'Indeed, I was now fond of the girl, though mine, you know, could not go beyond a platonick Love,' and Davies has to leave the area to get out of the relationship. However, when Davies finally finds her husband, twelve years later, living with a mistress, she has developed such a taste for the life that she persuades him to let her live with him as his brother, continuing in male disguise until the end of the war.[11]

The Female Soldier (1750) recounted the similar story of Hannah Snell, daughter of a Worcester hosier, who also followed her husband to war.[12] Born in 1723, Snell had married a Dutch sailor, James Summs in 1744. However, the marriage was not a success: Summs stole his wife's possessions to pay for prostitutes and then ran away, leaving her pregnant. When their baby died, Hannah cut her hair short, adopted her brother-in-law's name, James Gray, and went after her husband. Again, the adoption of a male disguise involves the heroine in a number of liaisons with women. When Gray's sergeant, Davis, confides his plan to rape a certain young woman, Gray warns the potential victim and consequently gains her friendship. Observing the cordial relations between the pair, Davis begins to suspect that it was Gray who betrayed him and has him whipped, ostensibly for neglect of duty. This reinforces the girl's gratitude and affection for Gray, but when an acquaintance from Snell's home arrives, Gray is forced to run away to escape exposure. Subsequent encounters with women are also presented as an attempt to maintain Snell's male disguise, although Snell's feelings for the women appear slightly confused. In Lisbon, Gray is required to flirt with a number of women in order to prove his masculinity to the other men. When Gray and his friend, Jeffories, woo two women, we are informed 'the handsomest ... was the favourite of our heroine'. This preference is subsequently denied, however, when Jeffories suggests tossing a coin to decide which man might court the handsome woman. Gray agrees, 'not caring how soon she should be rid of such a Companion'.[13]

Julie Wheelwright argues that the encounters between women described in these accounts were simply an attempt to mimic male behaviour and should not be interpreted as erotic: 'The need to prove their masculinity forced these women to mimic male power relations, flirting with, mocking or flattering their admirers … There appeared to be no room for any real sexual intimacy.'[14] However, Emma Donoghue disagrees, referring to the case of an English soldier reported in *The Gentleman's Journal: Or the Monthly Miscellany* in April 1692.[15] The journal offered an appreciative description of a soldier

> who served two years in the French army in Piedmont as a volunteer, and was entertained for her merit by the Governor of Pignerol in the quality of his Gentlemen of the Horse; at last playing with another of her sex, she was discover'd; and the Governor having thought fit to inform the King his master of this, he hath sent word that he would be glad to see the lady; which hath occasion'd her coming to Genoa, in order to embark for France: Nature has bestow'd no less beauty on her than courage; and her age is not above 26. The French envoy hath orders to cause her to be waited on to Marseille, and to furnish her with all necessaries.[16]

Although the article is more concerned with the soldier's service record and beauty than the circumstances of her exposure as a woman, Donoghue draws attention to the line 'playing with another of her sex, she was discover'd'. 'Any kind of "playing" which reveals anatomical sex', she suggests, 'deserves an erotic reading'.[17]

While the erotic significance of encounters between women remains difficult to interpret in many accounts of female cross-dressing, the case of Catherine Vizzani appears much clearer. Catherine Vizzani's biography was written in 1744 by Professor Giovanni Bianchi of the University of Sienna, who had performed her autopsy. In 1751, it was translated into English by John Cleland as *An Historical and Physical Dissertation on the Case of Catherine Vizzani*. While Bianchi's account demonstrates a clear liking for his heroine, who is described as surpassing 'Sappho, or any of the Lesbian Nymphs, in an Attachment to those of her own Sex', Cleland is shocked by this attitude, attributing it to the more relaxed approach of the Italians to sexual matters.[18] His opinion was shared by a reviewer in the English *Monthly Review* of March 1751, who declined to mention any further details than the book's title, out of consideration for the modesty of his female readers.[19] From Bianchi's account, Catherine Vizzani was born in 1718 or 1719 in Rome, the daughter of a carpenter. Her preference for her own sex emerged early in life:

> When she came to her fourteenth Year, the Age of Love in our forward Climate, she was reserved and shy towards young Men, but would be continually romping with her own Sex, and some she caressed with all the Eagerness and Transports of a Male Lover.[20]

She became particularly enamoured of one girl, Margaret, whom she attempted to seduce during their shared embroidery lessons. The two became close, continuing an affair for two years, during which time Catherine adopted the practice of dressing in boys' clothes in order to spend the night beneath Margaret's window. However, one night, she was discovered by Margaret's father, who threatened to report her to the city governor. Catherine was forced to run away. She adopted the male disguise of 'Giovanni Bordoni' and obtained work as a servant for a number of different churchmen. During this time, Giovanni developed a reputation as being both insatiable in his desire for women and highly successful in sexual encounters, for which he employed a strap-on dildo. This caused some difficulties with his clerical employers, one of whom complained to Giovanni's father about his son's lewd behaviour. However, both Vizzani's mother and father were supportive of their daughter's disguise and sexual nature:

> The carpenter, who could hardly keep his countenance during a remonstrance delivered with a dictatorial solemnity, calmly answered, that, to his dear wife's inexpressible grief, their son was a prodigy of nature, and that, in his very early childhood, they had observed some astonishing motions of lust, which had unhappily gathered vehemence with the growth of his body; that, however, since such was the case, and the vigour of his constitution was not to be repressed by words or blows, nature must e'en take its course.[21]

Ultimately, Giovanni began to court a young gentlewoman, the niece of a village minister, 'and prosecuted [his addresses] with such ardour and success, that they both grew passionately in love with each other'. The uncle, who was concluding an advantageous match for his niece, attempted to keep them apart, but after a number of clandestine meetings, the pair agreed to elope together to Rome. However, on the eve of their departure, the young woman, Maria, confided the plan to her younger sister, who threatened to reveal the intended elopement to their uncle if Maria and Giovanni did not take her with them. Giovanni agreed, but the presence of the young girl slowed the pair down and they were overtaken by the uncle's men on the Sienna road. After an initial stand-off, Giovanni surrendered, in the hope that when her sex was discovered, the elopement would be interpreted as a simple frolic between girls. The chaplain who led the uncle's men, however, was reluctant to accept Giovanni's surrender so easily and shot him in the thigh. Seriously wounded, Giovanni was taken to the hospital della Scala in Sienna, where he ultimately died of his wounds.

In many accounts of female cross-dressers, sexuality was assumed to be fluid, changing direction according to the gender adopted by the protagonist. Thus, in his account of Catherine Vizzani, despite the evidence that Giovanni was 'the most addicted to that alluring sex [women] of all the men in that part of the country', Bianchi expressed admiration for Vizzani's chastity. On her deathbed, Vizzani told Maria de Colombo, purveyor to the nuns of the order of the Immaculate Conception of the Blessed Virgin at Sienna, that 'she was not only a female but a virgin, conjuring her, at the same time, to let no person know it until her death, and then to declare it publicly, that she might be buried in a woman's habit, and with the garland on her head, an honorary ceremony observed among us in the burial of virgins'. For Bianchi, Vizzani's virginity was

> a proof of singular address and self-government, that in such
> a length of time, she should preserve her secret from detection, and
> be proof against any inclination or love for a man, though living
> continually in the utmost freedom with them, and often lying in the
> same bed; a passion universally natural to young women, and
> so vehement in its actings, as to violate the institutes of the cloister,
> or elope from the coercion of parents.[22]

Although John Cleland was less impressed by Vizzani's status as a virgin, referring, in an afterword, to her 'lewdness' and 'impurities', he also recognised that she possessed a 'violent inclination' towards women.

Female Husbands

In a number of cases, women who cross-dressed went beyond simply
courting other women and married them, or became 'female husbands'.
Historians have suggested a variety of reasons why women might have
done so. Lotte van de Pol and Rudolph Dekker have argued that taking
the role of a husband within the institutional framework of a marriage
enabled women, psychologically, to make sense of their desire to court
other women.[23] However, as Lillian Faderman and others have noted,
in this period it was possible for women to court other women as women
and cultural representations of female–female desire were relatively
widespread.[24] Two entries in a Cheshire marriage register in 1707 and
1708 suggest that it might even have been possible for women to marry
each other as women. The register for the parish of Taxal records:

> Hannah Wright and Anne Gaskill, Parish of Prestbury,
> 4th September 1707
> Ane Norton and Alice Pickford, Parish of Prestbury,
> 3rd June 1708 [25]

The register made no comment on the apparent gender of these couples,
leading Donoghue to speculate that '[r]eactions to marriages between
women ... seem to have been wholly at the discretion of the clergymen
who married them'.[26] However, no other evidence has been found
of marriages being openly celebrated between two women, and
cross-dressing appears to have offered the most accessible means
for those women wishing to enter into marriage with another woman.
Donoghue suggests that, while such relationships can certainly
be interpreted as erotic, female husbands married other women for
primarily social, rather than personal, reasons: 'Marriage was a refuge
that seemed to offer so much: social status, domestic privacy, economic
convenience, a sense of emotional stability, a "No Trespassers" sign for
any man casting an eye at that female husband's wife.'[27] Martha Vicinus
stresses similar motives, arguing that for some women the 'façade
of heterosexual marriage' with another woman offered security and
potentially social respectability.[28]

It is difficult to assess how widespread this practice was in the
seventeenth and eighteenth centuries, although a number of entries
in eighteenth-century London marriage registers voiced suspicions about

the groom's gender. Impoverished clergymen living in or around Fleet prison in London were well known for performing wedding ceremonies without enquiring too closely into the circumstances of the relationship and were notorious for marrying male fortune-hunters and young heiresses. Marriage registers in this area contain a number of references to possible female husbands. On 15 December 1734, a marriage certificate was refused to John Mountford, a tailor, and Mary Cooper, a spinster, both from Soho and the clergyman noted 'Suspected 2 Women, no Certif.' A few years later, on 20 May 1737, a clergyman married another two Londoners, John Smith and Elizabeth Huthall, but recorded his doubts regarding the groom:

> By ye opinion after matrimony my Clark judg'd they were both women, if ye person by name John Smith be a man, he's a little short fair thin man not above 5 foot. After marriage I almost co[ul]d prove [the]m both women, the one was dress'd as a man thin pale face & wrinkled chin.[29]

Although Lord Hardwicke's Marriage Act 1753 was intended to make Fleet weddings harder to obtain, by requiring parental consent if the bride was under twenty-one and requiring all weddings to be publicly registered to prevent fraud, reports of female husbands continued for the rest of the century.

Although nothing further is known about many of these cases, court records and newspaper reports provide more detailed information about a few female husbands. In 1766 the *Gentleman's Magazine* reported a case in Poplar, London, in which 'two women had lived together for six and thirty years, as man and wife, and kept a public house, without ever being suspected'. The magazine attempted to prevent any erotic interpretations of the women's relationship by assuring its readers that: 'Both had been crossed in love when young, and had chosen this method to avoid farther importunities.'[30] The subsequent issue elaborated on this version of events, reporting that when the younger woman, Mary, was sixteen, her suitor was discovered to be a highwayman and hanged. When the same misfortune befell her seventeen-year-old best friend, the two decided to pose as man and wife. After tossing a halfpenny to decide which of them would play the role of husband, Mary East adopted men's clothes and became 'James How'. The pair was financially successful: with their combined savings of £30, the girls bought James How's suit and embarked on life together. After thirty-six years as innkeepers, they had saved £3,000. The couple became pillars of their local community and James How served in a range of town offices and was widely liked and respected, despite a number of comments on his effeminacy. However, in 1750, an old acquaintance, Mrs Bentley, recognised James How as Mary East and blackmailed the couple. They gave her £10 and she left them alone for fifteen years before returning to demand more money in 1765. When the women did not pay, she sent two men, who dragged James How into a field and threatened him. According to the *Gentleman's Magazine*, Mrs How was, at this time, unwell and staying with her brother in Essex. Feeling that she was close to death, she sent for her husband, but James How did not come. Apparently abandoned, Mrs How confessed everything to her brother and left her share of the couple's fortune to her family, before dying. Meanwhile, James How confided the situation to a male friend, who brought a case for blackmail before the local magistrates. Although Mary East was forced to admit her disguise and resume female clothes, the local community supported her, sending witnesses to the court to testify to her good character. Mrs Bentley and one of the hired men were brought to court and the man was sentenced to four years in Newgate prison.

The case of another mid-eighteenth-century female husband, Mary Hamilton, was also widely publicised. Boddely's *Bath Journal* reported:

> We hear from Taunton, that at a General Quarter Sessions of the Peace ... *Mary Hamilton*, otherwise *George*, otherwise *Charles Hamilton*, was try'd for a very singular and notorious Offence: Mr Gold, Council for the King, open'd to the Court, That the said Mary, etc. pretending herself a Man, had married fourteen Wives, the last of which Number was one Mary Price, who appeared in Court, and deposed, that she was married to the Prisoner, some little Time since, at the Parish Church of St Cuthbert's in Wells, and that they were Bedded as Man and Wife, and lived as such for about a Quarter of a Year, during which Time, she, the said Price, thought the Prisoner a Man, owing to the Prisoner's using certain vile and deceitful Practices, not fit to be mentioned.[31]

Court records show that Mary Hamilton was born in Somerset and lived afterwards in Scotland. At the age of fourteen, she left home in her brother's clothes and became a travelling quack. In May 1746, she returned to Somerset and took lodgings in Wells under the name of 'Dr Charles Hamilton'. In July of the same year, she married her landlady's niece, Mary Price. However, three months later, Mary Price discovered the deception and reported her 'husband', who was arrested and convicted on a clause of the vagrancy act. Mary Hamilton was sentenced to public whippings in four Somerset towns and six months' imprisonment in Bridewell.[32]

Social Attitudes to Female Husbands

Reactions to Mary Hamilton's masquerade demonstrate the ambiguous social attitudes towards female husbands in this period. Many female husbands were celebrated in the press and in chapbooks or pamphlets as comic heroes or 'marvels'. Mary Hamilton herself was described appreciatively by *The Bath Journal* as 'very gay, with Perriwig, Ruffles, and Breeches'.[33] In 1746, Henry Fielding made her the subject of his anonymously published pamphlet, *The Female Husband*. Despite claiming to be 'Taken From Her Own Mouth', the pamphlet provides a highly fictionalised account of Mary Hamilton's story and Fielding does not appear to have either met Mary Hamilton or researched the court records or newspaper accounts of her case.[34] Instead, he embellished the story considerably with fictionalised details, often for comic effect. Fielding's Mary Hamilton, for example, was born not in Somerset, but on the Isle of Man, while many of the central characters were represented as caricatures. An earlier wife of Hamilton's, the widow Mrs Rushford, is satirised as a sexually insatiable older woman (a sexual stereotype of the period), while Mary Price is portrayed as an incredibly naïve ingénue, a familiar Fielding character. The pamphlet veers between a satirical account of a monstrous figure, who has committed crimes against nature and a grudging admiration for a heroine who has achieved a highly successful illusion. Terry Castle has suggested that these tensions in Fielding's account reflect both his own ambiguous attitudes towards his heroine and a conflict in the intended purpose of his pamphlet. While such accounts of female husbands had traditionally appeared in pornographic texts, in which sexual encounters were described in comic or titillating detail, Fielding's *The Female Husband* was also aimed at female readers, as a moral or cautionary tale, warning against being duped by, or tempted to become, such a trickster.[35]

Legal responses to female husbands were similarly unpredictable. Elsewhere in Europe, women could be executed for passing as men or having sex with other women. In England, there were no specific laws against either sexual encounters between women or cross-dressing. However, some female husbands were prosecuted under vagrancy or fraud laws. Mary Hamilton was charged with 'Imposing on his Majesty's subjects' under a clause of the vagrancy laws.[36] The use of financial fraud laws in other cases meant that a number of instances were interpreted, or represented, in financial, rather than sexual, terms. In 1694, the Oxford antiquarian, Anthony à Wood, reported the case of a female husband in a letter to a friend. He noted:

> Appeared at the King's Bench in Westminster hall a young woman in man's apparel, or that personated a man, who was found guilty of marrying a young maid, whose portion he had obtained and was very nigh of being contracted to a second wife. Divers of her love letters were read in court, which occasioned much laughter. Upon the whole she was ordered to Bridewell to be well whipt and kept to hard labour till further order of the court.[37]

This suggestion that the young female husband had married in order to obtain the young maid's 'portion' was a frequent theme in pamphlet and press reports of female husbands. An early-eighteenth-century pamphlet, *The Counterfeit Bridegroom*, recounted the story of a woman from Southwark who, in 1695, had advertised a dowry of £200 for any man who would marry her daughter. From amongst the suitors who presented themselves, her daughter chose 'a Young Smock fac'd [pale] pretended Youth, lately arrived from Ireland, under the disguis'd name of Mr. K_ a Squires Son'. However, on the wedding night, there was no 'real Performance, excepting now and then a kiss or two' and the wife eventually became frustrated and investigated with her hand, only to find that her husband was a woman. The following morning, the female husband had escaped with the £200.[38] On 5 July 1777, the *Gentleman's Magazine* reported the case of Ann Marrow, who had been sentenced to sit in the pillory and then to six months' imprisonment 'for going in man's cloaths, and being married to three different women by a fictitious name, and for defrauding them of money and effects.' The rubbish thrown at Ann Marrow in the pillory by an angry crowd blinded her.[39]

However, although some cases undoubtedly resulted in prosecution and imprisonment, there is no evidence of any systematic policing of female husbands. Valerie Traub has argued that such cases were often resolved at community level and 'It usually took some extraordinary circumstance to motivate a community to involve local officials or for such officials to embark on a legal proceeding.'[40] Cases often only came to court if the relationship between the two women themselves broke down and the wife reported her female husband to authorities. In 1760, *The London Chronicle* reported the case of Samuel Bundy, found to be a woman, Sarah Paul, who had been committed to Southwark Bridewell prison 'for defrauding a young woman of money and apparel, by marrying her'. The paper reported, ostensibly on Bundy's account, that she had begun cross-dressing at the age of thirteen, when a male abductor had forced her to wear male clothes. Subsequently escaping from the abductor, she had begun a life at sea, but given this up in her mid-teens to work as a painter. It was at this point that she was 'taken notice of by a young woman', whom she married at the age of nineteen. There were some financial strains upon the marriage:

> Quitting her master upon some dispute between them, she was obliged to depend upon her wife for support, who expended her money and pawned her clothes for her mate's maintenance, which is the fraud she is charged with: the adopted husband says, the wife soon discovered the mistake she had made, but was determined for some time not to expose the matter.

In an attempt to resolve the financial difficulties, Samuel Bundy had twice enlisted as a sailor, but ran away on each occasion, first to avoid discovery and then 'to return to the wife, whom (she says) she dearly loves'.[41] The wife apparently became unhappy with the situation at some stage, and reported Samuel Bundy to the authorities. However, the wife also reciprocated Bundy's feelings and soon changed her mind. The paper observed, 'there seems a strong love, or friendship, on the other side, as she keeps the prisoner company in her confinement'; and a follow-up report two weeks later noted that the case against Bundy had been dismissed because 'the prosecutrix, Mary Parlour, her bride, not appearing against her, she was discharged'. The judge simply ordered Samuel Bundy's clothes to be burned and Sarah Paul 'never more to appear in that character'.[42]

The attitudes and motivations of the wives in these cases are difficult
to assess. Contemporary reports tended to gloss over the wife's role
or assume that the feminine partners of female husbands were unaware
of their husband's true sex and had been duped into marrying them.
It is certainly possible that some women were initially unaware of their
husband's sex. Mary Price, the young bride of Mary Hamilton may not
have been aware of her husband's disguise. In Fielding's account of the
case, 'something of too vile, wicked and scandalous a nature, which was
found in the Doctor's trunk', was produced to the court in evidence
of Hamilton's deception. Mary Price's deposition, contained in the court
records of case, claimed that Hamilton's use of a dildo persuaded her
for the two months of their marriage that her husband was a man:

> The said pretended Charles Hamilton ... entered her Body several
> times, which made this Examinant believe, at first, that the said
> Hamilton was a real Man, but soon had reason to Judge that the
> said Hamilton was not a Man but a Woman.[43]

However, Emma Donoghue is unconvinced, suggesting that Mary Price,
like other wives of female husbands, discovered her husband's sex
at an earlier stage, but did not report him until the relationship began
to turn sour.[44] Other wives were apparently aware of the sex of their
female husbands, but maintained the deception as they were happy
in the relationship. In January 1760, *The London Chronicle* reported the
case of John Brown, who was recognised by a former acquaintance while
trying to enlist. Brown, formerly Barbara Hill, had disappeared from
York fifteen years earlier and had subsequently worked as an apprentice
stonecutter and as a London postchaise driver. Around 1755, Brown
had married a woman 'with whom she has lived very agreeably
since'. Brown's wife was clearly very contented with her marriage:
'On [Brown's] sex being discovered after her enlisting, her supposed wife
came to town in great affliction, begging that they might not be parted.'[45]

Many women may have escaped detection altogether and successfully
passed as men throughout their lives. This is particularly likely in the case
of middle-class women, whose social position may have assisted them
in maintaining their disguise. Female husbands and passing women were
previously associated largely with working-class women, as much of the
evidence focuses on women from lower down the social scale. However,
recent research suggests that this may simply have been the result

of higher detection rates amongst working-class women, while middle-
and upper-class women might have been able to use the privileges
of wealth and greater freedom to travel, to avoid detection.[46] This theory
is supported by the case of Mary Diana Dods, the illegitimate daughter
of the fifteenth Scottish earl of Morton, in the early nineteenth century.
Dods adopted a number of male pseudonyms before emerging on the
London social scene as Walter Sholto Douglas and marrying her
pregnant friend, Isabella Robinson. The two women were assisted
by Mary Shelley to hide from society until after the birth of the baby and
then escape to Paris under false passports. The Douglases were accepted
into Paris society as man and wife and remained in Paris until Dods'
death a few years later.[47] While this case demonstrates that women from
the middle and upper classes did also consider marriage to another
woman a viable possibility, by the late 18th and early 19th century, the
framework of romantic friendship offered them a more conventional
model for the expression of love and commitment between women.

Chapter 3
Romantic Friendship, 1700–1900

The term 'Romantic friendship' was first revived by Elizabeth Mavor, in her 1971 biography of the Ladies of Llangollen. Celebrated by some of the most illustrious people of their age, upper-class Anglo-Irishwomen, Lady Eleanor Butler and the Honourable Miss Sarah Ponsonby had eloped together to Wales in 1778. There they established a home at Plas Newydd, which they shared for forty years, sleeping in the same bed, signing their correspondence jointly and addressing each other as 'my Beloved'. Eager to distance the pair from the suggestion of lesbianism which might have occurred to twentieth-century readers, Elizabeth Mavor revived the eighteenth-century term 'Romantic friendship' to describe the women's emotional but allegedly non-sexual intimacy.[1] This view has been developed extensively by lesbian feminist historians such as Carroll Smith-Rosenburg and Lillian Faderman and has become central to historians' accounts of female emotional intimacy in the eighteenth and nineteenth centuries. Arguing that middle- and upper-class feminine women would have been unable to conceive of a same-sex sexual relationship prior to the emergence of a sexological discourse on lesbianism in the late nineteenth century, Faderman characterised romantic friendships as non-sexual and indeed widely socially acceptable. In doing so, she made a clear distinction between these women and the individual cases of cross-dressing or 'transvestite' lesbians who, she claimed, adopted a male persona in order to express and act upon desire for a woman.[2]

Although male friendships had been celebrated in literature and as an important social relationship since the classical period, female friendship was not widely discussed and friendship was largely defined as male in ancient and medieval texts. However, in the mid-seventeenth century, friendships between women began to enter the public domain in European countries, largely as a result of literature celebrating female friendship by women such as the poet Katherine Philips. Female friendships were enabled by the development of institutions such as girls' boarding schools and salons, which gave women access to relationships outside the family, and friendship circles began to develop around key women such as that centred on the court of Queen Henrietta Maria and King Charles I. During the eighteenth century, poetry, novels and other literature celebrating female friendship proliferated. Inspired by the rise of the Romantic Movement and the culture of sensibility, pure friendship came to be praised as an ideal for women. Romanticism encouraged women to feel empathy for others and to reflect on their own feelings, keeping diaries to record the true emotional self, which was thought to be hidden behind the veneer of social convention. Influential literature such as Jean-Jacques Rousseau's novel *Julie, ou la nouvelle Heloise* (1761) celebrated female friendship as a representation of pure feeling.[3] With increasing levels of female literacy, a growing number of English women writers were exploring the subject in their own published writings, representing women's friendships as faithful and beautiful, in contrast to the quick-burning but transitory flame of heterosexual passion.

Early literature on female friendship, in the late seventeenth and early eighteenth centuries, included passionate declarations of romantic love and detailed descriptions of the beloved's body. Anne Killigrew, a spinster and Maid of Honour to the Duchess of York, whose poems were collected and published by her father after her death from smallpox in 1686, wrote a number of poems on female friendship. In 'On the Soft and Gentle Motions of Eudora', Killigrew compared the way in which her beloved, Eudora, moved with the gentle notes of a lute.[4] The letters exchanged by writers Elizabeth Carter and Catherine Talbot during their lifelong romantic friendship also contained numerous expressions of romantic and physical love. Elizabeth Carter wrote of her 'wild emotion' for Talbot, claiming she is 'absolutely my passion; I think of her all day, dream of her all night, and one way or other introduce her into every subject I talk of'. Talbot returned her feelings, sending her a lock of her hair and playfully worrying on one occasion that Carter had 'fallen in love with another woman, and the first is forgot'. Physical tokens of love, such as portraits in lockets or bracelets were widely carried by romantic friends and often gazed at and kissed in public.[5]

Widespread acceptance of these relationships, in an era in which marriage and motherhood were increasingly being promoted as women's primary roles, was partly the result of the social function which romantic friendships performed. Male friendship networks had been important throughout the early modern period in supplementing kinship ties and consolidating power networks, and with the rise of the gentry class in the eighteenth century, female friendship networks performed a similar function. An eighteenth-century funeral monument in Westminster Abbey demonstrates the social value of romantic friendships. The monument to Mary Kendall, who died in 1709/10, was erected by her cousin Captain Charles Kendall and referred to her 'close Union and Friendship' with Lady Catherine Jones and her desire 'That even their Ashes, after Death, Might not be divided'. Kendall was interred in the family mausoleum of the Earl of Ranelagh, as a result, and the monument represented a public testament, not just to the friendship between the two women but to the consequent ties between the Kendall family and that of the Earl of Ranelagh.[6] Although some romantic friends did remain spinsters, romantic friendship was not regarded as incompatible with marriage and was therefore not usually seen as a cause for concern. Friendships were thought to afford young women an education in romance which would lay the foundations for their future heterosexual experience. Similarly friendships were thought to complement heterosexual love, as friends could act as allies in the courtship process and later as sympathetic listeners during the occasional difficulties of marriage. Comparing friendship and heterosexual love in his *The Friendships of Women* (1867), William Rounseville Alger claimed:

> In the lives of women, friendship is, - First, the guide to love; a preliminary stage in the natural development of affection. Secondly, it is the ally of love; the distributive tendrils and branches to the root and trunk of affection. Thirdly, it is, in some cases, the purified fulfilment and repose into which love subsides, or rises. Fourthly, it is, in some cases, the comforting substitute for love.[7]

Anne Lister's Diaries

The theory that middle- and upper-class women's intimate friendships in this period were not sexual was dramatically challenged in the 1980s by the discovery of Anne Lister's diaries. Conducting research in a Yorkshire archive in 1981, local historian Helena Whitbread uncovered the diaries of an early-nineteenth-century Yorkshire gentrywoman, Anne Lister, which recounted a succession of passionate physical relationships with other women from adolescence and through-out her adult life. The diaries were written in code, based on ancient

Greek, and Whitbread deciphered them with the help of local archivists, published excerpts in 1988.[8] Born in the late eighteenth century, Anne Lister was the oldest daughter of a retired captain and gentleman farmer. However, she lived for much of her life with her aunt and uncle at the family seat, Shibden Hall in Halifax, and having proven herself capable of managing it effectively, she ultimately inherited the estate on their deaths. Lister led an outwardly respectable life and her diaries record her participation in 'the cosy domestic universe of a Jane Austen novel', regularly visiting local gentry families, playing backgammon and whist with her aunt and uncle, doing needlework and playing the flute.[9] However, the diaries also point to a succession of sexual affairs with other women and record the occasions on which she experienced an orgasm, referred to in code as a 'kiss' and further identified by a cross in the margin of her journal. In an entry of 18 November 1819, Lister described a night of passion with her long-term lover, Marianna:

> From the kiss she gave me it seemed as if she loved me as fondly as ever. By & by, we seemed to drop asleep but by & by, I perceived she would like another kiss & she whispered, 'Come again a bit, Freddy.' For a little while I pretended sleep. In fact, it was inconvenient. But soon, I got up a second time, again took off, went to her a second time &, in spite of all, she really gave me pleasure, & I told her no one had ever given me kisses like hers.[10]

Lister's first affair had occurred at boarding school, with Eliza Raine, the daughter of a West Indian planter. By 1819, she was simultaneously engaged in three sexual affairs: one with Isabella (Tib) Norcliffe, one with Marianna Belcombe and another with Marianna's sister, Anne. At the same time she was amusing herself in a flirtation with a local girl, Miss Browne, whom she only succeeded in kissing before the girl became abruptly engaged. Isabella Norcliffe was a frequent visitor at Shibden Hall and was apparently devoted to Lister, suggesting in 1819 that they marry 'in disguise at the altar'. However, the affair was not a passionate one, and in October 1821, Lister noted:

> A kiss [orgasm] of Tib, both last night & this morning, but she cannot give me much pleasure & I think we are both equally calm in our feelings on these occasions.[11]

Marianna Belcombe, with whom Lister had been engaged in an ongoing
affair since 1812, was apparently the love of her life and the diary
includes numerous references to their passionate physical relationship.
However, Marianna was the penniless daughter of a doctor and was
therefore forced to marry for money, which caused some difficulties
for the women. Marianna worried that their affair was 'unnatural' and
was anxious about discovery, while Lister attempted unsuccessfully
to separate Marianna from her husband and complained in her diary
that Marianna sometimes lacked sensibility. Marianna's marriage was
clearly also problematic in itself and in 1821 Marianna and Anne became
infected with a venereal disease which they believed Marianna had
caught from her husband. The relationship waned in 1824, when Lister
set out on travels around Europe, during which time she had affairs with
two other women, Maria Barlow and Madame de Rosny. On her return
she established a long-term relationship with a local heiress, Anne
Walker, whom she lived and travelled with from 1832 until her own
death in 1840.[12]

The discovery of Anne Lister's diaries clearly refuted the argument
that before the late nineteenth century, women were unable to imagine
sexual relationships with other women and forced historians to reassess
the notion of romantic friendships as unquestionably non-sexual.
Subsequent research has uncovered further evidence that the distinction
between respectable, non-sexual romantic friendships and lesbian sexual
relationships was not as clear as Faderman and others had suggested.
While late-seventeenth- and early-eighteenth-century literature on female
friendship contained frequent references to the beloved's body, by the
mid-eighteenth century, such physical descriptions were beginning
to disappear from published literature. Martha Vicinus has argued
that in the second half of the eighteenth century, women's sexual love
became increasingly marginalised and intimate female friendships came
to be divided into two types: sensual romantic friendship and sexual
Sapphism. In England, the Romantic ideal of pure friendship was
contrasted with the sexual freedoms evident in the French court in the
years before the French Revolution. Rumours about Marie-Antoinette's
alleged Sapphic orgies, which were circulating in political pamphlets
and pornography in England in the late eighteenth century, made the
English gentry classes more cautious in the expression of same-sex love.
As a result, although the convention of sentimentalised romantic

friendship continued into the nineteenth century, friendships which
were based on a spiritual and not a physical love were regarded
as morally superior.[13]

Novels and other literature on female friendship increasingly made
a distinction between appropriate and inappropriate relationships in this
period. Late-eighteenth-century women's writing frequently explored
the theme of conflicting types of sensibility: heroines were depicted
attempting to discern the line between acceptably feminine, virtuous
sensibility and dangerous, impure, erotic sensibility. While sensibility
remained a virtue into the nineteenth century, novels warned against
immoderate sensibility which could become excessive and frequently
indicated illicit erotic desire. In Samuel Richardson's *Sir Charles
Grandison* (1753–1754), Miss Barnevelt epitomises the dangers of erotic
sensibility. Described as loud and assertive, with masculine features,
she exploits the conventions of romantic friendship to take inappropriate
liberties with other ladies. However, the heroine, Harriet Byron, is not
deceived and dislikes her from the outset. Describing an encounter with
Miss Barnevelt, she observes:

> Miss Barnevelt said, she had from the moment I first enter'd
> beheld me with the eye of a Lover. And freely taking my hand,
> squeezed it. – Charming creature! said she, as if addressing
> a country innocent, and perhaps expecting me to be covered
> with blushes and confusion.[14]

The absence of appropriate femininity was frequently used to distinguish
between acceptable and suspect romantic friendships in literature.
In Maria Edgeworth's *Belinda* (1801), the inappropriate romantic friend,
Mrs Harriot Freke, is represented as a comic oddity who cross-dresses,
while the Amazonian Miss Sandford and the bluestocking Lady
Cornelia Classick in Charlotte Lennox's *Euphemia* (1790) are depicted
as a strangely masculine pair who render men redundant. Historian
Katherine Binhammer has argued that pain and suffering also emerged
as a literary device indicating illicit erotic sensibility in this period.
'Pain', she argues, 'functions as sexual desire' in novels such as Mary
Wollstonecraft's *Mary*, where the heroine is depicted as going
to considerable lengths to care for her invalid friend Ann.[15]

Outside the realm of fiction, the distinction between virtuous and
illicit relationships was often less clear. Although the Ladies of Llangollen

were widely celebrated in their own time as the epitome of virtuous romantic friendship, even they were not entirely above suspicion. Despite having apparently maintained cordial relations with the women for some time, their neighbour, the diarist Hester Thrale Piozzi, privately referred to Ponsonby and Butler and their friends as 'damned sapphists' and claimed that this was why various literary women refused to stay overnight in their house unless accompanied by a man.[16] Their contemporary, Anne Lister, expressed similar doubts in her diary after a visit to Plas Newydd in 1822. She speculated:

> Foolscap sheet from M[arianna] … She seems much interested about Lady Eleanor Butler & Miss Ponsonby and I am agreeably surprised (never dreaming of such a thing) at her observation, 'The account of your visit is the prettiest narrative I have read. You have at once excited and gratified my curiosity. Tell me if you think their regard has always been platonic & if you ever believed pure friendship could be so exalted. If you do, I shall think there are brighter amongst mortals than I ever believed there were …'
> I cannot help thinking surely it was not platonic. Heaven forgive me, but I look within myself & doubt. I feel the infirmity of our nature and hesitate to pronounce such attachments uncemented by something more tender still than friendship.[17]

Despite her outwardly respectable life and accepted position amongst the gentry families of the locality, Anne Lister herself was also subject to occasional suspicion. In 1818, she recorded in her journal 'how the people generally remark, as I pass along, how much I am like a man'.[18] On another occasion she notes that, while on an evening walk along Cunnery Lane, some labourers had accosted her: 'three men said, as usual, "That's a man" and one axed "Does your cock stand?"'[19] As in fiction, a lack of appropriate femininity was often the focus for contemporaries' suspicions. As she grew older, Lister increasingly adopted a masculine style, dressing entirely in black and assuming 'gentlemanly' manners towards women. Lister's masculine appearance was a source of concern for her lover, Marianna, who apparently felt it might arouse suspicions of the type insinuated by the passing labourers in 1818.[20] The Ladies of Llangollen were subjected to similar suggestions in a local newspaper article. In a report on the couple in *The General Evening Post* on 24 July 1790, the pair was represented as a masculine/feminine couple. The journalist observed:

> Miss Butler is tall and masculine, she wears always a riding habit, hangs her hat with the air of a sportsman in the hall, and appears in all respects as a young man, if we except the petticoats which she still retains. Miss Ponsonby, on the contrary, is polite and effeminate, fair and beautiful.

As Eleanor Butler was in fact a short, plump fifty-one-year-old matron at the time of the article, the description was perhaps intended to indicate suspicions regarding the nature of the couple's relationship, rather than providing an accurate account of their appearance. The Ladies were certainly concerned by the implications of the article and wrote to the Tory politician Edmund Burke to request advice on how to prosecute the paper.[21]

The manner in which contemporaries interpreted individual relationships was clearly open to negotiation, and it was possible for astute women to manipulate their personal image. The Ladies of Llangollen apparently engaged in an ongoing and often highly successful public relations campaign intended to diffuse any potential scandal surrounding them. They cultivated friendships with influential figures of the age and, in particular, with literary individuals who would be likely to defend them in print. In 1796, Anna Seward published a poem entitled 'Llangollen Vale' praising the 'vestal lustre' of their 'sacred Friendship', while in 1824 William Wordsworth dedicated a sonnet to them, celebrating the 'Vale of Friendship':

> Where, faithful to a low-roofed Cot
> On Deva's banks, ye have abode so long;
> Sisters in love, a love allowed to climb
> Even on this earth, above the reach of Time![22]

The language of sisterhood employed by Wordsworth was widely used by writers on female friendship in this period to diffuse any suspicion regarding the nature of the relationship. Writers similarly drew on classical names and natural imagery in fictional representations in an attempt to lend the friendship a classical nobility and purity.

Class and Romantic Friendship

Although upper-class female relationships can no longer be seen
as straightforwardly non-sexual, class was nevertheless an important
aspect of romantic friendships. The new gentry class, which had emerged
by the beginning of the eighteenth century, used gendered notions
of respectability to distinguish itself from both a supposedly debauched
aristocracy and ill-mannered working class. Advice literature emphasised
virtuous conduct for women and appropriate female friendship
marked gentry women as well bred and therefore reinforced their
class status. Literature confirmed this notion of virtuous female
friendship as restricted to the gentry class. Sarah Scott's *A Description
of Millenium Hall* (1762) depicted a female utopia in which upper-class
female friends lived together in a close-knit community. While the
upper-class women are 'so strongly united' in affection 'that one could
not suffer without the other's feeling equal pain', the working-class
women who share the utopia live separately in individual cottages where
they get along 'better, than if we lived together', for they 'used to quarrel'
until 'the ladies … shewed us so kindly how much it was our duty
to agree'.[23]

Drawing on these perceptions of virtuous friendship as primarily
upper-class, individual women were able to use their class status
as a means of demonstrating the respectability of their relationships.
The Ladies of Llangollen and Anne Lister bolstered their class status and
therefore their respectability in a number of ways, such as demonstrating
wealth by carrying out improvements to their property and choosing
their company carefully. Eleanor Butler and Sarah Ponsonby took pains
to create a pastoral idyll at Plas Newydd, while Lister went into serious
debt in order to carry out renovations at Shibden Hall. Both built
reputations as literary and educated women and cultivated friendships
with upper-class friends. Anne Lister was apparently aware of the
importance of being seen to keep good company, observing in her diary,
after an incident in which an 'impertinent' carter had asked her if she
'want[ed] a sweetheart':

It will be a lesson to me to take care whom I talk to in future.
One can hardly carry oneself too high or keep people at too
great a distance.[24]

The Ladies of Llangollen were also sensitive in their relationships with people lower down the social scale, being overbearing with servants and notorious for paying low wages and making unreasonable demands. Butler and Ponsonby were equally conservative in their political views, expressing opinions which were more conservative than other women of their class and period. They were passionate royalists from the outset of the French Revolution, believed slavery improved the condition of Africans and were outspoken on issues of morality, advocating the branding of adulterers and expressing outrage at the supposed immorality of the French. Anne Lister was also both socially and politically conservative, complaining about Manchester's rioting workers at Peterloo and arguing that women should not learn the classics for fear of being polluted by them, despite having done so herself.[25]

However, although romantic friendship was widely associated with the upper-classes and much of the literature on the subject was produced by gentry women, emotional friendships also existed between working-class women. Charlotte Charke's account of her adventures as a cross-dressing actress, *Narrative of the Life of Mrs Charlotte Charke* (1755), refers to an actress friend who shared Charlotte's travels. The pair met in the 1740s and, when Charlotte left her troupe of actors in 1749 to take to the road as 'Mr Brown', her friend accompanied her as 'Mrs Brown'. Although there are few explicit references to the relationship between the two women, it is clear that the women regarded their relationship as a partnership, raising Charlotte's daughter together and supporting each other through financial difficulties. Such accounts of working-class female friendship are rare. However, Emma Donoghue argues:

> The problem seems to be one of different kinds of evidence.
> In general, middle-class women's romantic friendships were
> described in pious poems and novels, which did not give sexual
> details, whereas working-class women's lives were represented
> in the bawdier and more hostile genres of medical treatises
> and criminal biographies.

Nevertheless, she continues: 'I have found no reason to believe that friendship was limited to the upper-classes of women-loving women, nor sex to the lower.'[26]

Romantic Friendship and Conventional Femininity

The extent to which women were seen to fulfil conventional feminine roles and obligations was also central to the way that their friendships with other women were interpreted. Women who combined romantic friendships with spinsterhood or resisted marriage in other ways were more vulnerable to criticism than those who conformed to marital expectations. Historians have noted that, while spinster writers were increasingly careful to avoid celebrating the beloved's body in literature from the early eighteenth century onwards, some married women writers continued to do so throughout the eighteenth century. Nevertheless, marriage was not always sufficient to protect women's friendships from suspicion, particularly if women's commitment to marriage was open to question. The romantic friendship between Katharine Bovey, who died in 1727, and Mary Pope was celebrated in a monument erected by Pope after Bovey's death. After extolling the virtues of Katharine Bovey, it stated:

> This monument was erected With the utmost respect to her Memory and Justice to her Character, By her executrix Mrs MARY POPE Who lived with her near 40 years in perfect Friendship Never once interrupted Till her much lamented Death.[27]

Despite the fact that both women had previously been married, their friendship appears to have attracted some negative comment. It is likely that Bovey was the inspiration for the fictional 'Perverse Widow', criticised in *The Spectator* on 10 July 1711 as beautiful, accomplished, but uninterested in men. Richard Steele also satirically dedicated Volume II of *The Ladies Library* to her, explaining that the perversity of this woman resided in the fact that she ensnared men's hearts, only to reject them, while her female companion watched, a humiliation which had been experienced by his friend, 'Sir Roger de Coverley'. Donald F. Bond, editor of the Oxford edition of *The Spectator*, explained:

> Mrs Catherine Bovey (or Boevey), the supposed original of this character, became a widow in 1692, at the age of twenty-two, upon the death of her husband William Bovey. She thereupon lived

in retirement in the Manor of Flaxley, near Gloucester, devoting
herself to religious and charitable works, in company with a friend,
Mrs Mary Pope of Twickenham.[28]

Having been widowed at such a young age and without children,
Katherine Bovey might have been expected to remarry and her failure
to do so, despite having received offers of marriage, was sufficient
to draw negative comment on her friendship with Mary Pope.

   Although the majority of literature on female friendship in this period
tended to stress the role of friendship in preparing for and supporting
marriage, a number of texts by women writers in the late seventeenth
and early eighteenth centuries criticised marriage. Mary Astell, who came
from a family of wealthy Newcastle coal merchants, wrote two feminist
treatises advocating spinsterhood in this period. Both her *A Serious
Proposal to the Ladies* (1694–1697) and *Some Reflections upon
Marriage* (1700) proved very influential despite going quickly out
of print. Other texts specifically linked disdain for marriage with female
friendship, suggesting that women only had the time and freedom
to devote to female friends if they remained unmarried. Jane Barker's
Love Intrigues (1713) and *A Patchwork Screen for the Ladies* (1723)
depicted the adventures of a spinster heroine, Galesia, and the support
she received from numerous female friends along the way.[29] Other
literature by women writers bemoaned the marriage of female friends,
representing marriage as the 'tomb of friendship'. In fiction and personal
letters and memoirs, women described their fears that conformity
to a husband's demands and commitment to new interests would take
married women away from their female friends and cause them to forget
their love for each other. In a sonnet sequence addressed to her beloved,
Honora Sneyd, written over a period of several years before and after
Sneyd's marriage to Richard Edgeworth, Anna Seward described
her sense of betrayal at the marriage and her fears of further loss
in the future:

> Honora, should that cruel time arrive
> When 'gainst my truth thou should'st my errors poise,
> Scorning remembrance of our vanish'd joys;
> When for the love-warm looks, in which I live,
> But cold respect must greet me, that shall give
> No tender glance, no kind regretful sighs;

When thou shalt pass me with averted eyes,
Feigning thou see'st me not, to sting, and grieve,
And sicken my sad heart, I could not bear
Such dire eclipse of thy soul-cheering rays;
I could not learn my struggling heart to tear
From thy loved form, that thro' my memory strays;
Nor in the pale horizon of despair
Endure the wintry and the darken'd days.[30]

While these concerns continued to be expressed in personal letters and
private writings throughout the century, by the mid-eighteenth century,
overt attacks on marriage had almost disappeared from published works
by women writers. The promotion of marriage and motherhood as the
primary roles for women increased in the context of the expanding
British Empire, so that attacks on marriage came to be regarded as both
unfeminine and unpatriotic. Literature from the mid-century onwards
sought to justify spinsterhood rather than proclaim its advantages.
In Sarah Robinson Scott's *A Description of Millenium Hall* (1762),
the upper-class female characters are justified in their unmarried status
by their active role in promoting marriage amongst the poor girls of the
parish. Literary heroines and spinster writers alike defended themselves
by adopting the pretext of an earlier disappointment in love or referring
to a disability, which had ostensibly prevented their marriage. The
depiction of female friendships as part of a love triangle with a man also
became a common theme in women's writing. In Catherine Trotter's play
Agnes de Castro (1696), one of the women is emotionally torn between
her affection for a female friend and her love for a man. In Sarah
Fielding's novel *Familiar Letters* (1747), women's friendship overcomes
heterosexual rivalry, enabling a woman to put the future happiness
of her friend with a man before her own marriage chances.[31]

In the context of the increasing social pressure on women to marry,
women who wished to focus their lives on a romantic friendship faced
a number of practical difficulties. In a period in which the large majority
of women were financially dependent on male relatives, the lack
of economic means to establish a joint home was a significant obstacle.
The Ladies of Llangollen were fortunate – and unusual – in receiving
a small allowance from their families, sufficient to support themselves
in respectable independence. For others, such as the novelist Charlotte
Brontë and her lifelong romantic friend, Ellen Nussey, a joint home

remained an unattainable dream. The pair had met at school in 1831 and continued a close and passionate friendship throughout their lives, visiting each other frequently after leaving school, sharing a bed when together and exchanging letters complaining about their separation when apart. In the years after leaving school, the idea of living together was frequently discussed by the women. In 1836, Brontë wrote to Nussey:

> Ellen, I wish I could live with you always. I begin to cling
> to you more fondly than ever I did. If we had but a cottage
> and a competency of our own, I do think we might live and love
> on to Death without being dependent on any third person
> for happiness.[32]

Without an independent income, however, the women were unable to establish a joint home and continued to live in their respective family homes for much of their adult lives. For many unmarried women in this period, regardless of class, family responsibilities represented a further tie to the family home. Spinster daughters were widely expected to assume responsibility for caring for unwell or widowed parents and Charlotte Brontë's responsibility for her ailing father both tied her to live in his home and frequently prevented her even from visiting Ellen Nussey.

Social attitudes towards appropriate behaviour for women in this period also restricted women's freedom of movement. When Ellen Nussey wrote to suggest a short holiday together in Bridlington in 1839, Brontë replied: 'Your proposal has almost driven me clean daft ... The fact is, an excursion with you, anywhere, whether to Cleethorps or Canada, just by ourselves, would be to me most delightful.' However, a number of practical obstacles and family difficulties immediately arose, and when Nussey finally took matters in her own hands and appeared unexpectedly in a borrowed carriage to collect Brontë, their families were shocked. Ellen's brother, Henry, immediately sent an urgent message to some family friends, the Hudsons, asking them to meet the young women at the other end, thus limiting the possible impropriety of two young unmarried women travelling unaccompanied and independently. The Hudsons found Brontë and Nussey and took them to their house, where Ellen subsequently wrote that they were 'entertained and detained for a month', before finally being allowed one week's holiday alone in Bridlington.[33]

Although romantic friendships were widely accepted amongst schoolgirls and younger women as an educational precursor to marriage, as women became older their passionate relationships with other women were more likely to be regarded with social and familial disapproval. Charlotte Brontë increasingly worried in her letters to Ellen Nussey in the years after they left school that her feelings for Ellen were too passionate, and might be disapproved of. Similarly, *The General Evening Post* article on the Ladies of Llangollen in 1790 noted that Butler and Ponsonby's friendship had been the object of concern to their families even before their elopement to Wales. Eleanor Butler, the *Post* noted, had received and rejected several proposals of marriage and, as 'her particular friend and companion, [Sarah Ponsonby] was supposed to be the bar to all matrimonial union, it was thought proper to separate them, and Miss Butler was confined'.[34] As literature by women writers indicated, romantic friendships and marriage were often not as compatible as some male advice literature optimistically assumed. Romantic friendships could be a motivation for marriage resistance for some women, as in the case of Eleanor Butler. Charlotte Brontë also refused at least three proposals of marriage in her youth, while Ellen Nussey resisted marriage throughout her life. For other women, marriage to a romantic friend's male relation might appear a suitable compromise. When Ellen Nussey's brother, Henry, proposed to Charlotte in 1839, she wrote to Ellen that she had been tempted to accept in order to be able to live with Ellen, but ultimately she could not agree.[35] For Charlotte and other women, fears that marriage would limit their independence further and restrict their access to their female friends proved to be well founded. In 1854, Charlotte Brontë married her father's curate, Arthur Bell Nicholls, apparently with some reluctance and simply in order to ensure that her elderly father could remain living in his vicarage, while Bell performed his duties for him. Brontë wrote to her publisher, George Smith, shortly before her marriage:

> My expectations however are very subdued – very different I dare
> say, to what yours were before you married. Care and Fear stand
> so close to Hope I sometimes scarcely can see her for the shadows
> they cast.[36]

Letters written after the marriage suggest that she regretted the step and found Nicholls' restrictions on her time and friendships difficult to bear. Nicholls insisted that Brontë destroy the letters Nussey had written her over the years, objecting to their 'passionate language' and subsequently checked Brontë's letters before she sent them. He and Nussey were not on friendly terms and he prevented Charlotte and Ellen from meeting on several occasions before Brontë's sudden death from excessive morning sickness in 1855.

Romantic Friendship and the Construction of Identity

Ongoing research since the discovery of Anne Lister's diaries has enriched our understanding of romantic friendship in the eighteenth and nineteenth centuries. In place of the strict opposition of appropriate 'pure' romantic friendships with scandalous sexual relationships between women, a new picture has emerged of more fluid attitudes to female friendship in which factors such as the women's age, marital status and class background shaped the interpretation of individual relationships. Although women's outward behaviour and friendship models were, to an extent, constrained by contemporary norms of femininity, some individuals drew on these fluid notions of friendship and femininity to develop a personal sense of identity. Individual attitudes to sexual identity varied among specific women, with some developing a clearly sexual identity based around their same-sex desires, while other women created a more discreet and ambiguous identity which emphasised affection and love rather than desire.

Anne Lister's diary itself represents valuable evidence of this process, documenting Lister's painstaking construction of an individual sexual identity from the cultural resources available to her. Anne possessed a clear sense of her own sexual desires, claiming: 'I love, & only love, the fairer sex & thus beloved by them in turn, my heart revolts from any other love than theirs.'[37] Her diaries not only chart the course of her various love affairs with women, but also describe her methodical attempts to construct a sense of identity based on these desires. Although explicit literary references to female same-sex desire were scarce, Lister drew on a range of classical and Romantic literature to piece together a unique identity. Learning Latin and Greek for the purpose, Lister read widely in classical literature. In particular, the Roman satires of Juvenal and Martial and the poetry of Sappho provided her with an awareness of ancient homosexuality and a language in which to describe sexual practices. In her own era, the literature of the Romantics offered a model of male libertinism, which she was able to identify with. Rousseau's

Confessions enabled her to regard her passion for women as natural, while Byron's poetry, including *Don Juan*, reinforced her sense of herself as a romantic sexual adventurer and womaniser. Such careful construction of a sexual identity from a wide range of available sources demonstrates that it was possible for women to develop an identity based on their desire for other women, even in the absence of an explicit language of lesbianism.

Moreover, Lister's diary shows that her sources could also be used to identify sympathetic women. Lister described using classical references as a coded method of ascertaining other women's sexuality and reported similar enquiries being made of her. Suspecting that an acquaintance, Miss Pickford, may have had a sexual interest in women, Anne asked her if she was familiar with the Sixth Satire of Juvenal and interpreted her affirmative response as evidence of her sexuality. Some years later, while travelling in France, a fellow lodger of Lister's, Miss Mack, used a reference to Achilles to discreetly enquire about Anne's own sexuality. Such incidents suggest that, despite social conventions which emphasised the sexual innocence of women and their friendships, some women were both aware of the possibility of same-sex desire between women and able to develop a sexual identity based on that desire.[38]

Other women expressed their love for members of their own sex in a more discreet and less explicitly sexual way. The language of pain or illness was sometimes employed to articulate erotic bonds which women were otherwise unable to express. This seems to have been the case in the ambiguously erotic relationship between the Ladies of Llangollen. Eleanor Butler's journal carefully records a number of instances when Sarah Ponsonby went to considerable lengths to nurse Butler through migraines. An entry for 2 December 1785 notes:

> I kept my bed all day with one of My dreadful Headaches. My Sally.
> My Tender, My Sweet Love lay beside me holding and supporting
> My Head till one o'clock when I by Much entreaty prevailed with
> her to rise and get my breakfast.

Another on 6 December records:

> Rose at Eight after a tedious night Spent in coughing and with
> a most dreadful head ache. My dearest. My Kindest love did
> not sleep even for one moment the entire night but lay beside

me watching and lamenting my illness and soothing by her
tenderness the distressing pain of My Head.

In her biography of the women, Elizabeth Mavor speculated whether
'such meticulous recordings of migraines ... could be read as code;
as the only permissible expression of a yet more intimate relationship;
or as the unconscious expression of a desire for such a relationship'[39]
Katherine Binhammer agrees that this concern with illness is emotionally
significant, reflecting that 'While I would not call it a "code", concealing
a more authentic sexual relationship underneath, I do suggest that pain
and suffering here, and in other scenes of romantic friendship, unleash
erotic desire. The sickbed replaces the sexual bed as the space for that
exquisite desire.'[40]

Chapter 4
'New Women', 1850–1900

In the last decades of the nineteenth century, debates about gender
and female sexuality came to be dominated by the figure of the 'New
Woman', a term used by contemporaries who believed that they were
seeing the emergence of a modern type of woman, obsessed – supposedly –
with novel experiences and sensations, sometimes of a sexual nature.
A highly contested concept, the New Woman represented a number
of frequently conflicting ideas, to a range of different commentators. For
many feminists, who had been campaigning for expanding educational,
employment and political rights for women, the New Woman was an
independent and pioneering woman who fought for and embodied these
new opportunities. In the cartoons and articles of newspapers and the
periodical press, she offered a simple visual target for satirical attacks
which mocked feminism and the perceived threat to the conventional
gender order posed by New Women. Finally, she appeared as a familiar
character in the 'New Women' novels which burst onto the scene in the
1880s and 1890s. Between 1883 and 1900, over one hundred novels,
many of them written by New Women novelists, were published,
exploring current ideas about women's social role, sexuality and gender
identity. In the context of these conflicting notions of the New Woman,
it was frequently unclear even to contemporaries exactly who the
New Woman was, prompting the novelist Sarah Grand to ask:

> Who is this New Woman, this epicene creature, this Gorgon set
> up by the snarly who impute to her all the faults of both sexes
> while denying her the charm of either – where is she to be found
> if she exists at all? For my own part, until I make her acquaintance
> I shall believe her to be the finest work of imagination which the
> newspapers have yet produced.[1]

Mrs M. Eastwood made a similar distinction in her article, 'The New
Woman in Fiction and in Fact', which appeared in *The Humanitarian*
in 1894. She suggested that, while the 'New Woman' who appeared
in fiction threatened social disruption and was simply a product of some
women's overwrought imaginations, the real New Woman was in fact

much more suited to the real world and to undertaking necessary social and sexual reforms.[2] In both her fictional and actual forms, the New Woman offered a range of possibilities for the expression of desire between women. New Woman characters in fiction were often depicted in close, 'romantic' friendships with other women and possessed the masculine characteristics and appearance which were beginning to be attributed to female 'inverts' or homosexuals by sexual scientists. The financial independence and expanding social role sought by real New Women also promoted greater intimacy between women, enabling pioneering women to reject marriage and motherhood in favour of an intimate and supportive relationship with another woman. At the root of this emerging model of femininity were changing attitudes towards sexuality and the development of an organised feminist movement in the nineteenth century.

Victorian Sexuality

By the late eighteenth century, attitudes towards sexuality had begun to shift and take on greater social significance in British culture. The Victorian age has conventionally been regarded as synonymous with sexual repression, Puritanism and hypocrisy. However, in recent decades historians have argued that the picture is more complex and that in fact, as a result of the Victorians' energetic attempts to control sexuality, the nineteenth century saw an explosion of interest in, and debate about, sex. Jeffrey Weeks has claimed that in this period, sex 'acquires a peculiar significance in structuring ideology and social and political practices, and in shaping individual responses'.[3] He suggests that sexuality became a significant part of the social consciousness from the end of the eighteenth century, demonstrated by its appearance as a topic of parliamentary debate from the 1850s onwards, the emergence of birth-control propaganda and sexual advice manuals in the early nineteenth century, the development of pornography as a modern phenomenon in the mid-eighteenth century and increasing scientific categorisation of sexuality in the nineteenth century. However, attitudes to sexuality continued to be shaped by long-standing ideas, including the influence of religious codes of morality and chastity and the double standard in implementing these values, which enforced chastity on the female but allowed a large degree of sexual freedom to the male.

The debate intensified in the nineteenth century as new social conflicts arising from changing class and power relations were to a large extent expressed in terms of gender and sexuality.

One central focus of attention was the family, which took on increasing ideological significance in the nineteenth century, its growing social importance linked to a new perception of the family as the basic unit of society. While earlier models had located the family within a broader social network of neighbours and extended kin, the new modern version was a smaller, more inward-looking and emotional unit, with marriages increasingly founded on love and romance rather than social alliance. Changes in the family also reflected wider social changes during the Industrial Revolution, which facilitated the rise of the middle class to become the dominant class in British society by the nineteenth century. Differing social practices and ideologies became important in distinguishing between the classes, and the middle class increasingly emphasised morally ordered, loving homes, hard work and sensible spending. This new middle class ideology was bolstered by an evangelical revival in Methodist and Church of England communities in the late eighteenth century, which sought to 'rechristianise' the country and the family.[4]

The rise of this new domestic ideology had a significant impact on notions of women's social roles and sexuality. An emerging practical and ideological separation of home and work was linked with an emphasis on the home as a place of peace and refuge. As this notion of 'separate spheres' developed, middle-class women tended to withdraw from the workplace into the home, while the public spheres of work and politics were redefined in more narrowly masculine terms. Literary works and advice books reinforced the ideological emphasis on women's place in the domestic sphere and argued that men and women were naturally suited to the roles they were assigned in society.

In his influential poem 'The Angel in the House' (1854), Coventry Patmore defined women as innately emotional, nurturing and passive, dedicated to placing the happiness of their husbands and children before their own. Evangelical cultural commentator John Ruskin noted that these characteristics were complemented by the natural rationality and activity of men:

Now their separate characters are briefly these: The man's power is active, progressive, defensive. He is eminently the doer, the creator, the discoverer, the defender. His intellect is for speculation and invention; his energy for adventure, for war, and for conquest, wherever war is just, wherever conquest necessary. But the woman's power is for rule, not for battle,—and her intellect is not for invention or creation, but for sweet ordering, arrangement, and decision ... Her great function is Praise.[6]

Chastity, historically important in attitudes to female sexuality, became increasingly significant in the nineteenth century in the context of changing practices of property inheritance, reinforced in middle-class ideology through a belief in women's sexual passivity or asexuality.[7] While married women were expected to submit to intercourse with their husbands in the interests of producing children and satisfying male sexual desire, advice literature and medical texts widely assumed that women had little interest in sex on their own account.

Historians and contemporary commentators have noted an increasing trend towards homosocial structures in middle-class society as a result of the ideology of separate spheres. Ideas about the fundamentally different characteristics of men and women combined with social practices based around distinct spheres of influence meant that women spent the majority of their lives in the company of their own sex, while men socialised with other men at work, in gentlemen's clubs and in Parliament. These homosocial practices meant that men and women frequently found that they had few, if any, interests or pursuits in common, with the result that, as an anonymous writer observed in 1857, it was almost 'impossible ... [in the middle classes] for the sexes to break ground on any but the most commonplace topics of conversation'.[8] Instead, women frequently turned to each other for emotional support and understanding.

The Rise of Feminism

The confinement of middle-class women to the domestic sphere and the emergence of homosocial structures in middle- and upper-class society have been seen as important factors in the rise of feminism in this period. In 1792, Mary Wollstonecraft published her pioneering work, *Vindication of the Rights of Woman*, demanding equal educational, employment and political rights for women and an end to the sexual

double standard. She argued that women were made trivial and
incapable of true virtue by their lack of education and, unless they
were allowed to develop themselves, would never be able to take
a responsible role in society. In 1823, Harriet Martineau took up the
call for greater educational opportunities for girls and, by the 1850s,
a number of women's groups had been founded to campaign on this
issue. The campaign enjoyed considerable success, and a number
of significant advances were made in this area in the nineteenth century.
In 1858, a Royal Commission recommended the establishment of girls'
secondary schools, which would teach household management
to middle-class girls, and attendance at elementary schools, founded
and financed by the state for working-class girls, became compulsory
in 1880. Women began to gain access to higher education in the late
nineteenth century, with King's College, London, admitting women for
the first time in 1847. The Education Act (1870) allowed women to vote
and serve on local school boards and enabled universities to grant
degrees to women and a number of women's colleges, such as Bedford
College for Women (1849), were founded in this period.[9]

Employment opportunities became an important area of feminist
concern during the nineteenth century. While middle- and upper-class
women were raised in the expectation that they would marry and be
financially supported as wives and mothers, this was not a practical option
for all women, even supposing they wished it. A growing gender
imbalance in the population meant that women outnumbered men and,
by 1851, just under one quarter of women of marriageable age under
thirty were single.[10] The problem of these so-called 'superfluous women'
led to growing feminist pressure for greater employment opportunities
to enable unmarried women to support themselves. Occupational
choices for middle- and upper-class women were extremely restricted
in this period, with writing or acting as a governess, lady's companion or
seamstress, the only respectable options for women of this class. However,
by the late nineteenth century, employment opportunities for middle- and
upper-class women had begun to expand. The numbers of professional
women increased from 106,000 in 1861 to 429,000 in 1901, with women
increasingly working as teachers and as clerks in the Post Office. By 1895,
264 women were registered as doctors. Other opportunities opened up for
working-class women, as domestic servants and in laundries.[11]

Political rights for women, including the vote, were a further area
of feminist concern in the nineteenth century. Sporadic calls for the

enfranchisement of women began in response to the Reform Bill (1832), which was the first piece of legislation to explicitly exclude women from the vote. In 1865, the election of a reforming government held out the promise of suffrage reform and John Stuart Mill, a Liberal MP, tabled an amendment including women's suffrage to the Reform Bill (1867). He was unsuccessful, but suffrage societies were formed to support the campaign, and over 100,000 signatures were obtained on a petition asking for female suffrage. Many of these smaller suffrage societies came together to form the National Union of Women's Suffrage Societies (NUWSS) in 1897 under the leadership of Millicent Fawcett and continued to apply political pressure through parliamentary lobbying, working with both the Liberal and the Labour parties. In 1903, the NUWSS was joined by another significant group, the Women's Social and Political Union (WSPU), established by Emmeline Pankhurst, in conjunction with a number of women who had been working among the factory women of Manchester. From 1905 onwards, the WSPU made use of militant campaigning tactics, disrupting Liberal party meetings, breaking windows, starting fires and going on hunger strike. These tactics provoked considerable opposition to the suffrage cause and the government used this suffragette action to justify the continued exclusion of women from the suffrage. Nevertheless, in 1918, women over the age of thirty who were householders or the wives of householders were granted the vote and, in 1928, this was extended to include all women aged over twenty-one.[12]

The WSPU attracted a high proportion of single women, with almost all the full-time organisers and 63 percent of those making donations in 1913–1914 being unmarried.[13] For some single women who were attracted to other women, such as the suffragette Micky Jacob, the movement encouraged them to consider new options:

> Looking back, I think that the Suffragettes helped me to – get free. I met women who worked, women who had ambitions, and some who had gratified those ambitions. I looked at my own position, and began to think and think hard.[14]

Others met partners and lovers through the movement. The composer Ethel Smyth, who contributed the suffrage anthem, *The March of the Women*, was well known for her attraction to other women and may have had an affair with Emmeline Pankhurst. Edy Craig and Christopher

St John (Christabel Marshall), who lived together for forty-eight years from 1899 until Edy's death, were also active in the WSPU, committing militant acts and contributing to propaganda through plays such as *Votes for Women* (1909).[15]

Independent Women

These suffragists were among a number of women who took advantage of the emerging educational and employment opportunities in the late nineteenth century to lead independent lives and develop careers and relationships away from family networks. Constance Maynard left what Martha Vicinus describes as 'an usually narrow religious upbringing' to study at Girton College, Cambridge, in the 1870s.[16] Enjoying her studies, but finding it difficult to settle in a non-religious environment, she went on to found Westfield College in 1882, with the support of two Evangelical benefactors. The college was the first which specifically aimed to prepare its female students for University of London degrees, and Maynard acted as its mistress for thirty-one years. She was one of a number of women active in the new women's colleges founded in the late nineteenth and early twentieth centuries. Others followed a more accepted occupation for women: that of writing. Novel writing had been regarded as a respectable female occupation since the eighteenth century, but in the nineteenth century it became increasingly associated with feminism. New Women novelists regarded their writing as a liberating act of self-expression and many wrote New Women novels which advanced feminist ideas. One of the most popular occupational choices for middle- and upper-class women in this period was social work. For much of the nineteenth-century, women of this class had visited the poor and advanced their welfare through charities and religious organisations. By the late nineteenth century, this work was increasingly organised and professional: in 1893 it was estimated that approximately 20,000 women were 'maintaining themselves as paid officials in works of philanthropic usefulness in England'.[17] Women worked in hospitals or workhouses and served as poor-law guardians or on school boards. Earlier traditions of female philanthropy had centred on the importance of fostering friendships between women across classes and, in the 1880s, the settlement movement provided a new focus for this aim. Settlement houses were established in working-class and slum areas, from which middle-class residents could offer childcare centres, prenatal classes and girls' clubs to the surrounding community.

For women active in these emerging occupations, commitment to their work could be difficult to reconcile with the demands of marriage and motherhood, and many New Women looked instead to other women for support and encouragement. The Irish writer, Edith Somerville, noted:

> The outstanding fact, as it seems to me, among women who live by their brains, is friendship. A profound friendship that extends through every phase and aspect of life, intellectual, social, pecuniary. Anyone who has experience of the life of independent and artistic women knows this.[18]

Many New Women formed female residential communities, which provided alternative domestic structures to those of the family. Women's settlement houses often looked like an urban home, while women's colleges fostered a strong sense of fellowship and loyalty amongst their students and teachers.[19] While the shared residential space of women's colleges and settlement houses clearly promoted these friendships, Deborah Epstein Nord has highlighted the importance of female community even in the lives of pioneering women who lived outside residential communities. Focusing on one female network in late-nineteenth-century London, she traces the connections between Beatrice Potter Webb, her cousin Margaret Harkness and Amy Levy, who all lived and worked in London in the 1880s and were part of a broader network including the South African novelist Olive Schreiner and Eleanor Marx. Both Levy and Harkness also wrote novels, while Beatrice Potter Webb served as a Charity Organization Society worker and a rent collector in the East End. Deborah Epstein Nord suggests that although the women did not participate in an organised female community, their membership in this more fluid network 'sustained them and gave them identity and purpose' focused on their work, socially marginal status and resistance of marriage and family.[20]

While this particular female friendship network had broken apart by the end of the 1880s and Beatrice Potter Webb had married, other New Women chose to form long-standing supportive partnerships with other women. Edith Somerville and Violet Martin formed a lifelong partnership in the late nineteenth century, which lasted until Violet's death in 1915 and continued, for Edith, beyond the grave. The two women were second cousins but did not meet until their early twenties, when they found they enjoyed an intellectual and emotional sympathy. Edith was the eldest child in her family and was encouraged in her intellectual and physical activities by her family, who ultimately sent her to college in the 1870s. Violet had a strong interest in writing and, after meeting Edith, the two women collaborated on thirteen books together, including their first work, *An Irish Cousin*, published in 1889. Edith and Violet regarded their partnership as an alternative to marriage and Edith commented that, while for most young people, the flirtations of youth 'are resolved and composed by marriage', 'to Martin [Violet] and to me was opened another way, and the flowering of both our lives was when we met each other'.[21] After Violet's death, Edith believed that Violet continued to live and communicate with her on another plane and she went on to publish a further sixteen books in their joint names.

Katherine Bradley and Edith Cooper formed a similar emotional and writing partnership in the same period. Katherine was Edith's aunt and the two women had grown up in the same household. In 1878, Edith joined Katherine at University College, where they both studied classics and philosophy. Both women were feminists and rejected their female names as a symbol of their rejection of subordinate female roles. When they embarked on a collaborative writing career, they therefore adopted the joint pen-name of 'Michael Field', which may also have ensured that their work was treated with greater respect by critics than a work published under women's names. Katherine and Edith regarded their collaborative writing technique and their emotional intimacy as fundamentally linked. In a poem written in the 1890s, they explained:

My love and I took hands and swore,
Against the world, to be
Poets and lovers evermore.[22]

Both women regarded their relationship as a marriage and, in 1907, converted to Roman Catholicism in the hope of being reunited in an afterlife. The two died less than a year apart, with Katherine nursing Edith through cancer until Edith's death in December 1913, before herself dying of cancer in 1914.[23]

While these two pairs of women emphasised the importance of collaboration in their relationships, other women found the issue of equality more problematic. Constance Maynard engaged in a series of passionate relationships with other women during her career in teaching and as mistress of Westfield College. Within a year of founding Westfield, Maynard invited Anne Richardson, a young Quaker student from Newnham College, to transfer in the hope of sharing some of the responsibilities of Maynard's position. Richardson brought a friend, Frances Ralph Gray (Ralph), with her and the three women formed a close emotional bond. Constance ultimately fell in love with Ralph and the two were very close for two years before Ralph abruptly withdrew, first into a separate apartment outside of Westfield and later travelling away. However, in 1891 Ralph returned to Westfield, apparently hoping to renew their intimacy. Constance recorded their conversation in her diary:

> [Ralph] was not well, and I went up to see that she was rightly attended to. As I left she said with gentle hesitation, 'You never bite my fingers now, as you used to do.' 'Oh no, never,' I replied lightly. 'And you never snarl and growl like a jaguar when you can't express yourself. I never heard anyone growl as well as you.' 'No,' I said, 'it's useless. I've been cured of that.' The sweet low voice went on, 'And you never rock me in your arms and call me your baby.' 'No,' I said in the same even tone, 'I've been cured of that too.' 'Oh!' she said, with quite a new meaning, 'oh, I see.' Here was a spot too painful to be touched, and I said, 'Goodbye, dear,' and left the room. I will not go into the desolation I felt when alone again. I was like a pot-bound root all curled in upon itself, like an iron-bound bud that has lost the spring, and now no rain and no sunshine can open it.[24]

Martha Vicinus has suggested that the difficulties Constance and Ralph experienced centred on the power imbalance in their relationship. While Constance sought emotional support and advice in fulfilling her role as mistress of the college, she also expected both Ralph and Anne to submit to her authority and superior status. For Ralph, this lack of professionalism and restriction on her personal autonomy apparently proved too difficult to accept.[25]

Although Constance and Ralph found professional inequality problematic in their relationship, other women based successful partnerships on the career of one partner. The best-selling novelist Marie Corelli was supported both emotionally and professionally throughout her career

by her partner Bertha Vyver. Bertha was the daughter of a French
Countess and gave up her own career as a painter to help promote
Marie's career, encouraging Marie to regard herself as a talented novelist
and creating the successful persona of 'Marie Corelli'. Adopting
a motherly role towards Marie, who described herself to Bertha as 'Your
wee little one', Bertha kept house and nursed Marie's invalid father, while
Marie financially supported them both. Bertha's role was not, however,
a purely private one and the two women also attended public functions
together as a couple.[26]

The extent to which emotional partnerships between New Women
contained a sexual element is difficult to establish and must have
varied between individual couples, as with earlier romantic friendships.
Some relationships undoubtedly were sexual. Minnie Benson, wife
of Archbishop of Canterbury, Edward White Benson, had a number
of affairs with women friends. The sexual aspect of Minnie's relationship
with Lucy Tait caused her considerable feelings of guilt and, in 1878,
she wrote in her diary:

Once more and with shame O Lord, grant that all carnal affections
may die in me, and that all things belonging to the spirit may live
and grow in me. Lord, look down on Lucy and me, and bring
to pass the union we have both so blindly, each in our own region
of mistake, continually desired.[27]

Religious beliefs were clearly influential in shaping some women's
attitudes towards their friendships with other women. Lillian Faderman
argues that Edith Somerville and Violet Martin's partnership is unlikely
to have been a sexual relationship, citing Geraldine Cummins,
Somerville's biographer and companion from 1927, who claimed that
Somerville had 'definite views' on the 'evils of sexual immorality and
considered the Irish Roman Catholic Church wise in its condemnation
of misdemeanours of this kind'.[28]

The New Woman, Feminism and Sexuality

The connections between women's expanding social role and ideas
about female sexuality remained extremely contentious throughout the
nineteenth century. The Marriage Question emerged as a central concern

of both feminist and anti-feminist campaigners in this period, with attitudes ranging from a belief that marriage represented women's ideal and natural role to a condemnation of marriage as little more than legalised prostitution and slavery. Sexuality, both in itself and as a symbol of female autonomy, became a particular preoccupation for the second generation of feminists in the last decades of the nineteenth century.[29] Social purity feminists in the 1880s and 1890s protested against a value system that confined women to the private sphere on the grounds that their moral purity could therefore be protected by men, while men assumed power in the public sphere. In an era when concerns about syphilis and other venereal diseases had brought issues of sexual morality and prostitution into the realm of public debate, feminists drew attention to the double standard which enforced chastity on women while allowing men the sexual freedom to use prostitutes and pass venereal diseases to their wives. For many social purity campaigners, the solution was to enforce moral standards equally on both sexes, and Christabel Pankhurst campaigned widely under the slogan: 'Votes for women and Chastity for men.'[30]

New Women writers explored many of these issues in their novels, using their characters to put forward arguments about social and sexual change and bring these ideas to a wider audience. In Sarah Grand's novel *The Heavenly Twins* (1893), the character Evadne refuses to consummate her marriage, while Gwen in Iota's *A Yellow Aster* (1894) regards marriage as an experiment. In Grant Allen's novel, *The Woman Who Did* (1895), Herminia Barton has children out of wedlock. New Woman novels were frequently criticised for being sexually and socially irresponsible in advancing these ideas, as the novels were often extremely popular and critics argued that they could corrupt their readers. Marie Corelli referred to such concerns in her novel *The Sorrows of Satan* in which Satan, portrayed as a sadistic misogynist, describes New Women novelists as 'self-degrading creatures who delineate their fictional heroines as wallowing in unchastity, and who write freely on subjects which men would hesitate to name'.[31] *The Woman Who Did*, which ran into nineteen editions in its first year of publication, was particularly notorious as an example of New Woman arguments about free love. However, it was actually very different from the social purity theme of most New Women novels and was criticised by Sarah Grand and by leading feminists such as Millicent Garrett Fawcett, who regarded the novel as unrepresentative of their views and damaging to the feminist cause.[32]

A significant number of New Women novels featured same-sex relationships between women. Sally Ledger has argued that male writers tended to present such relationships in a different way from women novelists, explicitly pathologising their New Women characters as unmarried and lesbian, as in the case of Olive Chancellor in Henry James' *The Bostonians* (1886) and Cecilia Cullen in George Moore's *A Drama in Muslin* (1886). Women novelists, however, made greater use of a romantic friendship model in the representation of female relationships such as that of Hadria Fullerton and Valeria Du Prel in Mona Caird's *The Daughters of Danaus* (1894), Lucretia Bampfylde and Kitty Manners in Isabella Ford's *On the Threshold* (1895) and Rosalind Dangerfield and Leslie Ardent in Gertrude Dix's *The Image Breakers* (1900).[33] In many such novels by women, the partnership ends when one of the women marries. Kit Drummond and Susan Dormer in Edith Arnold's *Platonics* (1894) are described at the outset as having a relationship 'of such tenderness, such benign loving-kindness, as almost raised friendship into a sacrament'.[34] Kit is described in terms of the archetypal New Woman, standing comfortably in 'rough tweed clothes' with hands 'thrust ... deep into her pockets'.[35] However, when she meets a male suitor, Kit loses her masculine demeanour and marries, leaving Susan to fall into a fatal decline.

Nevertheless, female same-sex desire was explored in New Women novels written by both men and women. Thomas Hardy's *Desperate Remedies* includes a scene in which his two central characters, eighteen-year-old Cytherea Graye and forty-six-year-old Miss Aldclyffe, who has a 'masculine cast' to her countenance, go to bed together and kiss and hug passionately:

> The instant they were in bed Miss Aldclyffe freed herself from the last remnant of restraint. She flung her arms round the young girl, and pressed her gently to her heart.
> 'Now kiss me,' she said.[36]

Cytherea is bemused by this behaviour and confesses her love for a man, but Miss Aldclyffe is persistent and begs her not to let a man stand between them. In Elizabeth Wetherell's *The Wide, Wide World* (1852), a relationship between a schoolgirl and an older girl is also described in physical terms. The younger girl is excited about the prospect of spending two nights with her friend and when they meet, 'There was a long silence, during which they remained locked in each others arms.' The older girl tells the younger to 'Come here and sit in my lap again ... and let your head rest where it used to.'[37]

Other novels presented relationships between women in positive and central terms, such as that between Diana Warwick and Emma Dunstane in George Meredith's *Diana of the Crossways* (1885). Set in the 1830s and 1840s, the novel was loosely based on the experiences of Caroline Norton, a society hostess whose husband tried and failed to divorce her for an alleged affair with Whig Prime Minister Lord Melbourne and who was subsequently accused of passing a Cabinet secret, learned from an admirer, to *The Times*. However, the central relationship in the novel is one between two women, Diana Warwick (Caroline Norton) and Emma Dunstane. Diana is portrayed in the terms of a New Woman: she writes novels and is difficult to define in conventional gender terms. As a woman, she resists definition, indicated by the range of names she possesses, from her maiden name, Diana Merrion, to her pen-name, Antonia, and Emma's affectionate name for her, Tony. Her gender and sexuality are equally indeterminate. She possesses a masculine air and is accused by her first husband of 'using men's phrases' and by an admirer of being too interested in politics.[38] She is represented as being sexually cold but is simultaneously regarded by her fellow characters as a sexual predator. Her masculine characteristics are equally apparent in her relationship with the feminine invalid Emma, whom she treats in much the same way as an MP might his wife, visiting Emma at her house in the country as a break from acting as a political hostess in Westminster. The two make frequent declarations of love to each other, Diana writing:

> I long for your heart on mine, your clear eyes ... My beloved! I have an ache – I think I am wronging you ... It is not compassion I want, I want you ... Let me hear Emma's voice – the true voice ... I kiss this miserable sheet of paper ...
> Your Tony[39]

Emma is equally affectionate, telling a mutual friend, Tom Redworth, 'You know our love. She is the best of me, heart and soul,' and the women show physical affection, throwing their arms around each other and kissing.[40] Although both women are or were married, and Diana remarries and is pregnant at the close of the novel, their husbands are

represented as unimportant. Diana's husbands are both dismissed
as uninspiring men of commerce, while Emma's husband is a philanderer,
with whom she does not have a sexual relationship. In contrast, the
emotional intensity of Diana and Emma's love is at the heart of the
novel.

Passionate friendships and partnerships between women, such as
those portrayed in New Women novels, were clearly prevalent in feminist
circles in this period. Love between women may have been encouraged
by the all-female environment and the anti-male ethos of the feminist
movement in Britain. Certainly, several prominent lesbian couples have
been identified in the international feminist movement, highlighting the
extent to which other members were aware and tolerant of lesbian
relationships.[41] However, in a period in which conventional notions
of femininity emphasised women's sexual innocence and asexuality, any
public discussion of sexuality by women remained highly contentious
and continued to divide the feminist movement. In the 1860s, Josephine
Butler's campaign against the Contagious Diseases Acts, which sought
to reduce venereal disease rates in the military by confining infected
prostitutes in lock hospitals, had divided feminists for this reason. While
some women regarded the issue of sexuality and the double standard
as central to the wider cause of women's rights, others sought to distance
the campaign for the suffrage from an issue which might potentially
discredit their cause. Contemporary critics of the suffrage movement,
disturbed by the spectacle of independent women vociferously demanding their right to autonomy and blaming feminists for the perceived
obliteration of distinctions between the sexes, frequently attacked
deviant female sexuality as a means of discrediting the feminist cause.
The linking of female autonomy of the kind practised by 'New Women'
with 'masculinity' and sexual knowledge, led to frequent criticisms that
the feminist movement had been overrun by lesbians.

The New Woman as Caricature

By the 1890s, many of these anxieties and debates had become embodied
in the cultural icon of the 'New Woman', who emerged into the public
domain of the periodical and newspaper press and novels in a variety
of forms. In the satirical journal *Punch* she was frequently depicted
as a manly woman or Amazon, who affected such masculine pursuits

as smoking and riding bicycles. *Punch*'s 'Angry Old Buffer' complained about the perceived disintegration of conventional gender categories, for which New Women writers were at least partly to blame:

> ... a new fear my bosom vexes;
> Tomorrow there may be no sexes!
> Unless, as an end to all pother,
> Each one in fact becomes the other.
> Woman *was* woman, man *was* man,
> When Adam delved and Eve span
> Now he can't dig and she won't spin,
> Unless 'tis tales all slang and sin![42]

Cartoonists in *The Cornhill* represented the New Woman as a figure in manly dress, adopting an air of aggressive independence and strong opinions, with large hands and nose, a long stride and a discontented mouth. In particular, smoking, bicycling and the 'rational dress' adopted by some feminists to enable greater freedom of movement became easy visual targets for a satirical critique of feminist gender challenges. Cartoons portraying New Women engaged in these activities depicted them as simultaneously ambitious and threatening, but also inexpert and socially inept: they were shown lighting the wrong end of a cigarette or falling off their bicycles. A *Punch* article on rational dress included the verse:

> There was a New Woman, as I've heard tell,
> And she rode a bike with a horrible bell,
> She rode a bike in a masculine way,
> And she had a spill on the Queen's highway.[43]

This New Woman's humiliation was complete when, knocked unconscious by her fall, she had to be rescued by a young doctor who was so shocked by the sight of her rational dress, with its split skirt, that he covered her with a petticoat for modesty.

Connections were frequently made between the New Woman and an excessive interest in sexuality. As depicted in periodicals, she was simultaneously unfeminine and hyperfeminine, on the one hand possessing a masculine mind and body and on the other taking accepted ideas about women's inherently affectionate nature to excess. These

contradictory elements of her nature were illustrated most clearly
in her excessive interest in sexuality and sex. Hugh Stutfield
claimed:

> Emancipated woman in particular loves to show her independence
> by dealing freely with the relations of the sexes. Hence all the
> prating of passion, animalism, 'the natural workings of sex,' and
> so forth, with which we are nauseated. Most of the characters
> in these books seem to be erotomaniacs. Some are 'amorous
> sensitives'; others are apparently sexless, and are at pains to explain
> this to the reader. Here and there a girl indulges in what would
> be styled, in another sphere, 'straight talk to young men.' Those nice
> heroines of 'Iota' and other writers of the physiologico-pornographic
> school consort by choice with 'unfortunates,' or else describe
> at length their sensations in various interesting phases of their
> lives.[44]

Such connections between feminism, New Women, masculinity and
sexual deviance were increasingly made in the late-nineteenth-century
press and, in the 1890s, began to appear in descriptions of the female
homosexual offered by the new scientists of sex: sexologists.

Chapter 5
Sexology and the Science of Sex, 1880s–1920s

Sexology and Victorian Attitudes

In the late nineteenth century, sexual desire between women again became the focus of scientific interest, with the emergence of the new medical field of sexology. The term 'sexologists' has been used to describe a number of doctors and scholars who, in the late nineteenth and early twentieth centuries, set themselves up as experts in the field of sexuality. The nineteenth century had been characterised by its belief in science and in humankind's ability to make sense of, and control, society and the natural world through the application of scientific reason. From the mid-nineteenth century onwards, the field of medicine was emerging as a particularly powerful scientific discourse, with growing social and political influence. A number of developments in the profession – including the establishment of the professional body, the General Medical Council, in 1858 and the introduction of professional exams and qualifications for doctors – meant that medical professionals could claim increasing social authority as 'experts'. The appointment of John Simon to the new post of Medical Officer allowed the profession to have an increasing role in shaping government policy on social issues, such as public health and welfare, family and maternity issues and sexuality.[1] Within the context of these developments, sexologists sought to claim a unique expertise and understanding of sexual desire and behaviour. 'Deviant' forms of sexuality, they argued, should no longer be seen as a moral problem, but a medical one: sexual acts between members of the same sex were not wilfully committed sins, which the individual could avoid committing through moral control, but were evidence of an underlying pathology or sickness.

Through a wide body of literature, sexologists have been seen as making two significant contributions to thinking about sexuality. The first was to categorise or list a range of human sexual behaviours from same-sex desire or homosexuality to bestiality and foot fetishism. The second was the claim that certain types of people would perform specific types of sexual behaviour. Whereas sexual behaviour between women had previously, under the moral approach, been regarded as immoral and unacceptable behaviour which any woman was capable of if she failed to exert moral control over herself, the sexologists argued that specific types of people were likely to commit these types of acts. Michel Foucault, whose work on the history of sexuality has been particularly influential in shaping historians' views on sexology, argued: 'The sodomite had been a temporary aberration; the homosexual was now a species.'[2]

Medical theories on sexuality in the nineteenth century were strongly influenced by broader Victorian ideas about sex and gender. Gendered middle-class social roles, which reflected a belief that men were suited to the worlds of work, politics and war, while the appropriate female sphere was that of the home and the family, were widely believed to be 'natural' and nineteenth-century scientists reinforced this view. Herbert Spencer argued that the distinction between the sexes could be explained by their differing biological capacities and suggested that this difference was the result of an earlier arrest in the individual evolution of women: women's reproductive role demanded that their bodies conserve energy, rather than expending it on unnecessary intellectual functions.[3] By the end of the nineteenth century, this difference was being seen in genetic terms. Patrick Geddes and J. Arthur Thompson argued in their best-selling book, *The Evolution of Sex* (1889), that sexual difference was apparent in differences in cell metabolism. While male cells were katabolic, dissipating energy and therefore rendering men active, female cells were anabolic, storing energy and making women passive.[4] Victorian thinking about sexuality was closely interlinked with these ideas about the social roles of men and women, so that male sexual roles were also defined as active and female as passive. William Acton represented the more extreme end of this belief in the sexual passivity of women when he claimed: 'I should say that the majority of women (happily for them) are not very much troubled with sexual feeling of any kind.'[5] While other commentators accepted women's capacity for sexual pleasure, the view that women's sexuality was reactive, requiring a man to initiate sexual activity, was widespread. As Havelock Ellis expressed it: 'The female responds to the stimulation of the male at the right moment just as the tree responds to the stimulation of the warmest days in spring.'[6]

Inversions: Krafft-Ebing, Havelock Ellis and Freud

The assumption of the sexual passivity of women posed a conceptual problem for theorists considering desire between women in the Victorian period. The belief that women could only respond to, but not initiate, sexual encounters rendered it theoretically impossible for two women to interact sexually, in the absence of a man. Early sexological writings resolved this difficulty by arguing that women who desired other women possessed a masculine sexual desire. George Chauncey has noted: 'In the Victorian system, therefore, a complete inversion (or reversal) of a woman's sexual character was required for her to act as a lesbian; she had literally to become man-like in her sexual desire.'[7] Such women were termed 'inverts' and represented as sexually aggressive, in keeping with contemporary notions of male sexuality.

Sex and gender roles were assumed to be closely connected in Victorian ideology, so that individuals' thought, character and behaviour were thought to be linked to their sexual instincts. As a result, early sexologists represented the female invert as possessing masculine habits, corresponding with their masculine sexual role, and described the male invert as correspondingly effeminate. In his monumental study of sexual pathology, *Psychopathia Sexualis* (1886), Richard von Krafft-Ebing asserted:

> Uranism [inversion] may nearly always be suspected in females wearing their hair short, or who dress in the fashion of men, or pursue the sports and pastimes of their male acquaintances …
>
> The female urning [invert] may chiefly be found in the haunts of boys. She is the rival in their play, preferring the rocking-horse, playing at soldiers, etc., to dolls and other girlish occupations. The toilet is neglected, and rough boyish manners are affected. Love for art finds a substitute in the pursuits of the sciences. At times smoking and drinking are cultivated even with passion.
>
> Perfumes and sweetmeats are disdained. The consciousness of being a woman and thus to be deprived of the gay college life, or to be barred out from the military career, provides painful reflections.[8]

By the turn of the century, thinking about the relationship between sex and gender roles was beginning to change, with a shift towards a narrower definition of sexual roles. Sexologists began to separate transvestism and gender inversion from homosexuality, arguing that it was possible to combine desire for one's own sex with the outward

conventions of one's appropriate gender role. In 1905, in the first of his
Three Essays on the Theory of Sexuality, Freud made a distinction
between the sexual object, which was the focus of an individual's sexual
desire, and the sexual aim, or mode of sexual behaviour.[9] Whether or not
an individual assumed a passive or active role in sexual encounters was
therefore separated from the issue of sexual object choice. However,
these arguments focused primarily on male homosexuals, and sexologists
apparently found it much more difficult to break the link between sexual
and gender inversion in women. British sexologist Havelock Ellis, despite
explicitly arguing that transvestism and homosexuality were unrelated,
nevertheless claimed in his *Sexual Inversion* (1897):

> The brusque, energetic movements, the attitude of the arms, the
> direct speech, the inflexions of the voice, the masculine straight-
> forwardness and sense of honor [of the female invert] ... will
> all suggest the underlying psychic abnormality to a keen observer.
> In the habits not only is there frequently a pronounced taste for
> smoking cigarettes, often found in quite feminine women, but
> also a decided taste and tolerance for cigars. There is also a dislike
> and sometimes incapacity for needlework and other domestic
> occupations, while there is often some capacity for athletics.[10]

Female homosexuality continued to be widely linked with masculinity
and gender inversion until at least the 1930s. However, the earlier central
emphasis on the female invert's 'masculine' sexual role was increasingly
replaced in the early twentieth century by a focus on the invert's choice
of women as the object of sexual desire.[11]

The focus on the masculine female invert in early sexological writing
meant that her sexual partner was largely ignored. Influenced by the
powerful social model of marriage in the nineteenth century, early
sexologists found it difficult to conceive of relationships between women
outside a paradigm of masculine and feminine roles. Ellis therefore
distinguished between the 'actively inverted woman', possessing 'one
fairly essential character: a more or less distinct trace of masculinity'
and those women 'to whom the actively inverted woman is most
attracted'. The objects of the female invert's desire were described
as 'plain' in appearance, but 'always womanly'. In line with their
feminine gender traits, these women were imagined as primarily asexual,

but possessing a 'genuine, though not precisely sexual, preference for women over men'.[12] In assuming conventional feminine gender and sexual roles, these women were not regarded as inverts. Their interest in women was frequently represented as the result of seduction by a female invert, or a more general responsive interest in women, which could easily be transferred onto a man, if the opportunity arose. However, by the end of the nineteenth century, sexologists were expressing increasing concern about the true invert's feminine partner. Commentators began to consider relationships between feminine women, who had previously been considered asexual, and identified homosexuality in single-sex institutions such as boarding schools and convents. The new focus on sexual object choice, rather than gender inversion, meant that feminine, passive homosexual women could now be understood as pathological, because of their interest in women. In 1934, Lura Beam and Robert Latou Dickinson's American study of 600 women was the first to explicitly reject the model of masculine and feminine roles in homosexual relationships between women. Beam and Dickinson specifically asked their lesbian research subjects whether they assumed the male role in a relationship and found that the majority of women surveyed claimed that neither they nor their partner assumed a male role.[13]

While views on the characteristics of the lesbian shifted from the late nineteenth century to the early twentieth, similar debates occurred in the sexological literature as to the causes of homosexuality. Despite claiming to replace the idea of same-sex desire as a sin with a scientific and medical understanding of inversion, early works nevertheless maintained a link with antisocial behaviour. Inversion was understood as an acquired condition, which could develop as the result of some wilful abuse of the body or sexual instinct, such as masturbation. In his case history of twenty-nine-year-old Ilma S, Richard von Krafft-Ebing identified masturbation amongst other causes of her acquired inversion. At the age of eighteen, Ilma had a passionate affair with a man (her cousin) and, after they separated, practised masturbation and subsequently passed as a man. In explaining the cause of her condition, Krafft-Ebing cited a statement from Ilma:

The change of my feelings originated in this, that in Pesth, dressed as a man, I had the opportunity to observe my cousin. I saw that

I was wholly deceived in him. That gave me terrible heart-pangs.
I knew that I could never love another man; that I belonged
to those who love but once. Of similar effect was the fact that,
in the society of my companions at the railway, I was compelled
to hear the most offensive language and visit the most disreputable
houses. As a result of the insight into men's motives, gained in this
way, I took an unconquerable dislike to them.

Commenting on the case, Krafft-Ebing observed that: 'The antipathic
sexual instinct of this patient, which was clearly acquired, expressed
itself in a stormy and decidedly sensual way, and was further augmented
by masturbation.'[14]

For Krafft-Ebing and many of his contemporaries, inversion
was also understood in relation to the influential nineteenth-century
concept of degeneration. The work of Charles Darwin in the mid-
nineteenth century had demonstrated that different species evolved
in specific ways in response to the natural environment and that the
future of the human species was therefore unpredictable. While 'positive'
responses to this theory explored the ways in which human beings could
control the progress of the species and its natural environment towards
greater civilisation through manipulation of the evolutionary process,
pessimistic approaches focused on the potential degeneration of the
human race back down the evolutionary cycle towards primitivism.
The concept of degeneration was widely used to support hierarchies
of class and race in the context of Victorian imperialism. Drawing
on this theory, Krafft-Ebing argued that sexual morality formed the
basis of civilisation, so that human sexual relations must be based
on love and monogamy so as to maintain order. In his view, sexual
relations outside marriage represented a degeneration to an earlier,
lower state of evolution and therefore posed a threat to civilisation.
Other writers developed these ideas, attempting to demonstrate
a higher incidence of homosexuality in racial groups which were
considered more degenerate. Sexual theories of degeneration were
also applied along class lines by a middle class–dominated medical
profession. The working class were commonly assumed to be sexually
immoral and degenerate, and the nineteenth-century medical and
advice literature blamed servants for introducing sexual perversions
into middle-class homes, by showing the children in their care how
to masturbate.[15]

While an understanding of homosexuality as a sign of 'functional degeneration' appeared in the earlier work of Krafft-Ebing and others, by the end of the nineteenth century, sexologists were beginning to question this notion. Laura Doan and Chris Waters have argued that the publication of Havelock Ellis' work *Sexual Inversion*, in 1897, represented the first significant challenge to the established view that homosexuality was an acquired condition. They point to a review of *Sexual Inversion* in the British medical journal, *The Lancet*, which 'reiterated the prevailing belief that it was always an "acquired and depraved manifestation of the sexual passion"', despite Havelock Ellis' explanation of sexual inversion as a 'congenital anomaly'.[16] In Ellis' view, sexual inversion was an innate condition, which occurred naturally in a minority of individuals. The German lawyer, Karl Heinrich Ulrichs, whose work was circularised in Britain by Edward Carpenter, added to the congenital argument with his 'third sex' model of homosexuality. Ulrichs claimed that sexual orientation was innate in members of the 'third sex', explaining that 'the "germ" of same-sex desire is implanted *ab ovo* in the very physiognomy of the man-loving man', emerging at puberty.[17] As he developed his table of sexual types, Ulrichs added the category of the 'Urninging', or female 'Urning'. These individuals constituted a 'fourth sex', 'of persons built like females having woman–womanly sexual desire, i.e. having the sexual direction of men'.[18] The Urninging mirrored the Urning in every respect, so that their sexual orientation was similarly characterised as innate and displaying itself at puberty. This notion of a 'third sex' was reflected in the work of Edward Carpenter himself, who explained the female homosexual as a naturally occurring type for whom a female body enclosed a masculine soul and temperament.[19]

Notions of homosexuality as innate were often connected with suggestions of the need for an external catalyst to spark the development of a lesbian identity. For Havelock Ellis, specific environmental factors external to an individual's make-up could precipitate the 'latent condition' of inversion, although they did require a 'favourable organic predisposition' on which to act.[20] Stella Browne, whose writing on female sexual inversion in the interwar period was heavily influenced by Ellis' work, placed greater emphasis on environmental factors. Although she claimed that lesbianism was innate, she qualified this by arguing that homosexuality was in part also a result of society's repression of the 'normal sexual impulse': if society were to take a less prudish attitude towards women's sexual behaviour, the incidence of homosexuality would diminish.[21]

With the appearance of Freudian psychoanalytic approaches to sexual development in the early twentieth century, the notion of the homosexual as a special category of person was replaced with a new theory of universal infant bisexuality.[22] According to Sigmund Freud, homosexuality, like heterosexuality, represented a possible outcome of any individual's sexual development and was explained as the result of an inhibition of the 'normal process', which could be sparked off by the child's environment. In his 1920 case study of an eighteen-year-old lesbian, Freud argued that the girl had developed a castration complex, sparked by her awareness that she did not possess a penis.[23] He argued that, while the sexual instinct of all girls was initially directed towards the mother, with a corresponding focus by the girl on her own clitoris as the primary site of her sexual desires, this sexual instinct would normally be transferred to the father during sexual development. The transference would occur as the girl developed a desire for a penis, which only her father, and not her mother, could give. When this transference was achieved, the girl's sexuality would now be focused on her vagina, rather than her clitoris. However, in some cases, as in the subject of the 1920 study, this transference was not made and the girl's sexual development was arrested at the first stage. Freud's theory of arrested development resembled the earlier notion of acquired lesbianism and challenged the early-twentieth-century dominance of congenital theories. Although Freud himself tended to avoid any suggestion that homosexuality should be seen as inferior to heterosexuality, the notion of 'arrested development' implied that there was a healthier developmental norm and thus raised the possibility of attempts to 'cure' homosexuality. C. Stanford Reid and Thomas Ross, among the most prominent early followers of Freud's theories in Britain, were key proponents of the therapeutic value of psychoanalysis.[24]

Sexology and Feminism

The social and cultural impact of the sexologists' theories has been a subject of considerable debate amongst historians. In the 1980s, a number of lesbian feminist historians argued that sexology had a significant negative impact on social attitudes towards women and their relationships with each other. Sheila Jeffreys claimed:

> As part of their self-imposed task of categorising varieties of human sexual behaviour, the sexologists of the late nineteenth century set about the 'scientific' description of lesbianism. Their description has had a momentous effect on the ways in which we, as women, have seen ourselves and all our relationships with other women up until the present.[25]

Lillian Faderman has suggested that the major impact of sexology was the 'morbidification' of women's relationships: 'In the popular imagination, love between women was becoming identified with disease, insanity, and tragedy.'[26] In particular, sexology challenged the acceptability of emotional or romantic friendships between women. Faderman argues that, while romantic friendships between women had been widespread and acceptable throughout the eighteenth and early nineteenth centuries, women's growing independence rendered these relationships more threatening in the late nineteenth century. Expanding educational and employment opportunities for women and the emergence of political campaigns for women's economic and social freedoms were perceived by many contemporary commentators as a threat to conventional feminine roles. The female relationships which sustained many women in these new roles came under increasing scrutiny with the rise of the feminist movement in the second half of the nineteenth century and the debates about the New Woman in the 1890s. Anti-feminism and the morbidification of women's friendships, Faderman has argued, came hand in hand.

It is clear that late-nineteenth-century anxieties surrounding women's increasing social and economic independence did influence the views of many sexologists. Edward Carpenter, despite claiming to support the women's movement, identified a link between feminism and the rejection of conventional sex and gender roles. He claimed that feminists were

> naturally drawn from those in whom the sexual instinct is not preponderant. Such women do not altogether represent their sex; some are rather mannish in temperament; some are 'homogenic', that is inclined to attachments to their own sex rather than

the opposite sex; such women are ultra-rationalising and brain-cultured; to many, children are more or less a bore; to others, man's sex-passion is a mere impertinence, which they do not understand, and whose place they consequently misjudge. It would not do to say that the majority of the new movement are out of line, but there is no doubt that a large number are; and the course of their progress will be correspondingly curvilinear.[27]

This linking of the disease of inversion with women's political challenges has been seen as enabling commentators to explain a process of social change in a less threatening way and to simultaneously warn other women away from such pathological behaviour.[28] Some sexologists did this by suggesting that previously 'normal' women could be drawn into inversion through contact with pathological women in the feminist movement. Iwan Bloch, considered one of the founding fathers of sexology, asserted:

There is no doubt that in the 'women's movement' – that is, in the movement directed towards the acquirement by women of all the attainments of masculine culture – homosexual women have played a notable part. Indeed according to one author, the 'Women's Question' is mainly the question regarding the destiny of virile homosexual women … For the diffusion of pseudohomosexuality the Women's Movement is of great importance, as we shall see later.[29]

While Bloch suggested that it was contact with homosexual women in the feminist movement which might draw women into 'pseudohomosexuality', others suggested that sexual desire for other women would be an inevitable result of women's increased social and economic independence. Havelock Ellis asserted:

Having been taught independence of men and disdain for the old theory which placed women in the moated grange of the home to sigh for a man who never comes, a tendency develops for women to carry this independence still farther and to find love where they find work.[30]

In other works, inversion was linked with the rejection of motherhood by emancipated women.

However, recent research into the impact of sexological ideas has challenged the lesbian feminist view, suggesting that the influence of sexological theories on wider social attitudes towards women has been overstated. Closer historical scrutiny has questioned the scope of sexology's influence on popular opinion, suggesting sexological works occupied a much more marginal location within the field of psychiatry and wider scientific trends, as well as noting that these ideas did not easily become absorbed into popular culture. Many sexological works were published in private pamphlets or limited editions, so that their circulation would have been relatively small: John Addington Symonds' *A Problem in Greek Ethics* (1883) had a print run of just ten copies.[31] Although other works reached a larger audience, with Richard von Krafft-Ebing's *Psychopathia Sexualis* running into twelve editions between 1886 and 1903, they were not readily available to the wider public. Laura Doan has characterised the intended readership of sexological works as 'professionals in the medical and legal field': she draws attention to Havelock Ellis' instruction, in the foreword to his *Studies in the Psychology of Sex*, that the work be sold 'only to professional readers'.[32] In a number of texts, further precautions were taken to limit access to specific passages, in response to concerns that morally weak individuals might use the texts as a pornographic source of ideas about potential immoral behaviour. In Krafft-Ebing's work, certain passages were published in Latin, to limit their accessibility to just a small number of well-educated middle-class male readers, who were assumed to be sufficiently morally responsible to read the texts in the scientific spirit in which they were intended. Despite these precautions, sexological works continued to be regarded with suspicion by many contemporary authorities. While the use of scientific and medical language leant the works an air of professional authority in a period of growing medical influence, the medical profession as a whole was by no means unanimously supportive of the sexological project. In an 'Editorial on the publication of Havelock Ellis's *Sexual Inversion*' in 1896, the British medical journal *The Lancet* accepted the need for some medical discussion of the issue of sexuality, but objected to the mode of the work's publication:

But while we admit that the subject of sexual inversion has its proper claims for discussion we are very clear as to the propriety of limiting that discussion to persons of particular attainments. When Mr Havelock Ellis's book was sent to us for review we did not review it, and our reason for this neglect of the work of the Editor of the 'Contemporary Science Series' was not connected with its theme or wholly with the manner of its presentment ... What decided us not to notice the book was its method of publication. Why was it not published through a [publishing] house able to take proper measures for introducing it as a scientific book to a scientific audience? And for other reasons, which it would serve no purpose to particularise, we considered the circumstances attendant upon its issue suspicious. We believed that the book would fall into the hands of readers totally unable to derive benefit from it as a work of science and very ready to draw evil lessons from its necessarily disgusting passages.[33]

Further reviews of sexological works provided *The Lancet* with the opportunity to present the views of the British medical profession on this literature. An article in *The British Medical Journal*, comparing the work of Viennese sexologist Krafft-Ebing unfavourably with that of British sexologist Ellis, again raised the issue of access to the literature and also suggested that xenophobia played a significant role in the reception of particular texts. Sexological theories were frequently regarded within the profession as predominantly seedy European imports, with dubious scientific credentials. Moreover, the medical profession was not alone in expressing these anxieties. The British Library Reading Room kept their copies of these works in a locked cupboard and only allowed access to those readers who were able to prove their genuine professional interest in the subject.

The idea that sexological categories were imposed on unwilling women by a hostile body of 'experts' has also been challenged by recent research. Work on the biographical backgrounds of many leading sexologists has suggested a much closer interaction between individual figures and a homosexual or lesbian culture than was previously thought, so that it is difficult to argue that sexological notions of homosexual identity originated with sexologists and not with the homosexual men and women with whom they came into contact. The relationship between sexologist Havelock Ellis and his wife, Edith Lees Ellis, whom he included amongst his case studies of female inverts, has been one focus of discussion on this issue. Speculating 'One wonders how many romantic friends, who had felt themselves to be perfectly healthy before, suddenly saw themselves as sick, even though their behaviour had in no way changed, as a result of the sexologists' formulations', Lillian Faderman observed:

> Ellis's wife, Edith Lees, seems to have been a victim of those theories. From his own account, Ellis apparently convinced her that she was a congenital invert, while she believed herself to be only a romantic friend to other women. He relates in *My Life* that during the first years of their marriage, she revealed to him an emotional relationship with an old friend who stayed with her while she and Ellis were apart ... He thus encouraged her to see herself as an invert and to regard her subsequent love relations with women as a manifestation of her inversion.[34]

However, Liz Stanley has challenged this view, arguing that Havelock Ellis' account cannot be relied upon because of tensions within the marriage and that Edith Lees Ellis's own papers suggest that the category of inversion was not imposed on her unwillingly.[35] In a letter to the sexologist Edward Carpenter, Edith Lees Ellis recounted a conservation she had had with Carpenter's sister, Alice, concerning Edith's sexuality, in which Alice had informed her that there was some debate amongst their acquaintances on the subject. Edith apparently responded by including a statement on the subject of her own inversion in a public lecture she was giving that week, something which she also did during her 1914 lecture tour of America. Her willingness to discuss her sexuality in the public domain, in terms of inversion, suggests that Edith Lees Ellis was comfortable with this interpretation of her sexuality and, in a subsequent letter to Edward Carpenter, she discussed her feelings for a woman she had been overwhelmingly in love with.[36] This evidence, Stanley argues, demonstrates not only that Edith Lees Ellis found the concept of inversion helpful in making sense of her feelings for other women, but also that she considered another sexologist, Edward Carpenter, himself a homosexual, a supportive friend and confidant.

A number of other letters to Edward Carpenter suggest that individual women found the ideas of some sexologists helpful in thinking about their sexuality, but often as part of an ongoing process which had started prior to reading the literature. Liz Stanley identified four letters which were written to Edward Carpenter in the years following the 1908 publication of his work *The Intermediate Sex*.[37] In a letter dated 25 October 1915, a woman writing under the pseudonym Frances Wilder told Carpenter that reading *The Intermediate Sex* had made her realise 'that I myself belong to that class and made everything fall into place'. She was a feminist and in touch with many other feminist women and with two women who were physically lovers. Two other women, one of whom wrote on 21 July 1913 and the other on 16 March 1925, described an understanding of their attraction to other women which had predated their reading of Carpenter's work. The first described her early desire to wear boy's clothes, engage in outdoor sports and, later, to have a career, in the context of the women's movement. She described her relations with women as 'masculine' and the women she was attracted to as 'feminine' and 'possessing that wonderful maternal instinct'. The second woman also described her relationships with women in gendered terms. The writer referred to herself by a man's name, despite being 'physically a girl' and had been lovers for three years with a woman who was 'in almost every respect ... quite different from me – small, dainty and feminine'. She and her lover were in touch with six other 'boys' who were lovers in the same way. The fourth letter-writer had been encouraged to contact Carpenter by a friend, Charles Lazenby, who also called her 'the boy'. She described reading Carpenter's *The Intermediate Sex* as 'like being given sight' and went on to outline her plans for 'getting together a group of Uranian women to form the nucleus of a club'. Stanley has noted that none of the letters referred to the work of any other sexologist apart from Carpenter and claims: 'It was the work of gay men as scientists of homosexuality, supported by many other gay men and women, that promoted the idea of "inversion" and its accompanying "mannish" lesbian and "effeminate" gay male stereotypes.' Such letters suggest that some women at least welcomed the ideas of some sexologists, regarding them as useful in providing a name and framework for thinking about their desires for other women.[38]

This picture of a close, collaborative relationship between individual sexologists and inverts is also apparent from a number of organisations and journals which were established in the early twentieth century to debate these issues. The British Society for the Study of Sex Psychology (BSSSP), of which Edith Lees Ellis was a member, was established in 1913 to provide a forum for the discussion of new ideas in the field of sex reform. The society was originally formed by a group of men interested in homosexual law reform but soon broadened its interests to include any aspect of sexual psychology, including the issues of prostitution, inversion, sexual ignorance, disease and sexual aberrations. Members

attended monthly meetings, at which guest speakers, including Dora
Russell, Marie Stopes, Ernest Jones (a leading British follower of Freud),
and other sexologists gave lectures or members held open discussions.
The first woman member of the society was the militant suffragist
Cicely Hamilton, and she was soon joined by a number of other notable
feminists, such as Kathlyn Oliver and Stella Browne, and by Mrs Mary
Scharlieb, one of the first women to gain a medical qualification
in Britain. The membership of these women suggests that feminism
and sexology were not necessarily antithetical views in this period and
feminists did not reject the ideas of sexologists such as Havelock Ellis
and Edward Carpenter. Lesley Hall argues instead that: 'The attitude
of open-minded enquiry, and refusal to accept conventional dogma about
sex and gender, which permeated the works of these writers and the
BSSSP appears to have been highly congenial to women in revolt against
conventional assumptions.'[39] The society continued to meet throughout
the interwar period and, from the early 1920s onwards, had an office
and library in London. The library made works by Havelock Ellis, Iwan
Bloch, Krafft-Ebing and others available to members, and the society
also published its own series of pamphlets, including work by Edward
Carpenter, Norman Haire and Stella Browne.

While the BSSSP was formed to provide a forum for members
to discuss new ideas emerging in the field of sex reform, the journal
Urania offered a critique of sexological literature in the same period.
The journal was published between 1915 and 1940 by a small group
of feminist men and women, including Thomas Baty/Irene Clyde,
a respected legal scholar, and the feminist couple Eva Gore-Booth and
Esther Roper. Urania had a circulation of approximately two hundred
and was distributed by private circulation. The journal adopted a radical
position on gender, arguing that distinctions between masculine and
feminine genders were socially constructed, not natural, and supporting
greater independence in women and sweetness in men.[40] The journal
reported with approval instances of cross-dressing, same-sex marriage,
sex change and acts of courage or physical strength by women.
Influenced by the turn-of-the-century feminist critique of marriage
as oppressive to women, Urania expressed hostility for marriage and
heterosexuality more broadly and championed love between women.
The journal published a range of articles on romantic friendships, such
as that between the Ladies of Llangollen, love poetry between women
and accounts of cross-dressed women. In a 1929 review of Radclyffe

Hall's novel *The Well of Loneliness*, the author recognised love between women as natural and understandable:

> There will inevitably be spirits in each garb who prefer their own type to the other. Since it is generally agreed that the feminine type is the more attractive and agreeable ... it follows that feminine attachments must be expected. That they do not find expression in the violent and brutally limited physical form styled by the world 'perversion' is equally natural.[41]

Alison Oram has argued that this celebration of love between women, combined with a rejection of marriage and heterosexuality, represented a uniquely radical approach in this period:

> But *Urania* had moved on from suffrage feminism, since it directly promoted the naturalness and desirability of love between women in contrast to the negative relationship of marriage and hetero-sexuality. This was quite extraordinary in the context of interwar feminism, where discussion of same-sex love was almost entirely avoided.[42]

Urania's relationship with sexology was equally unique. The journal was exploring similar issues to the sexologists, such as relations between the sexes, the social significance of sexuality and same-sex relationships, in a period when sexology was becoming more influential in mainstream society. However, Alison Oram has noted that the journal never directly referred to the work of sexologists and developed a clearly distinct theoretical position. Despite the similarities of interest, '*Urania*'s project was fundamentally different; it aimed to resist exactly those categories of sex and sexuality which the sexologists were busy establishing. Through its own feminist theorising of sex and gender, *Urania* mounted a powerful, though indirect, critique of mainstream sexology.'[43] Sexology therefore emerged alongside a range of other ideas and discourses about gender and sexuality, which were increasingly being debated in the years leading up to and beyond the First World War.

Chapter 6
Sapphism and the First World War, 1914–1918

Cultural Anxieties about Female Sexuality

Many of the anxieties about female sexuality being expressed by cultural commentators in the late nineteenth and early twentieth centuries were exacerbated by the outbreak of war in 1914. Cultural responses to war encouraged a polarisation of gender roles, in which the hypermasculine figure of the soldier was complemented by a passive, nurturing version of domestic femininity. Wartime propaganda, essential in the early years of the war when the British army relied on voluntary recruitment, drew on images of women as both individually defenceless and more broadly symbolic of the home, in order to motivate men to fight. A number of recruitment posters were addressed directly to women, inviting them to encourage their menfolk to enlist, with appeals such as 'Women of Britain say Go!'[1] Sexuality represented a significant undercurrent in the recruitment process and both propaganda and popular entertainment represented the soldier hero as a romantic ideal. Music-hall songs performed by female stars such as Vesta Tilly and Clara Butt suggested that men who enlisted could expect a sexual reward from women. One popular song told men:

> Now your country calls you to play your part in war
> And no matter what befalls you we shall love you all the more ...
> Oh, we don't want to lose you
> But we think you ought to go ...
> We shall want you and miss you
> But with all our might and main
> We shall cheer you, thank you, kiss you
> When you come back again.[2]

Official propaganda similarly drew upon romance and sexual honour to recruit men. One poster asked the 'Young Women of London':

> Is your "Best Boy" wearing Khaki? ... If not don't YOU THINK
> he should be? If he does not think that you and your country are

worth fighting for – do you think he is *worthy* of you? Don't pity the girl who is alone – her young man is probably a soldier – fighting for her and her country – and for *You*. If your young man neglects his duty to his King and Country, the time may come when he will *Neglect You*. Think it over – then ask him to JOIN THE ARMY *TODAY!*[3]

Such propaganda employed women in a symbolic appeal, intended to motivate men and at most to encourage women to use private methods of persuasion with the men in their lives.

However, public recruitment gestures by real women prompted considerable anxiety, breaking conventions of appropriate feminine behaviour in public and challenging notions of women as naturally nurturing and peace-loving. In August 1914, Admiral Charles Penrose Fitzgerald organised a group of thirty women in Folkstone, who handed out white feathers, a symbol of cowardice, to young men not in uniform. The symbolic act was intended to publicly shame 'slackers' into enlisting and Fitzgerald warned the men of Folkstone that if they were found 'idling and loafing to-morrow', 'there is a danger [of public humiliation] awaiting them far more terrible than anything they can meet in battle'.[4] A number of women responded to the call to join 'The Order of the White Feather' and the practice was widely adopted across the country, continuing even after the introduction of conscription in 1916. However, despite the pervasive presence of official propaganda using women to recruit men, the giving of white feathers by women caused considerable outrage. This was partly due to the difficulty of identifying 'slackers' on the street: women frequently relied on the wearing of a uniform as an indication of men's courage and status as soldiers, but, as the war drew on, many soldiers at home on leave, or those discharged from the army with wounds, appeared in public in civilian clothes, leading to misunderstandings and confrontations. Moreover, the practice of women approaching strange men in the street also prompted widespread anxieties about female sexuality. Even propagandists who encouraged women to send their men to war, such as Major Leonard Darwin, opposed the practice of handing out white feathers, claiming that he was 'very far from admiring those women who go up to young men in the street … and abuse them for not enlisting, a proceeding which requires no courage on the woman's part, but merely a complete absence of modesty'.[5] In the context of middle-class ideals of feminine respectability, which continued to emphasise the importance of women being chaperoned in public places to protect them from sexual harassment, the practice of women accosting men was worryingly suggestive of solicitation by prostitutes.

Fears that war might make women brazen, or even sexually out of control, were also evident from the reaction to the 'khaki fever' epidemic, which was thought to be gripping young women and teenage girls in the first months of the war. The excitement and enthusiasm surrounding the outbreak of war in 1914 led to considerable public interest in uniformed recruits, and large groups of onlookers were reported to loiter around garrisons and recruitment stations. The young men in khaki held particular appeal for boys and young women, who were excluded by their age or sex from any active participation in the war effort and seeking the vicarious excitement of associating with soldiers. Widely perceived as a public nuisance, young working-class women were a particular focus of concern in this context and were often represented in predatory terms as a threat to the soldiers. One writer noted:

> Some of them certainly behaved themselves very badly, simply pestering the younger of the soldiers by their 'forthputfulness', lying in wait for them, seizing them by the arm as they passed. I once saw some young Colonials running for their very lives to escape from a little company of girls. One might have thought, to see them, that they had tigresses at their heels. Another day I saw some English Tommies, who were being pursued by girls, spring into an omnibus for safety. The girls sprang in after them, whereupon the boys promptly betook themselves to the top, although it was raining in torrents at the time.[6]

The spectacle of young women loitering in the streets in the vicinity of soldiers raised the spectre of illicit sexual activity. *The Englishwoman* was typical of many contemporary commentators when it claimed in a 1916 report:

> Headstrong, impressionable, undisciplined girls, hardly more than children, have made themselves a nuisance by running after soldiers without any thought of more than silly or perhaps vulgar flirtation, and, by turns tempters and tempted, have often ended by entangling themselves and their soldier friends in actually vicious conduct.[7]

Anxiety centred on the perceived rise in the 'amateur' who, unlike the more familiar figure of the nineteenth-century prostitute, was willing to engage in immoral sexual activity without expecting payment. This 'amateur' type therefore represented a worrying new development in female sexuality, challenging Victorian notions of women as essentially asexual and exhibiting, instead, an enthusiasm and desire for sexual encounters on her own account. As enthusiasm for the war waned and as greater employment opportunities for women offered an alternative outlet for female patriotism, the khaki fever epidemic abated. However, general concerns about female sexuality persisted throughout the war, evident from the frequent attempts to curb female drunkenness, control sexual liaisons with soldiers and prevent illicit sexual acts by soldiers' wives.

While many of these debates centred on anxieties about female sexual encounters with men, female same-sex desire was also a source of concern during the First World War, often viewed as a threat to the nation and the war effort.[8] This anxiety emerged dramatically into the public domain in the final year of the war, as a result of a libel trial involving the well-known dancer Maud Allan and Noel Pemberton-Billing, an MP. Pemberton-Billing had worked as an actor and barrister before becoming an MP in 1916 and, in 1917, had formed the Vigilante Society to promote 'purity in public life'. He held anti-Semitic views, blaming a German-Jewish conspiracy for undermining the war effort in Britain, and in early 1918 his papers, the *Imperialist* and the *Vigilante*, published a number of articles on this theme. The first (written by Pemberton-Billing's assistant editor, Captain Harold Spencer, a Canadian who had been discharged from the British army for insanity) claimed that a 'Black Book', listing the names of 47,000 British men and women open to blackmail for their 'sexual perversions', was in the hands of the Germans. The 'first 47,000', he claimed, included:

> The names of Privy Councillors, youths of the chorus, wives of Cabinet ministers, dancing girls, even Cabinet Ministers themselves ... In lesbian ecstasy the most sacred secrets of the state were betrayed.[9]

A few weeks later Spencer wrote again, prompted by a letter from the novelist Marie Corelli, who had seen an article in *The Sunday Times* advertising a forthcoming private performance of Oscar Wilde's play

Salome, and suggested securing the list of subscribers as a means of getting the names of some of the 'first 47,000'. Spencer's article, intended to provoke a libel case and therefore gain publicity for his conspiracy theories, was entitled 'The Cult of the Clitoris' and claimed:

> To be a member of Maud Allen's [*sic*] private performance in Oscar Wilde's Salome one has to apply to Miss Valetta of 9 Duke St., Adelphi. If Scotland Yard were to seize the list of these members I have no doubt they would secure the names of several thousand of the first 47,000.[10]

Spencer's ploy was successful and Maud Allan sued Pemberton-Billing for libel, resulting in a trial that lasted six days from late May to early June 1918.

The trial attracted considerable public interest, with hundreds queuing at the Old Bailey to get a seat and most of the major national and provincial newspapers reporting the case in detail. Maud Allan was a celebrated Canadian dancer, who had studied classical piano in Berlin before becoming a dancer in 1901. In 1907, she had performed a dance called 'the Vision of Salome' before Edward VII and in 1908 came to England to give a further 250 performances featuring the dance at the Palace Theatre. Although well connected, being patronised by royalty and high society, Allan was also a notorious figure. The dance itself, which drew on contemporary ideas of Oriental exoticism and eroticism, was regarded as sexually charged and had been banned by morality societies in Manchester, Liverpool and Bournemouth. The Palace Theatre's manager had contributed to this interpretation in an illustrated pamphlet used to advertise the London performances, which claimed:

> The pink pearls slip amorously about the throat and bosom as she moves ... The desire that flames from her eyes and bursts in hot gusts from her scarlet mouth infects the act with the madness of passion.[11]

Maud Allan's reputation was further compromised by her intimate friendship with Margot, Prime Minister Herbert Asquith's wife, who was rumoured to be part of a lesbian clique. Margot Asquith paid for

Maud Allan's apartment overlooking Regent Park, for twenty years, from 1910 onwards and Maud Allan continued to live there in the 1930s with her secretary and then lover, Verna Aldrich.

The libel case centred on the title 'Cult of the Clitoris', which Allan's lawyers suggested implied allegations of lesbianism and nymphomania. In a pre-trial hearing at Bow Street Police Court, her counsel Travers Humphreys claimed:

> I find words which I must read, although I see there are ladies in the court ... The cult of the clitoris ... the words themselves are the filthiest words it would be possible to imagine ... The cult of the clitoris can only mean one thing, and that is that the lady whose name is coupled with it ... approves of that which is sometimes described in ... less gross language as lesbianism, and a more horrible libel to publish of any woman ... it is impossible to find.[12]

In order to defend themselves against the allegation of libel, Pemberton-Billing's team needed to establish the truth of this accusation and the trial therefore became centred on the issue of Maud Allan's sexual morality and that of her dance. The defence used a number of strategies to discredit Allan, including implying that she was a German sympathiser because of her piano training in Berlin, alluding to her friendship with Margot Asquith and linking the play *Salome* and its author, Oscar Wilde, with sexual perversion. However, a central aspect of the defence case revolved around the word 'clitoris' and Maud Allan's knowledge of its meaning. Captain Spencer claimed that the word was a specialist medical term, which he had obtained by telephoning a doctor, and that it was intended to be intelligible only to medical or legal professionals. In admitting to being familiar with the term, Maud Allan demonstrated a detailed knowledge of sexual matters which exposed her to accusations of sexual immorality. The court cleared Pemberton-Billing of libel to scenes of loud cheering and pandemonium, and Maud Allan was publicly disgraced.

Although the trial attracted widespread public interest and patriotic support for Pemberton-Billing, it is uncertain how clearly people understood the sexual aspects of the case. A young officer, Duff Cooper, told his future wife, Diane Manners, that the case was being widely discussed by officers at the front and that Margot Asquith's sexuality was also a topic of debate. He claimed:

> One of my brother-officers … believed that Mrs Asquith
> was a "female bugger" that being as near as his limited
> vocabulary allowed him to get to Sapphist.[13]

Diane Manners, working as a nurse at Guy's Hospital in London, however, replied:

> The nurses are just the same as your subalterns – they ask me all the
> time about the case and are totally ignorant of any significations.
> They have a dim vision of Sodom and Gomorrah, which is built
> for them by the word "vice". But even that is hazy.

This vague understanding of the sexual details was encouraged by the press, which tended to avoid specific details in their reports in favour of more general euphemisms such as 'moral perversion'. As a result, confusion appears to have existed even amongst the educated upper-class and Diane went on to report a story that 'Lord Albemarle is said to have walked into the Turf [Club] and said "I've never heard of this Greek chap Clitoris they are all talking of"'.[14]

War and Expanding Employment Opportunities

Concerns about the effect of war on female sexuality were exacerbated by the impact of the First World War on women's employment and accepted gender roles. While working-class women had been employed before the war in occupations such as domestic service and the textiles industry, the peculiar conditions of the war brought about a change both in the number of women working and, more significantly, in the nature of the work they were employed in. The loss of a large proportion of the male workforce to the front, particularly after the introduction of conscription in 1916, forced the government to appeal for women to fill their places, while a large number of working-class women, having lost their male breadwinner, were obliged to work for financial reasons. As a result the number of women working in industry increased from 3,276,000 in July 1914 to 4,808,000 in April 1918. The most significant change brought about by the war was the mass exodus from traditionally feminine areas such as domestic service or textiles into munitions work, policing, bus driving and other jobs previously perceived as exclusively masculine. While the appeal of munitions work can be explained in part by the higher wages guaranteed by government interest in the industry, women entered other jobs for more complex reasons. In her article on women police in the First World War, Philippa Levine stresses the generally middle- and upper-class backgrounds of the women attracted to this work and refers to the initially strong involvement of the feminist movement in campaigning for women in the police force.[15]

Middle- and upper-class women wishing to work during the First World War for patriotic reasons found a number of options open to them. Nursing had long been regarded as an appropriate occupation for women, utilising women's perceived nurturing and caring qualities. The association of women with military nursing had been reinforced in Britain by the myth which surrounded Florence Nightingale, and as a result, nursing was a popular and acceptable way in which women could contribute to the war effort. By November 1918, 12,769 trained nurses and 10,816 partially trained or untrained nurses were working for the Queen Alexandra's Imperial Military Nursing Service and the Territorial Force Nursing Services, while a further 2,396 British nurses and 1,685 Voluntary Aid Detachment nurses worked for the Royal Army Medical Corps in August 1918.[16] Although women who worked as nurses remained under the control of largely male doctors and therefore posed no direct threat to established gender norms, the work exposed many sheltered young women to both the horrors and dangers of war. The pressure for qualified medical personnel also opened up a number of opportunities for women doctors who took over the civilian roles of male doctors who had joined the Royal Army Medical Corps or contributed directly to the war effort themselves. In May 1915, Drs Louisa Garrett Anderson and Flora Murray founded the Endell Street military hospital in London and from 1916 onwards, women doctors began to work in hospitals on the front line in Malta, Salonika, Egypt, India, East Africa and Palestine. The Scottish Women's Hospitals (SWH), founded by Dr Elsie Inglis, was the largest medical organisation run entirely by women. In October 1914, the SWH established a hospital in France, and further hospitals were later established in Serbia and Russia, eventually employing over 1,000 women as doctors, orderlies, nurses and ambulance drivers.[17]

Britain was the first of the European nations involved in the war to establish women's paramilitary services. In the spring of 1917, the Women's Army Auxiliary Corps (WAAC) was established. By November 1918, 40,000 women were serving in the WAAC, 8,500 of whom were sent abroad. The women were given ranks, regulations and uniforms, like the men who served in the regular army. However, the WAAC had an organisational structure independent from the army and women were classified as non-combatants. Their role was to free men to go to the front by working in support roles as cooks, clerks and mechanics. In the following year, parallel women's services were established to support each of the branches of the armed services. In November 1917, the Women's Royal Naval Service was established and recruits performed clerical work and dealt with household matters, storekeeping and electrical and engineering work. In April 1918, the Women's Royal Air Force (WRAF) was set up, again to perform clerical and domestic jobs, but some WRAF women also became drivers, fitters, welders and carpenters, working on the aeroplanes.

A number of voluntary women police organisations were also established by middle- and upper-class women, as an extension of the growing involvement of such women in social welfare and factory inspection work. At the outbreak of war, the feminist National Union of Working Women (NUWW) proposed a force of non-uniformed volunteer patrols, while a number of women from a more militant suffragette background, including Margaret Damer Dawson and Nina Boyle, established the uniformed professional Women's Police Volunteers (WPV). When a disagreement over the role of the WPV occurred soon afterwards, Margaret Damer Dawson and Mary Allen broke with Nina Boyle and established a further group, the Women Police Service (WPS). The central role of women police during the war was the policing and protection of women, with a focus on moral welfare work, in the context of widespread anxieties about female promiscuity. Women police patrolled parks, the perimeters of garrisons and other public spaces, separating men and women who were thought to be engaging in immoral or inappropriate behaviour and following suspect couples to prevent illicit sexual encounters. Continuing a practice of the late-nineteenth- and early-twentieth-century moral purity groups, women police also entered public houses and other sites of 'ill-repute'. By 1916, the WPS were also heavily involved in patrolling and inspecting munitions factories where women were employed, to ensure the moral conduct of the women factory workers.

Many of the early women police recruits were from the educated middle class and were drawn into the work through their involvement in feminist politics before the war. Both Nina Boyle and Mary Allen had been members of the militant suffrage group the Women's Social and Political Union (WSPU) and the WPS maintained a strong feminist outlook, campaigning for an independent professional women's police force with equal powers to policemen. The NUWW, however, increasingly distanced itself from its feminist roots, seeking to recruit women from lower down the social scale, for whom policing might represent a viable paid occupation rather than a political or patriotic commitment. The majority of women who served as women police were older, married women, considered best suited to the maternal role of supervising and ensuring the welfare of girls and younger women. Louise Creighton, one of those involved in the founding of the NUWW patrols, thought recruits should be 'women of tact and experience, between thirty and forty years of age'.[18] However, the unique circumstances of the war and the new choices becoming available to women in this and other occupations offered exciting opportunities for single women and those who wished to resist conventional feminine roles. Joan Lock, in her history of British policewomen, described Mary Allen's response to the outbreak of war in these terms:

> She was invited to join a needlework guild, a prospect which filled her with horror: she wanted action. While in this state of limbo, she overheard two people on a bus discussing the risible idea of women police. Mary was enchanted by the notion and immediately investigated and volunteered.[19]

Mary's enthusiasm was shared by Margaret Damer Dawson, and the two soon established a close professional and personal relationship, living together in London between 1914 and 1920.[20] When Dawson died in 1920, Allen was a major beneficiary in her will, continuing to live in Dawson's house, Danehill, throughout the 1930s and beginning a relationship in the early 1920s with another former WPS officer Miss Helen Tagart.

Other wartime occupations actively encouraged younger unmarried women recruits and a number of women who made a significant contribution to the war effort through their work were in relationships with other women. It is difficult to interpret the precise nature of women's

close friendships in the absence of explicit evidence as to how the women
themselves viewed them, however. Dr Elsie Inglis, founder of the SWH,
had lived with Dr Flora Murray for a number of years in Edinburgh,
and Drs Louisa Martindale and Louisa Aldrich-Blake also lived with
women.[21] Emily Hamer argues that Evelina Haverfield, founder
of a number of women's voluntary organisations, including the Women's
Emergency Corps and the Women's Volunteer Reserves, was a lesbian
and lover of the former suffragette Vera 'Jack' Holme. The two women
worked closely with Dr Elsie Inglis in Serbia during the war, and
when Haverfield died in 1920, Holme stayed in Serbia working
as an ambulance and relief lorry driver. Emily Hamer notes:

> After Evelina's death Vera Holme had to remove her belongings
> from the home in Britain which they had shared; the house had been
> owned by Evelina. Vera sent a list of her belongings, which were
> to be returned to her, to the executors of Haverfield's estate. A copy
> of this list survives among Vera Holme's papers. Among the things
> that Vera Holme wanted back were presents that she had given
> to Evelina and things with particular sentimental value. Chief
> amongst these was '1 bed with carved sides [inscribed with] E.H.
> and V.H.'[22]

Holme's friend Naomi 'Micky' Jacob, who ran a munitions factory
in Willesden during the war, was also a lesbian, while Lilian Barker,
superintendent of Woolwich Arsenal from 1916, had lived with
her lover Florence Francis since the outbreak of war.[23]

Contemporary Perceptions of Women's War Work

The increase in women's employment during the war and the lasting
effect this had on attitudes towards female employment were perceived
by many contemporaries as a threat to established values concerning the
domestic and maternal role of women. Hostility to women's war work
reflected the extent to which it was seen to pose a challenge to accepted
views on the place of women. Pre-war attitudes to women's employment
had centred on the issue of public health, with the fear that working
women placed the health of themselves and their family at risk. This
was reinforced by the Victorian belief that women should not be exposed

to public life as this could only have an adverse effect on their moral well-being and that of their children. Such views were apparent in the hostility experienced by women police officers from members of the public who felt that they were behaving in an immodest fashion. Attitudes towards women's employment were complicated during and after the war by fears, expressed most vociferously by the trade unions, that women were taking jobs away from men. The government's belief that working women would return en masse to their homes after the war meant that this conflict was never fully resolved; it continued well into the interwar period and was exacerbated by such legislation as the 1919 Sex Disqualification Removal Act, which granted women access to public office and civil and judicial posts. Hostility to the work women did during the war may also have been fuelled by a growing sense of resentment amongst soldiers at the front – that while they were suffering the horrors of war, women were enjoying the greater independence which higher wages provided. Women were therefore perceived to be encroaching not only upon traditionally male spheres of employment but also upon the masculine autonomy and freedom which accompanied paid employment.

One focus for contemporary debates about changing gender roles was women's dress and, in particular, the wearing of uniforms by women. With women participating in the war effort through an increasing number of voluntary organisations and paid occupations, uniformed women became a familiar sight throughout Britain. As *The Daily Express* observed in 1918, women could be seen

> In offices, shops, railway companies, banks, acting, writing, driving taxis, ploughing the land, taming vicious horses, felling trees ... [dressed] in khaki, blue, brown or grey, with slouch hat, round hat, or no hat at all, in skirts as short as ballet girls' or in masculine breeches.[24]

Women rarely wore trousers in public before 1939, and the incorporation of breeches into some women's uniforms during the First World War therefore represented a significant break with conventions of feminine dress. Uniforms, in particular worn by women, became 'emblems of [women's] direct involvement in the war effort ... Uniforms carried enormous social prestige and symbolism. A war-related uniform was an immediately recognisable emblem of patriotic engagement,

of dedication to the nation's cause. To wear such a uniform was
a statement at once political and moral.'[25] For some women who wore
them, uniforms provided them with a new authority, derived from the
masculine and official connotations of the uniform. Mary Allen, who
argued strongly for the right of women police to wear the masculine
military-style uniform designed for the WPS by Margaret Damer
Dawson, claimed:

> It was a notable fact that the policewoman in uniform (as soon
> as the newness of her appearance had worn off) was treated with
> respect by the most frivolous and incorrigible girls … The uniform
> also earned the instinctive respect of the young soldier, even when
> drunk and inclined to be violent … The uniform alone unnerves the
> offender, and shows to onlookers and possible sympathisers that the
> power and majesty of the law is behind the figure in official blue.[26]

Despite Mary Allen's claims, public responses to the sight of uniformed
women varied. Naomi Jacob recalled that 'women who wore uniform –
unless they were nurses – were regarded as something strange, eccentric,
and a fine target for jokes' and the Marchioness of Londonderry
claimed that wearing a uniform 'led indeed to some strange experiences.
Some people were always rude to a woman in uniform … they were
incredulous or laughed outright.'[27] However, the writer Mary Agnes
Hamilton disagreed, arguing:

> Women wore trousers or knickers and puttees in perfect immunity
> from the guffaws that once greeted the brave spirits who had
> clambered upon bicycles in divided skirts; the lift-girl in smart
> boots, the driver of official car and public taxi in neat breeches
> and leggings, the munition girl and the land girl in trousers and
> overalls were not so much remarked upon by anybody. They were
> in uniform: uniform was immune from jeer or sneer.[28]

The satirical journal *Punch* gently mocked the confusion arising from
the presence of women in uniforms but rarely made the women
themselves the target of the joke.

For some women beginning to articulate a sexual identity based
on their desire for other women, the social sanction which wartime
uniforms gave to the wearing of masculine dress by women could offer

exciting new possibilities. Emily Hamer has argued that 'lesbians seem to have often chosen to mark their lesbianism through their clothes, their shoes, their hair-cuts and their jewellery. They made themselves visible to their contemporaries, and ... [t]he most obvious way of dressing like a lesbian was dressing mannishly'.[29] Late-nineteenth- and early-twentieth-century sexological work had frequently blurred the distinction between lesbianism and female transvestism, and a number of sexologists referred to a link between masculine dress and female inversion. August Forel claimed: 'Female inverts have been known to wear men's uniforms and perform military service for years, and even behave as heroes.'[30] Radclyffe Hall suggested that uniforms worn in the First World War represented an important aspect of an emerging lesbian identity for some women. Writing about wartime female inverts in *The Well of Loneliness*, Hall suggested: 'One great weakness they all had, it must be admitted, and this was for uniforms – yet why not?'[31] In this context, uniforms offered some women a means of expressing an alluring sexual identity and indicating desire for other women. Naomi Jacob described Mary Allen's uniform as an erotic tool:

> I have seen hundreds of women in uniform in two world wars, but I have never seen one who carried it off better than Commander Mary Allen. Her uniform, a severe military 'frock coat' in dark blue, which fell just below her knees, breeches and riding boots, with a field service hat with a gold band round the peak, was both dignified and arresting. Her boots alone could have demanded respect.[32]

While women such as Mary Allen were able to take advantage of wartime fashions to express lesbian sexual identity with relative impunity, in the aftermath of the First World War, women's uniforms became increasingly suspect. By 1925, Joan Lock was describing Mary Allen's appearance as 'grotesquely masculine' and women who continued to wear Land Army breeches or other uniforms became the object of harsher ridicule in the pages of *Punch*.[33]

Mary Allen and the WPS became the focus of a particularly hostile attack on women's uniforms in the early 1920s. Despite Margaret Damer Dawson and Mary Allen having received the Order of the British Empire, and Superintendent Isobel Goldingham, a Member of the British Empire, from the king in 1918, the WPS was not included in post-war plans for a women's police service. The group's militant suffragette origins and continued commitment to the idea of an independent, equal women's police force were viewed with concern by the Metropolitan Police and, when the Metropolitan Police came to launch their own women's police force in 1918, they turned to Mrs Sophia Stanley, director of the less militant NUWW patrols. Despite being sidelined by the new Metropolitan Women Police Patrols, Mary Allen and Margaret Damer Dawson's WPS continued to patrol the streets of London in the years after the war, prompting increasing anger on the part of the Metropolitan Police. Although, as Laura Doan demonstrates, General Sir Neville Macready, Commissioner of the Metropolitan Police, could have used any number of arguments to prevent the WPS from patrolling after the war, he chose to focus his attack on the issue of their uniforms, arguing that they were excessively masculine and that the WPS might reasonably be mistaken for his newly formed Metropolitan Women Police Patrols (MWPP). Given that the MWPP uniforms had, in fact, been based on those designed and worn by the WPS, it is possible that Macready's objection was not to the uniforms themselves, but to the significance of such a uniform when worn by specific women. Macready was clearly suspicious of the WPS leadership, whose politics and masculine airs may have prompted suspicions of sexual inversion, and Mary Allen apparently interpreted Macready's hostility to her in these terms. When Mary Allen and Helen Tagart were introduced to Radclyffe Hall and Una Troubridge in 1930, Troubridge recorded in her diary that Allen thought 'the authorities were against her because she was an invert'.[34] In this context, Macready's particular objection to the WPS may have centred on a concern that sexual inverts in the WPS were patrolling the streets of London in uniforms which made them visible to the public as both policewomen and sexual inverts.

However, while uniforms and masculine dress may have indicated lesbianism in the eyes of some women and cultural observers after the war – and increasingly after the publicity surrounding Radclyffe Hall's novel *The Well of Loneliness* in 1928 – Laura Doan has recently argued that such associations remained extremely vague and ambivalent during the First World War.[35] Focusing on reactions to the women ambulance drivers who served in the First Aid Nursing Yeomanry (FANY) at the front during the war, she suggests that masculinity and gender inversion were not necessarily associated with sexual inversion in these years. Ambulance-driving near and on the front lines required women who

were physically strong, mechanical and efficient, as well as possessing
the more conventionally feminine attributes of gentleness and care
for the wounded. The women endured 'an extremely Spartan mode
of living' and therefore, as one driver told new recruits, 'it will be readily
understood that the butterfly woman is totally out of her element ...
The more solid and responsible woman, with plenty of grit and pluck,
is the only type who is likely to "stick it out"'.[36] The women who
worked in this environment were often attracted by a sense of adventure
and possessed a strong muscular physique. Contemporary commentators
referred to the women in their outfits of khaki breeches, flannel shirts and
fur coats as 'like splendid young airmen', while the novelist May Sinclair
described watching driver Mairi Chisholm strolling

> about the seat of War with her hands in her pockets, as if a battle
> were a cricket match ... and yet there isn't a man in the Corps who
> does his work better or with more courage and endurance than this
> 18 year old child.[37]

In the years after the war, a number of cultural links were made between
ambulance-driving and lesbianism. In *The Well of Loneliness*, Radclyffe
Hall depicted a sexual affair between two women ambulance drivers,
a passage which the judge at the novel's obscenity trial identified
as particularly disturbing:

> According to the writer of this book, a number of women
> of position and admirable character, who were engaged in driving
> ambulances in the course of the war, were addicted to this vice.[38]

Lesbian novelist Gertrude Stein claimed to have driven an ambulance
close to the front line, as did Dolly Wilde and Joe Carstairs. The relationship between Mairi Chisholm and Baroness de T'Serclaes (formerly
Mrs Elsie Knocker), who shared a private bedroom and double bed for
four years while stationed at Pervyse, has also come under closer scrutiny.
   However, during the war, neither cultural commentators nor many
of the women themselves appear to have made an association between
the ambulance drivers and lesbianism. In 1916, *The Times* referred with
approval to the evolution of a 'race of young Amazons' employed on war
work, regarding them as the daughters of New Women, for whom the
war had acted as a '"crucible" in which the dross was purged away, and

the pure gold of New Womanhood emerged'.[39] When F. Tennyson Jesse, a journalist for *Vogue*, visited a FANY camp in France, she also described the women as attractive and impressive, possessing a 'blessed freedom' from the usual feminine concern with appearance:

> It is a sort of splendid austerity, that pervades their look and outlook ... and in their bodies expresses itself in a disregard for appearances that one would never have thought to find in a human woman. It leaves you gasping. They come in, wind-blown, reddened, hot with exertion ... they come in, toss their caps down, brush their hair back from their brow in the one gesture that no woman has ever permitted herself or liked in a lover – and they don't mind. It is amazing, that disregard for appearances.[40]

She goes on to compare the women's behaviour with that of chivalrous young gentlemen, describing how they 'made me feel, in the beautiful way they shepherded me, that I was a silly useless female, and that they were grave chivalrous young men; they watched over me with just that matter-of-fact care'. Despite this depiction of the women as attractive, manly and chivalrous, however, Jesse made no suggestion of sexual deviance in connection with the women, admiring them instead as 'touched with something finer, some quality of radiance'. Personal accounts suggest that the women themselves may also not have interpreted their masculine appearance and occupation as significant in terms of their gender or sexual identity. FANY member Pat Beauchamp recorded her surprise and bemused pleasure when she overheard a local Belgian observe: 'Truly, until one hears their voices, one would say they were men,' while Elsie Knocker donated the diary in which she recorded her four years in Pervyse with Mairi Chisholm to the Imperial War Museum with no apparent sense that their relationship might be interpreted in sexual terms.[41] Such evidence suggests that, while some connections were beginning to be made between masculinity, sexual knowledge and lesbianism by some individuals during the First World War, these ideas remained ambivalent and unclear until the 1920s.

Chapter 7

Identity Crisis? The Emergence of the Modern Lesbian, 1918–1939

The interwar period has been seen as a critical era in the development of modern notions of lesbianism. The increasing popularisation of the work of late-nineteenth-century sexologists meant that the medical model of sexual categories was gaining wider currency in the early decades of the twentieth century. Widespread fears regarding the growing independence of women in the wake of the suffrage movement, and the impact of the First World War on gender boundaries, fuelled debates about female sexuality. In such an atmosphere, it has been argued that close woman-to-woman relationships, of the kind which abounded in the eighteenth and nineteenth centuries, became increasingly suspect. In 1921, an attempt was made to introduce legislation against lesbian sexuality for the first time. A number of novels were published in the years after the First World War, which tackled the theme of lesbianism and brought the issue to a wider audience. The most influential of these was Radclyffe Hall's novel *The Well of Loneliness*, published in 1928, whose trial and subsequent banning for obscenity was the subject of widespread press attention. The decade also saw the formation of explicitly lesbian communities such as the expatriate lesbian community of the Parisian left bank, while individual self-identified lesbians, including Radclyffe Hall and the artist Gluck, employed clothing and mannerisms to express themselves as lesbian. These changes have prompted lesbian historians to focus upon the 1920s in particular as the decade in which a defined concept of lesbian identity began to emerge into mainstream culture. However, as recent work on the notorious interwar cross-dresser Colonel Barker and others has demonstrated, popular ideas about the links between gender and sexual identity continued to lack clarity throughout the period, remaining confused at least into the 1930s.

The Criminal Law Amendment Bill (1921)

In August 1921, three MPs attempted to introduce a clause which would have made sexual acts between women criminal in the same way

as similar acts between men had been since 1885. The clause
proposed that:

> Any act of gross indecency between female persons shall
> be a misdemeanour and punishable in the same manner as any
> such act committed by male persons under section eleven of the
> Criminal Law Amendment Act, 1885.[1]

The clause was introduced as a proposed amendment to the Criminal
Law Amendment Bill (1921), a piece of legislation primarily designed
to protect children under the age of sixteen from indecent assault. Added
at the committee stage, to what was an agreed Bill – and could therefore
not be significantly altered due to time constraints – the clause effectively
destroyed the Bill. Many commentators and historians have suggested
that the clause was introduced in an intentional attempt to block a Bill
which was perceived by some as an attempt to control middle-class male
sexual behaviour.[2] The clause bore very little relation to the primary
purpose of the Bill, and the Lord Chancellor, in his preface to the Lords'
discussion of the new clause, referred to its introduction as:

> the extraordinary proceeding, as it appears to me, under which,
> in the early hours of the morning in another place [the Commons],
> there has been introduced an Amendment of the Criminal Law ...
> having no relation at all to the subject matter of the Bill in which
> it has been incorporated, and being most highly disputable upon
> its merits.[3]

Laura Doan has suggested that the clause may have arisen as a result
of a misunderstanding at the committee stage. It was first tabled during
a meeting of a Joint Select Committee on the Criminal Law Amendment
Bill in October 1920. A London Metropolitan Police magistrate, Cecil
Maurice Chapman, had been called to give expert testimony to the
committee and, during the discussion, apparently passed a note proposing
the amendment to the chairman, Lord Muir Mackenzie. However,
Chapman was an active member of the British Society for the Study of Sex
Psychology (BSSSP) and shared the organisation's liberal stance opposing
legislation against sexual behaviour between consenting adults of the
same sex, and it therefore seems unlikely that he would have proposed

such a clause. Doan suggests, instead, that the clause emerged as a result of a lack of understanding of the concept of lesbianism or 'sexual inversion'. Parliamentary etiquette, established since the nineteenth century, prevented speakers from using explicit terms to refer to behaviour which was regarded as sexually deviant; vague euphemisms such as 'gross indecency' had, for decades, been employed in parliamentary discussions and in the drafting of legislation, to refer to same-sex practices. If, as was likely, the other members of the committee were less informed on current thinking about female sexuality and sexual inversion than Chapman was, it was possible that Chapman could have proposed the introduction of a clause aimed at sexual assaults by adult women on young girls, but that the committee had misunderstood and interpreted 'gross indecency' as referring to consenting sexual acts between adult women.

Despite this continued confusion over language, the fact that the clause was discussed, for the first time in parliamentary history, is an indication of a growing awareness of the possibility of desire between women. The views expressed during the debates give an insight into the attitudes of the establishment towards lesbianism in the interwar period. Parliamentary conventions regarding the etiquette of discussing sexual deviance in the House were maintained throughout the debate, and speakers in both houses employed euphemisms such as 'gross practices' to refer to lesbianism. Sir Ernest Wild, in a speech outlining his arguments for introducing the clause, excused himself from going into details about the offence he was attempting to legislate against on the grounds that 'We do not want to pollute the House with details of these abominations.'[4] Equally, every speaker in both debates expressed their distaste for the subject of lesbianism. Frederick A. Macquisten, MP, one of the Tory lawyers who introduced the clause in the Commons, referred to lesbianism as 'this horrid grossness of homosexual immorality', while the Earl of Malmesbury initiated the debate in the Lords with the apology: 'I am extremely sorry to raise a discussion upon what must be, to all of us, a most disgusting and polluting subject.'[5]

Many of the speakers argued that desire between women was an issue of concern because of the threat posed by lesbians to established gender norms and the role assigned to women within society. Macquisten argued that lesbian relationships were responsible for the break-up of marriages, implying that they were a common feature of divorce cases. He presented lesbians as sexual predators who preyed upon vulnerable married women, causing devastation to innocent husbands, and cited cases from his own experience to support his argument:

> In the course of my experience I have seen happy homes wrecked in this way. Only tonight I was speaking with a man whom I have known for a comparatively short time, and who told me how his home had been ruined by the wiles of one abandoned female, who had pursued his wife, and later some other misconduct happened with a male person which enabled him to get a divorce.[6]

Lesbianism was presented as a threat not only to heterosexual marriage but also to the maternal role of women. Sir Ernest Wild claimed:

> This vice does exist, and it saps the fundamental institutions of society. In the first place it stops child-birth, because it is a well-known fact that any woman who indulges in this vice will have nothing whatever to do with the other sex.[7]

Both Macquisten and Wild, who had proposed the clause together with Howard Gritten, apparently felt that in drawing attention to the threat posed to the patriarchal institutions of marriage and the family, they would encourage their colleagues to consider lesbianism a serious issue. Speakers were also unanimous in asserting that the lesbian minority was a pathological one. Frederick Macquisten and Sir Ernest Wild both relied upon medical expertise to support their argument for legislation. Macquisten suggested that questions of the cause or manifestations of lesbianism were 'more a matter for medical science and for neurologists', arguing that the duty of MPs was simply to implement legislation to control its disastrous effects.[8] Wild also referred to medical experts to support his claim that lesbianism was prevalent in society. He suggested to his fellow MPs that:

> If they were to consult any neurologist, any great doctor who deals with nerve diseases, they would be told that this is a very prevalent practice. I have the authority of one of the greatest of our nerve specialists – I do not wish to mention names – who has told me with his own lips that no week passes that some unfortunate girl does not confess to him that she owes the breakdown of her nerves to the fact that she has been tampered with by a member of her own sex.[9]

He concluded his point by referring them to the works of sexologists Richard von Krafft-Ebing and Havelock Ellis and drawing their attention to the apparently large numbers of lesbians in lunatic asylums.

However, despite broad agreement between the speakers that lesbianism was distasteful and pathological, both houses rejected the clause and therefore the entire Bill. The most significant reason for this, offered by speakers in the Lords, was the fear that legislation would only draw attention to the offence. This concern was based on an assumption that lesbianism only existed in a very few pathological cases and that the vast majority of the female population were unaware of the possibilities of lesbian sexual expression. The Earl of Desart, in his speech, suggested that such activities were practised by 'at most, an extremely small minority'.[10] Similar comments were made throughout the debates in both houses, with only Sir Ernest Wild claiming that 'this is a very prevalent practice', in an attempt to scare the Commons into accepting his amendment.[11] He later qualified his assertion, commenting that: 'It is idle to deny, although I will not say the vice is rampant in society, that there are people in society who are guilty of it.'[12] In contrast, the majority of the female population was represented as sexually innocent. During the Lords debate, a number of speakers referred to the natural timidity and nervousness of women, and their rejection of autonomy. The Earl of Malmesbury declared that:

> the domestic habits of men and of women are entirely different. Women are by nature much more gregarious. For instance, if twenty women were going to live in a house with twenty bedrooms, I do not believe that all the twenty bedrooms would be occupied, either for reasons of fear or nervousness, and the desire for mutual protection. On the other hand, I know that when men take shooting boxes the first inquiry is that each shall have a room to himself if possible.[13]

Focusing on the supposed innate nervousness and fragility of women, Malmesbury's comments defined women's feelings for each other in primarily 'sisterly' terms. The Earl of Desart agreed that women were potentially hysterical but was less sure of women's sexual innocence, suggesting that 'the sort of romantic, almost hysterical, friendships that are made between young women at certain periods of their lives' might be open to interpretation as manifestations of lesbianism.[14] The majority of speakers, however, were insistent on women's fundamental innocence. The Lord Chancellor claimed: 'I would be bold enough to say that of every thousand women, taken as a whole, 999 have never even heard a whisper of these practices.'[15] Such assumptions led many of the speakers in the two debates to conclude that if passed into law, the clause would serve only to advertise the existence of the offence. The Earl of Desart declared:

> you are going to tell the whole world that there is such an offence, to bring it to the notice of women who have never heard of it, never thought of it, never dreamed of it. I think that is a very great mischief.[16]

A similar point was made less sympathetically by Lieutenant-Colonel Moore-Brabazon during the Commons debate:

> There are only three ways of dealing with perverts. The first is the death sentence. That has been tried in old times, and, though drastic, it does do what is required – that is, stamp them out. The second is to look upon them frankly as lunatics, and lock them up for the rest of their lives. That is a very satisfactory way also. It gets rid of them. The third way is to leave them entirely alone, not notice them, not advertise them. That is the method that has been adopted in England for many hundred years, and I believe that it is the best method now ... To adopt a Clause of this kind would do harm by introducing into the minds of perfectly innocent people the most revolting thoughts.[17]

This fear that legislating against lesbianism would simply advertise the phenomenon and thus corrupt innocent female minds was the central objection to the clause. In an attempt to maintain a long-standing official silence on the issue, the Bill was rejected.

The Well of Loneliness Affair

Despite the attempt by Parliament to restrict public awareness of lesbianism, less than a decade later, the issue had again become the focus of public debate. In July 1928, Radclyffe Hall, already a well-known author, published *The Well of Loneliness*, a novel depicting the experiences of a female invert, Stephen Gordon, in a hostile society. Hall presented Stephen Gordon as an honourable individual whose sexual identity was innate and therefore outside her control. Strongly influenced by the views of late-nineteenth-century sexologists, Hall portrayed her heroine unambiguously as the stereotype of a 'mannish lesbian', while the plot represented misery, isolation and lack of fulfil-ment as the inevitable lot of the lesbian in Western society. The central message of the novel was an explicit plea for toleration on behalf of all homosexuals. By August 1928 it had been the subject of vitriolic attacks in some segments of the tabloid press, led by *The Sunday Express* and *The Daily Express*. Although the novel had initially received favourable reviews from *The Daily Telegraph* and *The Morning Post*, amongst others, on 19 August, James Douglas, editor of *The Sunday Express*, published an article entitled 'A Book that Must Be Suppressed', in which he declared:

> I would rather give a healthy boy or a healthy girl a phial of prussic acid than this novel. Poison kills the body, but moral poison kills the soul.[18]

Douglas demanded the novel be suppressed and the Home Secretary Sir William Joynson-Hicks agreed, instructing the Department of Public Prosecutions to take legal action against the novel. By the end of November, *The Well of Loneliness* had been officially banned as obscene. However, the uniquely popular medium through which Hall chose to disseminate her message, and the unprecedented publicity the novel received as a result of the press campaign and subsequent trial meant that lesbianism was again forced into the realm of mainstream debate.

Literary critics and historians have identified a number of reasons for the critical attention which *The Well of Loneliness* received. The novel's challenge to social attitudes was rendered unusually explicit to the reader by Radclyffe Hall's use of traditional literary conventions. The basic structure follows a conventional narrative of personal development and social integration, but in reverse, describing instead a pattern of increasing exclusion and isolation. At her birth, Stephen Gordon is the much-wanted child of a respectable and socially secure couple, but the story of her childhood traces her increasingly problematic relations with her mother and her peers, while the death of her father at the end of part one represents the loss of her only genuine and affectionate tie to society, culminating in her exile from the ancestral home. Her subsequent career as an independent woman is a tale of increasing isolation, declining from a socially valid life as a novelist and ambulance driver in the Great War, through the difficulties as an exile and an invert of finding a place in society, to her ultimate renunciation of her lover, Mary, to a man and retreat into loneliness and despair.[19] Again, in her treatment of the various romantic interests in Stephen's life, Hall employed conventional romantic modes. Stephen's socially acceptable but personally disastrous relationship with Martin is portrayed in conventional terms: Martin falls in love with Stephen in the fruitful spring – a season traditionally associated with romance and procreation – but is rejected by an outraged Stephen. However, during Stephen's love affair with Angela Crossby, while Stephen attempts to adopt conventional courtship patterns – introducing Angela to the parental home and buying her a ring – her abortive efforts are juxtaposed with and parodied by the socially approved and successful courtship of her neighbours, Violet and Alec. Finally, Hall employs traditional symbols of femininity and masculinity in her descriptions of Stephen's parents in order to emphasise Stephen's isolation from established gender roles. Lady Anna, her mother, is continually linked with Nature and enjoys a special bond, as a 'real' woman, with the procreative beauty of the natural world, while Stephen experiences a sense of restlessness, the product of her essential sterility, when she confronts Nature. She is similarly excluded from her father Sir Philip's masterful relationship with his natural surroundings by her problematic position as a woman in the male world of the hunt. This use of traditional literary forms allowed Radclyffe Hall to make her meaning explicit to the wider public. As a result, despite a desperate attempt by her publisher's defence lawyer, Norman Birkett, to deny that Stephen's affairs were lesbian during the obscenity trial of the book, it was impossible to do so.[20]

Despite Hall's own lesbianism and her participation in a wider lesbian social circle, the model of lesbian identity which she presented in the novel was strongly influenced by sexological theory. Hall's protagonist, Stephen Gordon, possesses the masculine physiology and characteristics labelled by the sexologists as those of the 'true female invert'. Michael Baker, in his biography of Hall, noted that she spent some time, while preparing the novel, researching the works of Havelock Ellis and Richard von Krafft-Ebing.[21] The 1928 edition of the novel also included a foreword by Ellis, endorsing the book, in which he stated:

> I have read 'The Well of Loneliness' with great interest because – apart from its fine qualities as a novel by a writer of accomplished art – it possesses a notable psychological and sociological significance. So far as I know, it is the first English novel which presents, in a completely faithful and uncompromising form, one particular aspect of sexual life as it exists among us today.[22]

As Ellis noted, Hall offered a faithful reproduction of the sexologists' 'man trapped in a woman's body' in her depiction of Stephen. Physically, Stephen's body possesses only the genital features of a woman: she is 'a narrow-hipped, wide-shouldered little tadpole of a baby' and matures into a tall, strong woman who looks ill at ease and faintly ridiculous in feminine finery.[23] As a child and adolescent she enjoys conventionally masculine activities, such as riding and fencing, so that her schoolroom is cluttered with riding whips and dumb-bells and she acquires 'absurd little biceps'.[24] Her prowess at the hunt is a source of pride to her father and envy to their neighbour, Colonel Antrim, who wishes his own son and daughter were such natural riders. However, Laura Doan has argued that Radclyffe Hall did not simply reproduce the arguments of the sexologists, instead using them selectively to fit her own account. As a result Stephen's physical signs of masculinity are also combined with other arguments explaining Stephen's masculinity: not only do Sir Philip and Lady Gordon name their daughter Stephen, but as a young child Stephen dresses up in masculine clothes as the young Nelson and announces to the female servants: 'I am a boy.'[25] Hall continues to emphasise Stephen's essentially masculine nature throughout the novel, giving her an excessive smoking habit and other stereotypically masculine features in maturity. Stephen's fine intelligence and strong moral code are similarly based on the work of Havelock Ellis, who attempted to defend inverts by arguing that they were often compensated for their lack of 'normality' by a greater than average intelligence and sense of morality. Ellis' portrayal of inverts suggested that they could make an important contribution to society, an argument which Hall exploited in the novel to further her message of tolerance.

Literary critics have offered a number of explanations for Radclyffe Hall's acceptance of the sexological stereotype of the mannish invert, despite the availability of alternative models of love between women. Lillian Faderman has suggested that the adoption of a congenital explanation of lesbianism was part of a strategic defence against demands for inverts to be cured: if their condition was understood as innate and incurable, society had little choice but to accept inverts as potentially productive citizens.[26] In addition, Esther Newton has suggested that sexological theory was the only available cultural model which allowed Hall to break with the asexual notion of romantic friendship and give Stephen an active sexual identity.[27] With the increasing dominance of medical models of sexuality, sexological theory was also the most explicit language Hall could use to convey Stephen's message to a wider audience.

Radclyffe Hall's application of patriarchal gender categories to the other characters in the novel serves to reinforce this message. Traditional binary gender roles and gendered power relations are accepted unquestioningly throughout *The Well of Loneliness*. Sir Philip, who represents the ultimate symbol of patriarchy in the novel, is idealised by his daughter, who responds to his question regarding the nature of honour, 'You are honour.'[28] The novel acknowledges the social privileges enjoyed by men, but rather than resenting a system which grants such rights unequally to men but not to women, Stephen is made to regret the fact that she is a woman.[29] This inequality in gender relations is particularly apparent in Stephen's romantic affairs. In her relationship with Mary, Stephen is 'all things to Mary; father, mother, friend and lover, all things, and Mary is all things to her – the child, the friend, the beloved, all things'.[30] The importance to Stephen of playing a dominant masculine role in their relationship is emphasised by the distress she feels at being unable to protect Mary from social disapproval, the first duty of a 'husband'. She complains: 'I cannot protect you, Mary, the world has deprived me of my right to protect; I am utterly helpless, I can only love you.'[31] In contrast, Mary is represented as stereotypically wifely and passive:

> Mary, because she was perfect woman, would rest [in Stephen's arms] without thought, without exultation, without question; finding no need to question since for her there was now only one thing – Stephen.[32]

Their life together is a replica of a conventional heterosexual relationship, in which Mary superintends the running of their home, while Stephen works in her study, emerging only to sleep or eat the meals placed in front of her. Ultimately, however, Stephen accepts her inadequacy as a husband and gives Mary away to 'another' man for her own good, as if she were a possession.

Contemporary reactions to *The Well of Loneliness* as a lesbian and potentially obscene novel were further shaped by attitudes to Radclyffe Hall herself. Hall came to be closely associated with her heroine so that Hall's own lesbianism and the manner in which she expressed it had important implications for her novel. As Emily Hamer comments: 'The prosecution of *The Well of Loneliness* cannot have been unaffected by the outrageous public spectacle of Radclyffe Hall's life.'[33] As a financially independent woman, Hall could afford to risk social disapproval by being open about her sexuality, and she began to do so as soon as she reached maturity. However, it was not until 1918, when she began her lifelong relationship with Una Lady Troubridge, the former wife of Lord Admiral Troubridge, that Hall's lesbianism became notorious. As the wife of an admiral, Una Troubridge held an important social position, and her desertion of her husband for a woman inevitably caused a scandal.

The couple's personal appearance was also a subject of comment in the 1920s. Like her character Stephen, Radclyffe Hall's personal image closely reflected the model of female inversion offered by the sexologists. *The Birmingham Post* described her in April 1927 as:

[A] well-known figure at all the interesting parties and public occasions and [she] is easily recognizable by her distinctive appearance, tall, slim, and very well groomed. Miss Hall affects a mannish mode of dress, and has what many people consider the best shingle in London. Her hair is of gold, and cropped as closely as a man's, a natural ripple in it being the only break in its sleek perfection.[34]

The Birmingham Post echoed many other media commentators of the period in noting Radclyffe Hall's masculine look. However, as Laura Doan has stressed, mannish tailored fashions for women were the height of modern fashion in this period and Radclyffe Hall was able to buy her

masculine evening suits from the ladies' tailors at Harrods. In this
context, press comment such as that in *The Birmingham Post* may have
been intended to stress Hall's chic modernity rather than her lesbianism.
The multiple cultural meanings carried by masculine dress in this period
enabled Radclyffe Hall, Una Troubridge and others to play with this
ambiguity and simultaneously appear as both a lesbian and a woman
of fashion. By 1928, however, the masculine tailored fashion was
beginning to be replaced by a return to more feminine styles. The
association of the look with Radclyffe Hall and therefore with lesbianism
may have been a factor in this shift, and women who continued to wear
masculine styles in the late 1920s and early 1930s were increasingly
identifiable as lesbians.[35]

The growing significance of the masculine image in conveying
lesbianism is clear from the media representations of Radclyffe Hall
during the *Well of Loneliness* trial. Newspapers which were hostile
to the novel's cause used masculine images of Hall, while the more liberal
press presented her in a more feminine light. The picture of the novelist
used by *The Sunday Express* in its initial article attacking the book,
was a three-quarter length portrait, showing Hall in a tailor-made suit
with tie, one hand in her pocket and the other holding a cigarette.[36]
The picture used by *The Daily Herald* in an article defending the novel,
on the other hand, showed only the novelist's head and shoulders, with
a hat hiding the short hair, and a pair of earrings giving a more feminine
impression.[37] The editors of both papers clearly felt that the image
presented by Radclyffe Hall would be important in swaying public and
official opinion either in favour of or against her novel. Hall's masculine
image was considered an indication of the lesbian nature of her novel
and, in the aftermath of the trial, masculinity and lesbianism were
increasingly linked.

For lesbians themselves, Radclyffe Hall and *The Well of Loneliness*
represented a defining image of lesbianism for much of the twentieth
century. Lesbian readers responded to the novel itself with a range
of reactions. For some readers, such as Eileen Carty, the book would
'always be my vade mecum: it explained "me" to me in the far off days
when the subject was very taboo, and there were certainly no books
easily come by'. Writing to a lesbian magazine in 1967, she commented:
'The style nowadays could be called pedantic, I know; but John
[Radclyffe Hall] had the courage to say "it all" in the first place.'[38]

Miss C. M. W. also described the novel's significance in defining her own sense of lesbian identity:

> I have a French edition, and ever since I first read it, in the greatest secrecy, at 18, I regard it as my bible. Stephen Gordon may not seem 'with it' to the 1967 Lesbian, but her code of honour is an outstanding example to each and every one of us.[39]

Others, however, found the novel dull or alienating. Rosanna Hibbert described it as 'a pretty awful book', which taught her nothing about lesbianism because Stephen was 'so grotesquely male'.[40] The novelist Mary Renault described reading it aloud to her lover 'accompanied by … rather heartless laughter', while on holiday in a French fishing village in 1938. *The Well of Loneliness*, she claimed, carried 'an impermissible allowance of self-pity, and its earnest humourlessness invites irreverence'.[41]

Orlando

Despite the unprecedented furore caused by the novel, *The Well of Loneliness* was not the only lesbian-themed novel to be published in the interwar years. The 1920s were boom years for lesbian literature, seeing the publication of a large range of texts from virulently anti-lesbian works, such as Compton MacKenzie's *Extraordinary Women* (1928), through relatively traditional celebrations of romantic friendship, such as Elizabeth Bowen's *The Hotel* (1927), to radical modernist texts with encoded lesbian themes, such as Virginia Woolf's *Orlando* (1928). The growing fears surrounding female autonomy and the increasing awareness of lesbianism prompted by the work of the sexologists had a considerable impact on female and lesbian literature throughout this decade, while the scandal caused by the *Well of Loneliness* affair arguably revolutionised the genre of women's literature from 1928 onwards. A number of lesbian literary critics have discussed this change, tracing the transformation from pre-1920s novels which innocently portrayed close, passionate friendships between women to novels written during and after the decade, where an increasing awareness of potential misinterpretation led novelists to either emphasise the heterosexuality of their heroines or employ negative stereotypes in their presentation of explicitly lesbian characters.[42] Vera Brittain's *Testament of Friendship* is evidence of this trend: writing in 1940 about her friendship with Winifred Holtby, Brittain explicitly denied that their relationship was lesbian, the necessity of which would not have occurred to an author writing twenty years earlier.

However, while much of the lesbian-themed literature published at this time was increasingly negative, some lesbian novelists were able to depict same-sex desire in literature without attracting the attention of the censors. A number of these works were produced by members of the expatriate literary community who lived and worked in Paris during the interwar period.[43] American and English novelists such as Gertrude Stein and Bryher, poets such as Hilda Doolittle, and publishers such as Sylvia Beach all developed different and unique ways of expressing themselves both as lesbians and as exiles in the absence of lesbian literary and artistic traditions in the decades before the Second World War. The circumstances of their community – to some degree removed from English and American social constraints by their status as expatriates in Paris, relieved from the need to consider the opinions of publishers by their greater access to more sympathetic and liberal publishing houses, and slightly distanced from the negative effects of societal oppression by their membership of a supportive lesbian community – meant that they were able to make a unique contribution to the early-twentieth-century lesbian artistic tradition. Within the United Kingdom, the highbrow novelist Virginia Woolf was also able to present same-sex desire in her modernist novel *Orlando*. Her social position, as an established novelist and critic, a married woman, and a member of London society, placed Woolf in a potentially more vulnerable situation than her expatriate contemporaries. Despite this, Virginia Woolf's *Orlando*, published only months after *The Well of Loneliness* and treating the subject of lesbianism in a much more positive light, escaped suppression to become a mainstream best-seller.

The novel was written for, and dedicated to, Vita Sackville-West and was subsequently described by Vita's son, Nigel, as 'the longest and most charming love-letter in literature'.[44] Historians and biographers continue to be divided over the extent to which Vita and Virginia's relationship was lesbian. While Nigel Nicolson's honest and sympathetic biography of his parents' marriage and numerous extra-marital same-sex affairs made it impossible to question Vita Sackville-West's interest in women,

the degree of Virginia's commitment to Vita has been disputed. Quentin
Bell argued that:

> There may have been – on balance I think that there probably
> was – some caressing, some bedding together. But whatever may
> have occurred between them of this nature, I doubt very much
> whether it was of a kind to excite Virginia or to satisfy Vita. As far
> as Virginia's life is concerned the point is of no great importance;
> what was, to her, important was the extent to which she was
> emotionally involved, the degree to which she was in love. One
> cannot give a straight answer to such questions but, if the test
> of passions be blindness, then her affections were not very
> deeply engaged.[45]

However, Virginia Woolf's own diary entries and her frequent letters
to Vita suggest that she did care passionately for her. In one letter
she declared:

> But I do adore you – every part of you from heel to hair. Never will
> you shake me off, try as you may …
>   But if being loved by Virginia is any good, she does do that;
> and always will, and please believe it –.[46]

She wrote to Vita up to four times a week during the height of their
relationship, and although Virginia was particularly circumspect about
their meetings, even in the privacy of her own diary, their private
correspondence gives some indication of the nature of their relationship.
Virginia Woolf's letters reveal a playful coyness:

> Should you say, if I rang you up to ask, that you were fond of me?
> If I saw you would you kiss me? If I were in bed would you –
> I'm rather excited about Orlando tonight: have been lying by the
> fire and making up the last chapter.[47]

Other letters used literary metaphors which appear to imply sexual
desires. In a letter dated 6 March 1928, she wrote:

> Goodnight now. I am so sleepy with chloral simmering in my spine
> that I can't write, nor yet stop writing – I feel like a moth, with

heavy scarlet eyes and a cape of down – a moth about to settle
in a sweet, bush – Would it were – ah but that's improper.[48]

As Nicolson's comment suggests, *Orlando* can also be read
as evidence of Virginia's affections. The eponymous hero/heroine was
based quite closely upon Vita and of the five photographs of Orlando
which illustrated the novel, three were of Vita herself, including the final
picture captioned 'Orlando at the present time', which showed Vita
in her ordinary clothes with her two dogs. In the early months of writing
the novel, Virginia's letters to Vita contained a number of requests that
they meet to discuss how Vita would react in a given situation as part
of Virginia's research, suggesting that Orlando's personality was
based closely on Vita's own. Woolf also drew upon Vita's physical
characteristics in describing Orlando. Virginia's diary entries and letters
show that, of all Vita's physical features, she particularly admired Vita's
legs, which were apparently long and shapely; while the novel contains
few references to Orlando's appearance, the shapeliness of his/her legs
is remarked upon on several occasions. Orlando's adventures were
closely modelled on episodes and fantasies in Vita's own life, while many
of the other characters were based on real people, including Vita's
husband, Harold Nicolson. Perhaps the most significant episode,
in a lesbian reading of the novel, is Orlando's first love affair with Sasha,
a Russian princess. Based on Violet Trefusis, with whom Vita had her
first serious lesbian affair, many aspects of this character's relationship
with Orlando reflect Vita and Violet's relationship. The social
disapproval, which was an important feature of the real relationship,
manifesting itself in increasingly desperate attempts by Violet's family
to marry her off, is reflected in the fictional relationship where Sasha's
'inferior' nationality is an impediment to social approval of their
relationship. Violet and Vita went abroad together on several occasions,
ultimately 'eloping' to France immediately after Violet's marriage
and having to be followed and brought home by their respective
husbands; in the novel, Orlando and Sasha make plans to run away
together.

Given the clear parallels between Orlando and Vita and the obvious
intensity of Virginia and Vita's relationship, which appears to have
reached a height in the period during which *Orlando* was being written
and published, the novel might have been expected to attract some

Illustrations

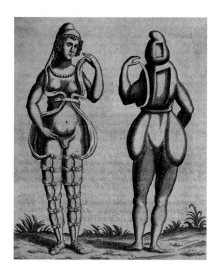

1. Front and back view of a hermaphrodite (engraving), c.1690.

2. Jacopo Amigoni (1696–1752), *Jupiter and Callisto*.

3. Sailors drinking the health of Hannah Snell, who dressed as a soldier in the 1740s.

4. Irish adventuress and cross-dresser Mrs Christian Davies, *née* Cavenaugh, alias Mother Ross (1667–1739).

The Rt Honble Lady Eleanor Butler and Miss Ponsonby.
"The Ladies of Llangollen."

From an original Drawing.

5. 'Romantic friends' Lady Eleanor Butler and the Honourable
Miss Sarah Ponsonby, known as the 'Ladies of Llangollen', who lived
together for forty years.

6. 'Passionate female literary types': a cartoon from *Punch* magazine, 2 June 1894.

THE NEW WOMAN.

7. A 'New Woman' joins the men in the smoking compartment of a railway train, from *Pick-Me-Up* magazine, *c.*1900.

8. Celebrated dancer Maud Allan
(1880–1956) performing the 'Vision
of Salomé'.

9. Edward Linley Sambourne (1844–1910),
Two Nude Models (albumen print), *c.*1890.

First Officer (in spasm of jealousy). "WHO'S THE KNOCK-KNEED CHAP WITH YOUR SISTER, OLD MAN?"
Second Officer. "MY OTHER SISTER."

10. *Punch* cartoon satirising women in uniform, 29 May 1918.

11. Vita Sackville-West (1892–1962), for whom Virginia Woolf wrote her novel *Orlando* (1928).

12. Lady Una Troubridge and Radclyffe Hall at a French bulldog show, 28 March 1928, a few months before the sensational appearance of Hall's novel *The Well of Loneliness*.

13. Union Hotel, corner of Princess Street and Canal Street, Manchester, 1970: a popular lesbian and gay venue from the 1950s to the present day.

14. Susannah York, Beryl Reid and Coral Browne in a scene filmed in the Gateways Club, London, for the movie *The Killing of Sister George*, 1968.

15. 'Bridegroom' 26-year-old Violet Ellen Katherine Jones and her 'bride', 21-year-old Joan Mary Lee, September 1954, Catford, London. After admitting making false statements to obtain a marriage certificate, both were fined £25.

16. Lesbian wedding, Clapham Common, South London, 1965.

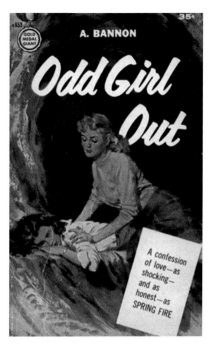

17. Cover of Ann Bannon's lesbian pulp fiction novel *Odd Girl Out* (1957).

18. Anne Heywood and Sandy Dennis in the movie *The Fox*, 1968.

FEB. 1966
VOL 3 No. 2.

Arena Three

Contents

- - - - - - - - - - - - -

Vol. 3 No. 2
February, 1966

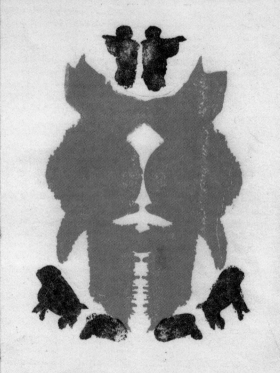

ARENA THREE is published monthly by Esme Langley
(MRG) Limited at 98, Belsize Lane, London. N.W.3.

19. Cover of the February 1966 issue of lesbian magazine *Arena Three*,
edited by Esmé Langley.

20. Jackie Forster, a founder member of the 1970s lesbian magazine *Sappho*.

21. Members of the Gay Liberation Front outside Bow Street Magistrates' Court in February 1971, demonstrating in support of the WLM women arrested at the 1970 Miss World Competition.

22. Lesbian and Gay Pride, London, 1983.

23. Lesbian women at Birmingham Pride, 1999.

24. Lesbian Avengers hijack a bus in Piccadilly Circus, London, in protest against Stagecoach boss Brian Souter's support for Section 28 (February 2000).

adverse attention. Virginia Woolf was apparently concerned about this possibility and wrote to Vita before beginning the book:

> But listen; suppose Orlando turns out to be Vita; and its all about you and the lusts of your flesh and the lure of your mind ... suppose, I say, that Sibyl next October says "There's Virginia gone and written a book about Vita" and Ozzie [Dickinson] chaws with his great chaps and Byard [of Heinemann] guffaws, Shall you mind?[49]

However, Virginia's fear that the publication of *Orlando* would produce unpleasant gossip about herself and Vita appears to have proved unfounded and their relationship never received the public vilification experienced by Radclyffe Hall. One reason for this was clearly that while Radclyffe Hall openly lived with a woman and adopted an explicitly lesbian public image, both Virginia Woolf and Vita Sackville-West were 'respectable' married women, who conformed to conventional feminine dress and behavioural codes, in public if not in private.

Virginia Woolf's use of modernist techniques may also have enabled her to express a lesbian theme in positive terms without risking prosecution for obscenity. The novel challenges realist representations of time – Orlando's life, in the novel, spans the period from the last years of the reign of Elizabeth I to the present day (1920s), at which point she is still a young woman – and critiques conventional notions of gender difference. Orlando's spontaneous change in sex from a man to a woman half-way through the novel allows Woolf to question the 'naturalness' of masculinity and femininity as well as enabling Orlando to have love affairs with both men and women. The physical aspect of the sex-change is given little emphasis. Orlando himself shows no signs of discomfiture upon making the discovery that he is a woman, and Woolf gives few details of Orlando's change in appearance, beyond the observation that 'No human being, since the world began, has ever looked more ravishing.'[50] We are informed that Orlando remains the same person, as a woman, as he was when a man:

> Orlando had become a woman – there is no denying it. But in every other respect, Orlando remained precisely as he had been. The change of sex, though it altered their future, did nothing whatever to alter their identity.[51]

In allowing Orlando to remain essentially unchanged by his/her change in sex, Woolf places the entire emphasis on gendered notions of behaviour and dress. When Orlando makes the discovery that he is a woman, she dresses in conventional female clothes and it is this, rather than any change in herself, which prompts the other characters to treat Orlando differently. We are told:

> Orlando had bought herself a complete outfit of such clothes as women then wore, and it was in the dress of a young Englishwoman of rank that she now sat on the deck of the Enamoured Lady. It is a strange fact, but a true one, that up to this moment she had scarcely given her sex a thought.[52]

As a plot device, Orlando's sex-change enabled Virginia Woolf to represent Vita's lesbian affairs without explicitly portraying her hero/heroine as homosexual. Although Orlando only has affairs with women when a man, and men when a woman, the fluidity of his/her gender allows the affairs to be interpreted as either heterosexual or homosexual by different audiences. Woolf implies that the ostensibly heterosexual nature of Orlando's love interests is motivated more by convention than desire: when Orlando becomes a woman she adapts her behaviour so as to focus her romantic attention on men in much the same way as she gradually adopts the other conventions of femininity. Moreover, by emphasising the fact that Orlando's identity remained unchanged by the sex-change, and allowing the female Orlando to remember all the experiences of the male Orlando, Woolf refuses to undermine Orlando's sexual experiences with women. In the early stages of her womanhood, Orlando is conscious of, and apparently unconcerned by, the fact that all her sexual experiences have been with women, and as Sasha, the Russian Princess, was the great love of the male Orlando's life, so she remains the great love of the female Orlando:

> And as all Orlando's loves had been women, now through the culpable laggardry of the human frame to adopt itself to convention, though she herself was a woman, it was still a woman she loved; and if the consciousness of being of the same sex had any effect at all, it was to quicken and deepen those feelings which she had had as a man. For now a thousand hints and mysteries became plain to her that were then dark. Now, the

obscurity, which divides the sexes and lets linger innumerable impurities in its gloom, was removed, and if there is anything in what the poet says about truth and beauty, this affection gained in beauty what it lost in falsity.[53]

The ambiguity of Orlando's gender enabled Woolf to allow him/her to have sexual experiences with and to feel sexual desire for women without explicitly portraying sexual acts between women. Just as Virginia Woolf's feminine clothing, her status as a married woman, and the private, implicit form of expression she adopted with regard to Vita prevented her relationship with Vita Sackville-West from being interpreted as lesbian, so her rejection of traditional literary styles and deconstruction of gender categories in *Orlando* prevented the lesbian theme from becoming explicit to a mainstream audience and enabled her to portray lesbianism positively without attracting the attention of the censors.

Colonel Barker's Masquerade

While Radclyffe Hall was able to make use of the new ideas of the sexologists to articulate an explicit lesbian identity in *The Well of Loneliness* and Virginia Woolf employed modernist techniques to play with conventional ideas of gender and sexuality in *Orlando*, popular notions of same-sex desire and lesbianism remained confused for much of the interwar period. The case of Colonel Barker, widely reported in the popular press in the 1920s and 1930s, demonstrates the extent to which the precise connections between biological sex, gender and sexual identity had yet to be fixed in the years before the Second World War. Colonel Barker first attracted the attention of the tabloid press in March 1929, following his arrest for contempt of court, after failing to appear for an earlier bankruptcy hearing. During a medical examination in Brixton Prison, Barker was discovered to be a woman, Valerie Arkell-Smith. Barker had been living as a man since 1923, working in a range of occupations and having a number of relationships with women, including Elfreda Haward, whom he married. Following the discovery of Barker's sex, Valerie was charged with two counts of perjury for falsely signing the marriage register in the marriage to Haward and sentenced to nine months' imprisonment in a women's prison. On release, Barker continued to live as a man under a number of names and was subsequently arrested for theft on two other occasions. In 1937, Barker appeared with his 'bride' in a peep-show at Blackpool which invited spectators to watch the couple lying on neighbouring single beds during their honeymoon. Spectators were informed that Barker had agreed to a £200 wager that he would not consummate the marriage for the duration of the Blackpool summer season. The show was one of the highlights of the 1937 season, apparently attracting 'more than a million' people, drawn by ongoing curiosity about Barker's 'true' nature.[54]

During the first trial in 1929, the court had attempted to impose some clarity on Barker's identity, insisting on her sex as female and implying that her relationship with Haward was sexual and lesbian. However, subsequent hearings were more confused. In the 1934 trial, the chairman of the court insisted on trying Barker under the name John Hill, which he had given when arrested, in an attempt to exclude the issue of Barker/Hill's gender identity from the proceedings. This intention was undermined by the defence who persistently raised the issue, presenting the desire to maintain his masquerade as Hill's defence for committing the crime. Further confusion arose during the 1937 trial, when Barker was referred to by the court as Valerie Arkell-Smith, but appeared dressed variously in masculine or a combination of masculine and feminine clothing. James Vernon has argued that the idea of the 'masquerade' as a performance which masked a true reality was popular in the interwar period and this was the way in which Barker's experiences were primarily represented in the press.[55] Newspapers ranging from *The News of the World* to *The Daily Telegraph* reported the case, investigating and reporting Barker's previous exploits in detail and marvelling at the success of Barker's masquerade as a man. However, despite the attempts of the law and the press to clarify or reveal Barker's true gender and sexual identity, popular opinion remained confused. During Barker's appearance at Blackpool in 1937, the social survey organisation Mass Observation interviewed the landlady at Barker's lodgings in an attempt to resolve the mystery. Mrs Gallimore, the landlady, informed them that she and her husband, Jack, had challenged Barker 'to prove that he was either a man or a woman' and Barker had responded by asking 'them all to go upstairs and he would show them'. However, the revelation did not resolve the issue and Mrs Gallimore was reported as saying:

'I don't know its a mystery, he's a man and a woman. You know he's got all that a woman has, big-busted, and he's gettan one o them theer that a mon cant do without.' Here she giggled and looked at the Observer … 'I cant tell what he is, I call him a Gene, Jack calls him a Moxphrodite, Jack says he can be a man one minute and then be a woman, Christ knows how he does it. They should lock up that sort of person, they're no use to anybody.'[56]

Barker himself did little to resolve the confusion in a succession of interviews and life-stories. Rejecting the increasingly influential medical categories of the lesbian or transvestite, he continued to draw, instead, on the more ambiguous earlier language of the masquerade.

Responses to Colonel Barker suggest that contradictory and confused ideas about gender and sexuality continued to exist throughout the interwar period. While the increasing influence of medical ideas about inversion and lesbianism provided one explicit language describing female same-sex desire, other, more ambiguous concepts continued to be employed. However, despite attempts by Parliament to restrict public awareness of desire between women in the early 1920s, widespread reporting of the *Well of Loneliness* affair and the Colonel Barker case meant that, by the 1930s, it was increasingly difficult to avoid discussion of the issue.

Chapter 8
Lesbian Bars, 1920s–1970s

Commercial bars and nightclubs have played an important role in the development of identities and communities based around same-sex desire. A male homosexual subculture in Britain has been traced back at least as far as the eighteenth century, and in the twentieth century a growing number of venues began to cater to men from a broad range of different economic and class backgrounds. In contrast, a lesbian subculture does not appear to have developed until the twentieth century, due to the social restrictions which women have historically faced. Limitations on women's freedom of movement in public places, a lack of financial resources and social disapproval of women's public consumption of alcohol were all factors in delaying the emergence of a lesbian bar culture.

Lesbian Bars in the 1920s and 1930s

Nevertheless, there is evidence that British lesbians participated in a commercial bar and club scene in the 1920s and 1930s, if not earlier. Radclyffe Hall referred to lesbian bars in Paris in her 1928 novel *The Well of Loneliness*, and other British lesbians were also aware of these venues in the interwar years. Barbara Bell, a teenager from Blackburn in the 1930s, was introduced to the Paris scene by her queer friend Cyril, the accountant at the dairy where she worked.

> Cyril had given me a couple of addresses where, he'd said,
> 'You'll find your sort of company. You must go to this square
> where they have stalls and find the soup stall. It's famous for
> its French onion soup. If you stand there, I'm sure someone
> will approach you'. So we went to this onion soup stall and
> up came a fella and said, 'You like girls? You like girls club?
> Come, you follow me.'
> We wove in and out, round about, for about five minutes,
> trusting him. Gave him a good tip and he shoved us in a doorway.
> I didn't know but it was a famous club – Le Monocle.[1]

Barbara entered through a red curtain and found an 'old-fashioned and theatrical' club, with plush settees and photographs of famous patrons on the walls.[2] Stools were lined up in front of the bar, facing a large mirror, which enabled those who sat down to observe the room behind them. For Barbara, this visit to Le Monocle was her introduction to the lesbian scene. The experience was a revelation:

> I couldn't tell whether they were men or women sitting on these
> stools. They were really very butchy and very fem. We fitted
> in with it all ... We soon made friends, and they showed us to a tiny
> table in another room through a wideish doorway. There were
> so many tables, with little lamps, so many women, all lesbian,
> no men at all. Oh God, was I thrilled! It was out of this world.
> It was paradise. It was everything I had dreamt of.
>
> When we first arrived, they all flocked round. We were quite
> a curiosity. There were about forty women – two or three German
> girls and the rest French. Some of the girls were sitting at the bar
> working as hostesses. If you wanted you could choose a girl and take
> her upstairs. I know because I went there later on, after the war.
>
> ... That was a wonderful initiation into lesbian life and
> I remember it so clearly. The dance floor was about six foot square
> so you couldn't really dance, you just held each other and waggled
> about. To see women kissing when they were dancing, I thought,
> God! Where am I? I knew I was in Paris but I felt I was on another
> planet.[3]

Although British lesbians were clearly visitors to the Parisian clubs in this period, a number of venues also existed in London. Radclyffe Hall had a wide lesbian social circle, who met at private parties, in salons and in clubs. In his biography of the novelist, Lovat Dickson claimed:

> These parties were all girls. Only on some occasions was a man
> with them. The sight of women dancing together at the Cave
> of Harmony or the Orange Tree Club or the Hambone aroused
> neither amusement nor alarm.[4]

Emily Hamer suggests that the Forum Club became an important venue for wealthy lesbians in the 1930s and 1940s. Established by Alice Williams in the mid-1930s, the Forum Club provided a women-only equivalent to the traditional gentleman's club. Hamer argues that, 'although it did not advertise itself as a lesbian club, a significant proportion of its members were lesbians.'[5] Alice Williams herself lived with the singer Fanny Mowbray Laming until Fanny's death in 1941, and the two were recognised as a couple both publicly and within the social functions of the Forum Club. Located on Hyde Park Corner in Knightsbridge, the club catered to a wealthy, professional clientele, and members included Dame Lilian Baker, Mary Allen, Ethel Smyth and Eleanor Rathbone.

Barbara Bell, working as a policewoman in London just before the Second World War, stumbled across another club in Mayfair:

> In the course of my duties in Mayfair, I accidentally found a lesbian club … It was a very high-class club in Hertford Street – beautiful club, beautiful clients, all women. It was secluded and secretive, very posho, rather like Le Monocle. Red plush and comfortable and luxurious …
>
> The police raided the Mayfair club one night when we were in and took our names … They didn't take anybody away. They just had a poke around to see if there was anything going on that shouldn't be – non-members who hadn't been signed in by a member.[6]

The women who frequented these clubs were primarily professional or independently wealthy women and were often regarded by their contemporaries as sexually experienced and predatory. Mrs C. Chesterton, founder of the Cecil Homes for homeless women and girls in London, described her observations of these women when visiting lodging houses, casual wards, restaurants and nightclubs in the capital in her book *Women of the London Underworld*. She claimed:

> You will find in the more expensive ill-run night club a type of woman expensively dressed, well groomed, of early middle age and with a curiously unsexed look about them. They may have a mannish suggestion about their dress, or they may be feminine and fluffy in appearance. But male attention leaves them unmoved, though the sight of a pretty girl with a soft complexion and the look of genuine inexperience brings a light to their eyes. This type of woman is on the look-out for companions of her own sex.

Abnormal desires in the sex direction can always be gratified – given
money and opportunity – and an appetite for abnormality
can readily be satisfied in many night clubs in that quarter.

... As a matter of fact, wealthy women of abnormal tastes do not
often seek recreation from chance encounters in the street, or other
public places.

It is at the gateways to the underworld, fascinating little café
bars, dance clubs, feverish centres of excitement and emotional
stimuli that you will find them.[7]

Barbara Bell also described meeting such upper-class women, while
socialising in the West End with her friends from the police:

We used to meet up after a work, sometimes a little gang
of us which was super. There was a place we used to go for
amusement, called Gunter's, off Park Lane. It's gone now. A lot of
women used to go there. It was expensive, and posh, rather colonial
style. Real tearooms but you could always pick up – if you wanted –
some bored rich woman dripping with gold and jewels. I never did,
but I had plenty of opportunity. The little waitress would come over
and say, 'The lady over there – would you like to join her for tea
at her table?'

'Yes, certainly' – crikey.

But I'd just have tea and thank them and then buzz off.[8]

However, while wealthy women dominated many of the clubs
in Knightsbridge and Mayfair in the 1930s, a number of other clubs
existed which catered to a more mixed clientele. Ellen, a West End dancer
in the late 1930s, recalled a number of clubs around Tottenham Court
Road, which were frequented by lesbians and homosexual men as part
of a broader bohemian and arty clientele:

Then I went to Paris with a show, and I met an English girl there –
she's dead now, I'm afraid, all dead, dear – called Nancy Wallace,
who was very well known in the clubs, and she was the one who
took me to the place called the Coffee Ann in London. It was most
famous, and from there I met loads of people. I went to a club in
Gerrard Street, and it was 42 Gerrard Street, and called The 42nd.
It was probably about the time of '42nd Street'. And all the girls

used to gather there, night after night. This is where I met
Marion – 'Billy'. She lived in Croydon, and was a secretary
in quite a well-known furniture company.[9]

Pat James also went to the Coffee Ann during the war and remembered
that it had 'wooden gates when you went in which you had to push,
like a sort of stable or something, and there were pebbles on the ground'
She described it as 'a very arty sort of place. People went in, but they
weren't homosexual or lesbian necessarily – they were arty types mostly,
or seemed to be.' A number of clubs existed in the Tottenham Court
Road area in this period, and Pat recalled visiting another club, called
the Jubilee, on the first floor of a building in Tottenham Court Road,
where you could get spam and chips very cheaply.[10]

After the Second World War: The Emergence of a Subculture

The Second World War gave further impetus to the bar culture in the
capital. Many women travelled or lived away from their home towns
during the war, working in the women's armed services or in other
wartime employment. Distanced from their families and local
communities, and with a new disposable income gained from their
war work, these women experienced a new freedom and independence.
Attitudes towards women and public drinking had also relaxed in the
interwar and war years, so that it became increasingly acceptable for
women to frequent pubs and bars without a male escort. In London,
Manchester, Brighton and other towns and cities around Britain,
women took part in a vibrant emerging bar scene alongside male
homosexuals and visiting servicemen and women. Pat James remembers
the wartime years as a period of great excitement at the Gateways club
in Chelsea:

> I know I went to the Gateways around 1944 … The club was
> in Bramerton Street, down a flight of stairs. They had a trio there.
> It was usually women playing at that time. There was an old
> Colonel who ran the Club, and it was very difficult to get in – I had
> to be taken in. You couldn't become a member, it was very exclusive
> in its way. They were arty types going down there, it wasn't really
> a lesbian club when he had it …

When I went to the Gateways, the atmosphere was fantastic. For a start we had women from overseas coming in, because they were stationed here, so you had all sorts of different people. Very interesting, very crowded, very packed. You got sightseers, of course, coming to look at all these people. People danced, especially during that war period when they were extra-enjoying themselves.[11]

Opened in the 1930s by a retired colonel, the Gateways club on Bramerton Street in Chelsea was the longest-running lesbian nightclub of the twentieth century. A middle-class bohemian club in the years before the war, the club had genteel and sedate clientele. Jill Gardiner, in her oral history of the club, claims that it became a registered members' club in 1936 as a means of getting around the restrictive licensing laws. Ted Ware took over the Gateways in 1943, and the clientele was diverse in the 1940s and 1950s. Lesbians came in increasing numbers in the evenings, but the club continued to attract a largely straight clientele during the daytime. Chelsea was known for its artistic, bohemian air, and visitors to the club included actresses Joan Collins and Diana Dors, Jamaican-born singer Noel Brown and pianists Jack London and Chester Harriott, as well as prostitutes and petty criminals.[12]

However, it was in the 1950s and 1960s that the Gateways became an almost exclusively lesbian club and a major fixture on the London lesbian scene. Ted Ware retired during the 1950s, and management of the club was taken over by his wife, Gina Ware, in conjunction with an American ex-air force woman, Smithy, herself a lesbian. Although Jill Gardiner argues that Ted was always welcoming to the lesbian clientele, his retirement seems to have been the final prompt to make lesbians the dominant clientele in the club. A small dark venue, the Gateways only had a capacity of about 200, but it was regularly packed and attracted visitors from far afield at the weekend. As the club was a members-only club, women had to apply in advance for membership and pay an annual fee of 10 shillings, but its status as a private club seems to have protected it from police attention. The increasing popularity of the Gateways in the 1950s and 1960s was part of a wider shift in lesbian venues from the centre to West London in this period. In Notting Hill Gate, lesbians were regular customers at The Champion pub on the corner of Wellington Terrace and Bayswater Road.[13] In the 1960s, Maureen Duffy and her

friends used to meet at The Cricketers pub in Battersea, on the corner
of Battersea Park Road and Albert Bridge Road. The other popular
lesbian club of the period, the Robin Hood Club on Inverness Terrace
in Bayswater, was also located in West London.[14]

By the 1950s and 1960s, many of the towns and cities outside London
had at least one bar which was frequented by gay men and lesbians.
The Union pub in Manchester, which was located next to the canal
in the red-light district, was a popular meeting place for local lesbians.
Luchia Fitzgerald recalled her first encounter with the Union clientele
as an amazing experience:

> These women would come along – really big women, they looked
> like Desperate Dan – and they would go into the pub and really
> young boys. Then I started to realise that what I thought was young
> boys was women dressed up like men … Honest to God, I will
> never forget till the day I die, the smell of lipstick and Angel face
> powder and as soon as I got close to these blokes they were caked
> with make-up and their beards were showing through the make-up
> and they were built like brick shit-houses, these blokes.[15]

Jose Pickering confirms Luchia's memory of the Union's mixed
clientele, recalling:

> There was a really good atmosphere in the Union – there was a real
> mixture of people. There were servicemen, there were barrow boys,
> there were prostitutes, there were drag queens who would get up on
> stage and do a turn … and we thought this is like Wonderland.[16]

While gay bars existed in many towns around Britain in this period,
Brighton was unique in possessing a variety of different clubs and bars
and a visible lesbian and gay population. Sandie, who used to visit
Brighton in this period, remembered:

> We came down on holiday, a week's holiday and it was the freedom
> in Brighton. There were so many gay people and they seemed
> to be accepted and there were clubs for gay people … ohh,
> wonderful! It was absolutely Mecca because it was very gay then.
> Brighton's gay now, but it was very very gay then.

> We'd never seen gay people en masse like that before and clubs
> that everyone knew were clubs for gay people which was unknown,
> even in a great city like Birmingham, but there you are.[17]

Siobhan described nights out in Brighton as pub crawls around a series
of small pubs and clubs.

> It was like a round of going from place to place, visiting Brighton.
> I was never in a big club, I was always in these little tiny places that
> were like people's lounges. You'd go down into them and there'd
> be a little bar in the corner and you'd just all sit there and drink
> until you got drunk and then you'd move on to someone else's.[18]

Lesbians frequented the Spotted Dog on Middle Street, run by a widow
called Flo Taylor, who had moved down from the north of England.
A working-class pub, the Spotted Dog had a back bar, where the gay
crowd used to go, and a front bar, which was 'normal'.[19] Another pub,
Pigott's, was also popular with women in the 1950s. Sheila remembered:

> I started going to Pigott's in 1950 when I was twenty and it was
> mostly girls but there were one or two men there, some of the boys
> were there. Dolly played the piano. This little lady used to play
> at the piano with her jangling bracelets; cigarette hanging on her
> mouth. And we used to have this sing-song, the old tunes, 'Don't
> laugh at me cos I'm a fool' that's right, 'Freight Train', that was
> Laurie's tune. Oh yes, they used to stand up at the piano. It's not
> a very big pub. I think the bar went in a sort of a half moon and
> there was only one entrance. It was terribly small, there was room
> enough for a piano, and there weren't many seats. It was quite tatty,
> all really dark brown. It was just ordinary working-class. There
> weren't any professionals there, they probably had their own
> places to go.[20]

The Queen of Clubs, another lesbian venue in Brighton in this period,
had more cheerful décor. Harriet recalled the club as 'nice and bright and
above ground. It was fairly cheerful. They had lights on and it wasn't
all dingy and sort of under cover, I didn't like that.' Opinions were
mixed, however, and Sandie described it as 'a bit sleazy. I remember
the décor wasn't very brilliant and the carpet always seemed to be very

sticky.'[21] Valerie remembered the regulars of this relatively quiet club as a tight-knit community of older women, giving it the atmosphere of a social gathering rather than a nightclub.[22] While many of the bars and clubs were very small venues, with room for little more than drinking and a piano, the Variety Club on Middle Street was a much larger venue. Spread over three or four floors, the club had a disco in the basement and was a very popular venue with both gay men and lesbians.

Women who lived in or visited Brighton in the 1940s and 1950s found the bar culture to be very mixed, with gay men and lesbians socialising alongside each other in many of the venues. The Lorelei coffee bar, which opened on a Saturday night, selling coffee after the clubs had closed, was a particularly mixed venue. Sandie commented:

> There was a real sense of comradeship then; you know, 'We're all in this together and let's make the best of it. Let's have fun, make a joke of it.' And there was a song around at that time, we used to go trotting through all those little lanes in Brighton, the little twittens, we used to go, two o'clock in the morning, running down these little lanes, singing, 'Frankfurter sandwiches, frankfurter sandwiches.' You know, the boys and the girls together. And other daft things we did. But oh, it was fun. It was harmless fun, too. In the sixties, there was more of a sort of family feeling. I don't know how else to express it. Because we used to say, then, 'Oh, he's family or she's family.' That was an expression that used to be used then, meaning, 'That's another gay person.' Even if you didn't know them. And that immediately gave you a feeling of closeness because being gay was being one of a minority group.[23]

In the early 1960s, a brief attempt was made to open a club for women, but this closed almost before it had opened. Jacaranda was a basement club opened by an older woman known as Big Kay. Considerable work had already been put into decorating and setting up the club, when Big Kay decided to hold a pre-opening party, while waiting for her licence to come through. The party was raided by the police and, although no arrests were made as the occasion was simply a private party, the incident was enough to prevent Big Kay from being granted a licence: the club never opened. Sheila and Sandie remembered this incident as the closest Brighton came to having a women-only venue. However, Margaret, who visited Brighton in the 1950s, recalled the British Legion

Club as an alternative women-only venue, frequented by middle-class lesbians:

> And at the same time we heard of another one on the seafront and it was in the British Legion Club, I think, 76 Marine Parade it was. Somebody said if you go down to the British Legion Club on a Friday night, gay women take it over or have it for the evening. So then we started coming down to Brighton on a Friday after work to go to this place. Now that place was the best place of all. Because when you went in the drinking clubs there was an element of rough, rough girls but these were more sort of professional. They seemed to be nicer types of people that went to the British Legion Club. It was only on a Friday night, and they were really nice, very friendly. You could have a drink, coffee, dance – that must have had a jukebox – just sit and chat, and then the fellow that ran it closed and moved, moved to Hastings. And that was the end of the British Legion Club.

Margaret's description of the British Legion women as 'professional', in contrast to the 'rough' girls who visited other drinking clubs, suggests that class may have been an important factor in determining which bars and clubs women frequented and the types of culture which emerged in those venues.

Butch/Femme Culture

Little research has been undertaken into the communities which were located in the lesbian bars and nightclubs in Britain after the Second World War. However, in the United States, extensive work on lesbian communities of the 1940s, 1950s and 1960s has demonstrated the importance of public bars and other commercial venues to lesbian community building and identity formation there. This body of literature offers a useful line of reference in making sense of the post-war British lesbian bar culture. Davis and Kennedy's oral history of the lesbian bar community in Buffalo, New York, and a number of other recent studies have expanded historians' understanding of the importance of class, ethnicity and geographical location in shaping unique lesbian bar communities throughout the United States.[24] These histories occupy a controversial position within US lesbian historiography, highlighting class and political tensions within the broader lesbian community. Located in the poorer and rougher parts of town, these bars were patronised almost exclusively by working-class lesbians and shunned by middle-class lesbians for whom, Davis and Kennedy argue, the pressures of professional work and social ties meant exposure as a lesbian was too great a risk. Katie Gilmartin develops this argument further, suggesting that the practices and values of the working-class bar culture were anathema to a middle-class lesbian identity based on discretion and small, close friendship circles. Her interviews with middle-class lesbians in Colorado Springs demonstrated that these women did not share a notion of community or sense of belonging with the working-class bar lesbians of their neighbourhood.

Unlike the working-class lesbians studied by Kennedy and Davis, they did not root their identities as lesbians in bar culture; on the contrary, their identities were rooted in the class-based distinctions they drew between themselves and those they considered regulars at the bars.[25] Gilmartin argues that class identities were therefore fundamental to the distinctions between different lesbian communities in 1950s' Colorado Springs.

Current research in Britain suggests that although class does appear to have been a factor in determining women's choices about which venues, if any, to frequent and in shaping their reactions to the bars, there was no clear class divide, as in the United States, between a working-class bar scene and middle-class private friendship networks. Well-known lesbian venues, such as the Gateways, were frequented by a range of clientele from across the class spectrum, as were other larger venues in Brighton. In the United States, class divisions were widened by, and exemplified in, the practice of butch/femme culture within the working-class bar community and butch/femme culture also clearly dominated British bars in this period. An organising principle for community life, butch/femme culture dictated personal image and identity, behavioural codes and the presentation of the lesbian culture to mainstream society.[26] Butch lesbians were recognisable by their adoption of a masculine image, based on jacket and trousers, worn with a shirt and tie, and they often had short hair, slicked back away from the face. Femme lesbians, on the other hand, adopted a hyper-feminine image, wearing dresses or skirts and blouses, with high-heeled shoes, handbags and make-up. Rene Sawyer, a butch lesbian in the 1950s, described the dress code:

> Now if you were a butch – one butch always knew another butch because it was the mirror image of yourself. It would be shirts or casual sweaters; trousers; and jackets. That would be the butch. And the femme always but always wore skirts, blouses, high-heeled shoes. Always carried a black patent leather handbag – or it needn't be black patent, but it was definitely a handbag – earrings, make-up. Butches never wore make-up. Femmes always wore make-up. So you never had any problem in those days because you always knew who to ask for a dance.[27]

Jose Pickering, a married woman who frequented the Union pub in Manchester as a femme in the 1960s, described how she and her friend used to get fitted in tailor-made feminine dresses by a dressmaker for their nights out:

> She would pin on the nearly finished dress to do the neckline and we'd be saying 'cut more off, cut more off' so it would be lower at the front and then the backs would be cut away with long sleeves … I used to have a false front in the dress, which was made of lace, to cover the cleavage and, as soon as we got out, off it came and into the handbag till you got back. You had to remember to put your front back on before you got in because you weren't meant to be showing all that.[28]

Butch/femme culture governed behaviour as well as image and conventions existed about whom women could dance with or have an affair with. While strong friendship bonds existed between butches and between femmes, feelings of sexual attraction towards another butch or another femme were regarded as inappropriate. Butch women were expected to be attracted only to femmes and vice versa. In a public environment, such as a bar, butches were expected to take an active role and it was the butch who invited the femme to dance. Existing relationships were considered exclusive, and if a butch wanted to dance with a femme who already had a lover, she was expected to ask the permission of her butch rival before approaching the femme. Such conventions were inevitably flouted on occasion, and in some venues fights between butch lesbians were a fairly regular occurrence.

Butch/femme culture was widespread in lesbian bars and clubs across Britain from the 1940s to the 1960s, and women who wished to be accepted by the bar community were expected to conform to a role. Pat James claimed that: 'There was role-playing and that was the way it was. If you weren't one way or the other, if you didn't conform, they derided you for it and said you didn't know what you were.'[29] However, by the 1970s, butch/femme culture was beginning to give way to the less gender-specific fashions assumed by feminists and the young women of the hippy counter-culture. This transitional period was a difficult time for a number of lesbian bar communities, with tensions between the older and younger generations occasionally flaring up in arguments and confrontations.

Subsequent accounts of butch/femme culture have been shaped by the hostilities which came out of this period of transition with the result that historical debates about the significance of butch/femme have been surrounded by controversy. For some middle-class lesbians of the 1950s and 1960s, the visibility of butch lesbians in particular posed a continuing threat, while for the lesbian feminists of the 1970s, butch/femme was simply a replication of the unequal gender balance inherent in heterosexual relationships. Lesbian feminist and Gay Liberation movement critiques of butch/femme culture in the 1970s meant that its significance in lesbian history was downplayed in the 1970s, but the debate resurfaced in the 1980s and 1990s, in response to a renewed popular interest in butch/femme.[30] One of the most vocal defenders of butch/femme in the United States, Joan Nestle, argued:

> Butch–fem women made Lesbians visible in a terrifyingly clear way in a historical period when there was no Movement protection for them. Their appearance spoke of erotic independence, and they often provoked rage and censure both from their own community and straight society. Now it is time to stop judging and to begin asking questions, to begin listening.[31]

For Nestle, a prioritising of middle- and upper-class models of lesbian identity, by middle-class historians at the expense of working-class lesbian histories, lies at the heart of the denial of lesbian bar culture. However, recent histories of lesbian bar communities have begun

to reassess butch/femme culture as a visible challenge to the oppression
of mainstream society. Davis and Kennedy claim that the members of this
community have been unfairly stereotyped 'as low-life societal discards
and pathetic imitators of heterosexuality' by '[p]opular culture, the
medical establishment, affluent lesbians and gays, and recently, many
lesbian feminists'. However, they argue that this has been a gross
misrepresentation and that the butch/femme communities should
be understood within a longer-term process of political resistance,
which culminated in the Gay Liberation movement of the 1970s.[32]
They suggest:

> By finding ways to socialize together, individuals ended the crushing
> isolation of lesbian oppression and created the possibility for group
> consciousness and activity. In addition, by forming community
> in a public setting outside of the protected and restricted boundaries
> of their own living rooms, lesbians also began the struggle for
> public recognition and acceptance.[33]

The Bar Communities and Wider Society

This understanding of lesbian bar communities as sites of resistance
is influenced by evidence that the bars faced ongoing hostility from
a threatening outside world, characterised by violent attacks by outsiders
and police involvement. The role of lesbian bars in 1950s' America
in providing a focus for homophobic violence has been well documented.
Leslie Feinberg, in her semi-autobiographical novel about the lesbian
butch/femme community in New York state, has portrayed the threat
of violence as a constant theme in lesbians' lives at this time.[34] While
local heterosexual men were frequently responsible for directing these
attacks at the butch members of the community, they were by no means
the exclusive perpetrators of violence. Feinberg also records a systematic
campaign of persecution by the police which took the form of organised
raids on lesbian bars as well as more spontaneous assaults on the street.
Kahn and Gozemba also draw attention to the importance of the
Massachusetts bars in attracting both public and police attention, and
thus violent assaults, on the lesbian community. Davis and Kennedy,
however, argue that police raids were present in this period more
as a threat than as a regular occurrence. They suggest that owners

were often able to stave off raids by a combination of pay-offs and
discretion. 'The law', they claim, 'loomed in the background, shaping
the boundaries of what was permitted and standing guard against
"going too far" '.[35]

Although few accounts of violent attacks on lesbians by local straight
men exist in Britain, there is evidence of police raids and corruption.
Claire Andrews described frequent raids on her regular club, the Casino,
in the early 1960s. There, the police would enter the club, separate the
men from the women in two lines and collect names and addresses before
marching them to the police station:

> The police attitude towards us was to show power … they
> were there to abuse us; they had the power to take us down to [the
> station] … they'd do the same procedure again and say, 'It says it's a
> boy,' or 'It says it's a girl,' and they'd keep you in the cell till the
> morning so you don't go back to the club.[36]

Alkarim Jivani argues that 'many club proprietors had an arrangement
with the police so that, in return for an inducement, they would be left
alone', while others went to court to contest prosecutions for keeping
a disorderly house.[37] In September 1962, David Browne, owner of the
Kandy Lounge in Gerrard Street, appeared in Bow Street Magistrates
after plain-clothes police observed men dancing the twist together.
In February 1964, George Munro Wilson pleaded not guilty after
plain-clothes police visited his club, the Witches Brew, and saw 'women
were dancing together and so were two effeminate men'.[38] However,
attempts to defend such charges were rarely successful and most
proprietors sought to avoid attracting police attention.

Attempts to avoid the attention of the police and hostile members
of the public meant that lesbian venues in this period were frequently
located in obscure places, in basements and on narrow side streets.
Venues were not advertised until the development of the lesbian and
gay press in the 1970s, and women were dependent on word of mouth
to find out where to go. Sometimes women were lucky enough to meet
other lesbians who told them where to go. Siobhan recalled:

> When I was twenty-one, I had an Irish friend who worked
> in an office and she came back and said, 'Guess what, we've got
> a lesbian working in our office.' I just wanted to know everything

that this lesbian did, everything. Every day that I saw this Irish friend, we just talked about Rita all the time. And then I asked her if she'd arrange for me to meet Rita and so this was arranged … I asked her if she would take me down to her club, 'cause I knew she went to a club. And she said, 'No,' she didn't think so 'cause she really wanted to persuade me not to be a lesbian, as it's a very lonely and hard life. If she could talk me out of it, she'd rather do that. And I said, 'I don't want talking out, I want to go to the club. Would you take me to the club?' So she said, 'Yes.'[39]

Others, however, had to resort to quite extreme measures to find bars and clubs. Janice described her attempts to find lesbian clubs in Brighton:

Although people had said that Brighton was the gay centre of the south, I didn't know where to go. A girl I worked with used to tell me how her sister was gay. She was frightened to invite me back there for tea because of this lesbian sister … [The sister] went to the Variety Club in Brighton but I didn't know that's what it was called or where it was. And I remember doing my cloak and dagger stuff here. I had a little car by this time, a little Morris, and the girl lived in Worthing. My friend said, 'Oh, she goes every Saturday night to this club'. So, come Saturday night, the following Saturday night, I actually drove round to her house and parked outside and waited for this girl and followed her. Would you believe this, I actually followed her to the Variety Club but I lost her, I lost her when she went up this little side road 'cause I couldn't get up there in the car, so I was foiled yet again. But at least I felt I was a step nearer.[40]

The hidden and enclosed nature of many of these venues meant that, even when women found them, they could be quite intimidating environments. Cynthia Reid, who was taken to the Gateways in the 1960s by an acquaintance, described the experience as extremely alienating:

It was just that it was a totally alien environment. There were all these very masculine-looking women, dancing with their partners who, to me, were very feminine looking women. It was all very butch femme in those days and not at all what I had envisaged. There didn't seem to be any people like me – sort

of ordinary quiet shy middle-class girls. And everybody seemed
to be so frightfully self-confident, knowing all the latest dances and
the latest pop tunes. Knowing each other obviously so very well,
totally in their environment, whereas I felt like a fish out of water.
And as I say, very, very shy and very, very frightened.[41]

Close-knit communities developed in small bars and clubs, so that
newcomers needed both to make sense of butch/femme culture and
to break into localised friendship networks. Valerie claimed that this
was particularly the case outside of London, where the women in local
bars all knew each other well:

> I used to go to the Queen of Clubs with friends. It was quite nice
> but to me it wasn't quite like the London clubs, it was much sort
> of quieter and I was surprised to find a lot of older people there,
> which you tend not to find in the London clubs and I always
> felt a little bit out of it because everybody knew everybody else.
> I eventually got to know some of the people there and used to end
> up on visiting terms with them. But it was much more like a social
> gathering than anything else, whereas the London clubs tended
> to have much more of an accent on dancing and picking people
> up and that sort of thing.[42]

By the 1970s, however, the lesbian bar scene around Britain was
beginning to open up to new cultural influences. By the 1970s, the
Gateways was having to contend with competition from a number
of new venues. Louise's, a central London venue with a girls' bar at the
back, opened in 1973. The same year, another venue opened in central
London, the New Oasis. Only surviving for a year, it was replaced
by Matty's club, which, by 1975, was the Gateways' only competitor for
the women-only club market. Women also frequented several mixed
clubs in London, including the Rehearsal, the Vortex, the Masquerade,
the Showplace and the Festival Club, as well as a number of south-east
London disco nights, such as the Moulin and 'She'.[43]

As social attitudes began to change, the lesbian and gay scene
became more open, advertising in the gay press and developing as part
of a broader emerging youth culture in the 1970s. Women were less likely
to socialise exclusively in one venue and frequently visited both mixed
and women-only spaces. Increased discussion of and information about

lesbian and gay bars and clubs meant that they became accessible to a wider range of women and different venues began to be associated with feminists, students or other social groups. Perhaps most significantly, the development of new political perspectives and organisations, such as the Gay Liberation Front and Women's Liberation, had a major impact on ideas about lesbian and gay identity and community in the bars and on the ways in which these venues were used.

Chapter 9
Lesbian Social Organisations, 1960s–1970s

In the 1950s and 1960s, a renewed sociological and medical interest
in homosexuality resulted in increased discussion about male homosexuality and lesbianism. A number of studies of female sexuality
and lesbianism appeared in this period, often representing lesbians
as neurotic and depressed individuals. Albertine Winner, a physician
who had served as a medical officer in the Auxiliary Territorial Service
(ATS) during the war, told the Psychiatry Section of the Royal Society
of Medicine in 1947 that:

> In dealing with large numbers of Lesbians one of the most striking
> things is the recurrent traits of immaturity, mainly emotional, but
> showing themselves in many unexpected ways, that one meets
> in women of high intellectual or artistic development. This certainly
> bears out the view that the homosexual relation is an immature one,
> an arrest of normal sexual development at an adolescent stage.[1]

She went on to divide the lesbians she had encountered into two different
types. The first type was a woman whose significant emotional attachments were with women and whose relationships were sincere and
faithful but often not sexual. However, the second 'more dangerous' type
she described was the 'promiscuous Lesbian', whose aim was primarily
sexual. 'Such women', she claimed, 'are usually dominant and forceful
personalities and may often seduce weaker and more pliable women
who are otherwise perfectly normal heterosexuals'.[2] This second notion
of lesbians as aggressive and sexually promiscuous became increasingly
influential in the post-war decades, and medical commentators drew
on the ideas of Freud to explain these personality traits. Dr George
W. Henry's American study *Sex Variants*, which was published in the
United Kingdom in 1950, emphasised poor relationships with parents,
histories of mental instability in the family and tomboyish or sporty
behaviour in childhood as common lesbian experiences.[3] Eustace
Chesser, a Harley Street psychiatrist and gynaecologist and a prolific
author of popular sex manuals in this period, published five books
between 1949 and 1971 which dealt with the subjects of female sexuality

or homosexuality and aimed to introduce the British public to notions of lesbians as masculine, immature and sexually aggressive.[4]

The Homophile Movement

Much of this new interest was sparked by ongoing debates about homosexual law reform. Acts of 'gross indecency' between men had been prohibited by the Criminal Law Amendment Act 1885 and as a result male homosexual encounters, particularly those occurring in the public domain, were policed throughout the first half of the twentieth century. However, in the years after the Second World War, a series of public scandals around homosexuality had drawn attention to the law and raised concerns about its continued usefulness and the role of the state in policing private behaviour. The sensational trial in 1954 of Lord Montagu of Beaulieu and Peter Wildeblood, diplomatic correspondent for *The Daily Mail*, marked an important turning point in public opinion. The men were convicted of gross indecency solely on the testimony of the two airmen with whom the acts had been committed and the trial exposed various unsavoury facts concerning police tactics, such as the practice of searching premises without a warrant, the use of witnesses who were granted immunity from prosecution themselves and the use of police agents provocateurs. As a result, there were calls in Parliament for legal reform. The Wolfenden Committee was established to consider the case for reform and, in 1957, issued its report in favour of decriminalising sexual acts between consenting adult men in private. It would be another decade, however, before the committee's recommendations were acted on and in the intervening years, a number of organisations were established to campaign for legal reform.

The Homosexual Law Reform Society (HLRS) was established in 1958 by two friends, A. E. Dyson, a lecturer at the University of Wales, and the Reverend Andrew Hallidie Smith. Its Executive Committee included a number of well-known figures of the day, such as Victor Gollancz, Dr E. B. Strauss and Kenneth Younger, MP, most of whom were not themselves homosexual, but regarded the issue as one of social concern. Using conventional lobbying tactics, the organisation sought to persuade MPs of the need for reform, by demonstrating the respectability of the majority of homosexuals. In May 1958, the HLRS established a separate organisation and registered charity, the Albany Trust, to deal with social and psychological issues relating to homosexuality and, in the late 1960s, the north-west branch of the HLRS renamed itself the Committee (later Campaign) for Homosexual Equality and continued to lobby for legal and social change. Although organisations such as the HLRS and the Albany Trust focused their work on improving the legal and social position of homosexual men, a number of women, some of them lesbians, were involved. Joy Blanchard worked at the HLRS offices on Shaftesbury Avenue as assistant to Antony Grey, the Secretary of the HLRS from 1962 onwards. Although, in keeping with the culture of discretion prevalent in societies such as the HLRS at this time, she never discussed her sexuality with Antony Grey, he believed her to be 'emotionally and temperamentally' a lesbian, if not so in practice. Cynthia Reid, a young London lesbian, contacted the HLRS in the early 1960s in the hope of meeting other lesbians and, although she did not find the social organisation she had hoped for, she nevertheless attended a number of the HLRS's meetings.

Leila J. Rupp has described a similar pattern in the United States, where women were heavily involved in campaigning for greater tolerance towards homosexuals through the homophile organisations of the 1950s and 1960s. The Mattachine Society, founded in 1950, 'included women but was dominated by men'.[5] Originally modelled on a Communist-style organisation, Mattachine initially argued that homosexuals represented a cultural minority and worked to resist police harassment and publish a magazine, called *One*. However, Rupp has argued that as a result of an internal power struggle in 1953, the organisation was remodelled along more respectable lines, replacing the idea of homosexuals as a cultural minority with the argument that the homosexual was 'no different from anyone else except in the object of his sexual expression'.[6] Although the national organisation was dominated by men, local branches of the organisation included more women. Despite tensions caused by the predominantly middle-class nature of the organisation and the working-class culture of the bar communities, bar lesbians in Buffalo, Philadelphia and Cincinnati joined local branches of Mattachine, and the Philadelphia branch, established in 1961, had a lesbian president. However, US women were not only organising as part of a mixed homophile movement in the 1950s and 1960s. In 1955, four lesbian couples, including Del Martin and Phyllis Lyon, formed the first national US lesbian organisation, the Daughters of Bilitis. Originally conceived as a social organisation, the Daughters of Bilitis later developed a political agenda, inspired by the Mattachine Society, and worked to demonstrate lesbians' respectability and right to acceptance within society.

In Britain, the homophile movement provided a similar focus for early lesbian organising. The HLRS's public profile as a homosexual campaigning organisation made it an obvious point of contact for women like Cynthia Reid, seeking to meet other lesbians and establish a social group in this period. In 1963 Antony Grey of the HLRS was also approached by Esme Langley for advice on setting up a magazine for lesbians. She wrote, 'I think it would do many people a power of good to be able to contribute to their own magazine, even if anonymously, and say what they have always wanted to say without let or hindrance.'[7] Antony Grey was able to put Esme in touch with Cynthia Reid and her partner Julie Switsur, and they subsequently made contact with a further two women, Diana Chapman and Patricia Dunckley. The Minorities Research Group (MRG) was founded later that year. It was agreed that the first task of the MRG would be to launch Esme's proposed magazine for lesbians, and the first issue of *Arena Three* was published in January 1964 (although due to delays in printing, it did not actually appear until the spring).

Arena Three

Arena Three represented the first magazine, specifically targeted at lesbians, to be published in Britain and it appeared monthly until 1971. The majority of subscribers were lesbians, although the magazine was also read by a number of gay men and by social and medical workers with a professional interest in homosexuality. In keeping with the professional background of its founding members, the readership was predominantly middle-class in the early years. This tendency was reinforced by an early advertising campaign in publications such as *The New Statesman*; but as an increasing range of newspapers agreed to carry advertisements, the class base of the readership broadened. Tony Geraghty, MRG's Press Officer, claimed that an article on the magazine in *The News of the World* in December 1964 had been a turning point in introducing working-class readers to the magazine.[8]

The content of the magazine was wide-ranging and changed over the years of publication. In the first year, many of the articles were written by the five co-founders, often under a variety of pseudonyms, but gradually readers began to contribute material and some ongoing series were launched. In the May 1964 issue, Clare Barringer launched a book review section, which continued until September 1965. Barringer reviewed a number of classic lesbian texts, such as Djuna Barnes' *Nightwood* and Radclyffe Hall's *The Well of Loneliness*, as well as introducing readers to any new lesbian-themed literature. Nancy Spain's autobiography *A Funny Thing Happened on the Way* was reviewed in July 1964, and readers were directed to a number of novels by US pulp fiction authors Tereska Torres and Shirley Verel. In a January 1965 article entitled 'The Fringe Benefits of Marginal Reading', Barringer reflected on the relative benefits to lesbian readers of badly written or negative portrayals which directly addressed a lesbian theme and a range of more generally conducive books without explicit lesbian content.

A number of articles on lesbian history were contributed by Lorna Gulston, including 'Passion in Park Lane', relating the story of eighteenth-century murderess Marguerite Diblanc and biographical accounts of Colonel Barker and Queen Christina of Sweden. Regular features such as these were supplemented with short stories, poetry, autobiographical accounts, humorous articles and political and current affairs pieces. The magazine also took on an increasingly political tone with reports on the Ford machinists' strike and other feminist issues in the late 1960s and an enthusiastic engagement with an emerging politics of gay liberation in the United States and Britain from 1969 onwards.

While series such as Lorna Gulston's historical articles were enthusiastically received, the majority of readers preferred to contribute to the magazine through the letters pages. An ongoing and increasingly important aspect of the magazine throughout its existence, these pages represented a fascinating insight into the readers' individual views and experiences. Olive Ager, who worked in the MRG offices for some years during the 1960s, described being inundated with letters from an amazing range of different women:

Then the letters started coming in. Loads and loads of letters, some with money in – quite a few people sent us money. The letters had to be answered, and that seemed to be what I did, an awful lot of answering letters, and an awful lot of sitting and having people

weep on my shoulder, listening to their stories. There were those who
came from small villages and small towns who really thought they
were the only ones, that there was nobody like them and that there
was something wrong with them. They were thoroughly delighted
when they knew there were hundreds of other people in the world
like them. There were those who had found out that they were
lesbians and they were deeply ashamed of it, and thought it was
wrong. They wouldn't accept it – you had to work and work and
talk to them to make them accept it. There were those who were
suicidal about it. There were those who were thrilled to bits –
thought it was absolutely marvellous, and what could they do? They
were bursting to do something to help. There were those who were
married and hadn't found out until then. It was very sad – they had
children – and wanted to leave their husbands but could not, or
would not, because of the children – they were very sad cases. Every
day somebody came. And the letters – there were stacks of letters.[9]

Many of these letters were reprinted in the magazine, opening up a
dialogue between different readers and enabling the *Arena Three*
community to offer advice and comment on each other's experiences.

However, while the letters' pages provided some sense of connection
between the readers, many subscribers wanted more direct contact, and
soon after the magazine was launched, requests began to be sent into
Arena Three calling for social meetings to be arranged. Although early
meetings took place in people's homes, the group soon outgrew this
possibility and an alternative venue was sought. The first of these public
meetings took place in the Shakespeare's Head on Carnaby Street
in May 1964. Locating a venue for a lesbian social meeting was difficult,
as Diana Chapman discovered:

> We eventually found a central venue for monthly meetings
> at Shakespeare's Head pub in Carnaby Street. Again we had
> to practice deceit and convey to the management and curious
> drinkers at the bar that we were a sort of business women's club
> on a spree without our men![10]

Meetings were held once a month and usually began with some form
of discussion or talk, before opening out into a more social gathering.
While these early meetings were held in London, where the founding

members and the magazine were based, readers from other areas
of Britain were soon calling for their own social meetings. By September,
volunteers had been identified to organise social meetings in Brighton,
East Anglia, Devon, Nottinghamshire, Cheshire, Salisbury and Bournemouth. Barbara Bell became the MRG representative for the South Coast
and described her role in befriending isolated and unhappy local lesbians:

> My job was to support lesbians who were having trouble with
> their relationships or make contact with those who felt isolated.
> The organisers would write to me from London or phone me
> if somebody wanted help or wanted to come and see me. Finding
> out about this club seemed like a salvation to these women – before
> then they were floundering around not knowing.[11]

However, while MRG representatives fulfilled an important
counselling function, local groups were also important as a focus
for social activities. Barbara Bell explained:

> We got a nice little social group going in the end. We would do the
> rounds of each other's homes, rarely more than eight or nine of us
> but it was a wonderful thing because you could just let your hair
> down and be natural … We used to periodically put on these do's.
> We'd dance our heads off – I suppose you'd call it having a disco
> nowadays.[12]

These social groups existed across Britain and, in London, groups had
formed in local areas such as Kensington and Richmond and catered
to a range of interest groups such as outdoor sports, indoor games,
musicians, metaphysics and a literary circle.

For many women, these first encounters with other lesbians provided
them with an affirmation of themselves and a sense of belonging
to a wider community. However, the experience of forming a lesbian
community could also be problematic, forcing women to acknowledge
a diversity of lesbian identities and images. The MRG social meetings
led almost immediately to one such dispute, which Diana Chapman
later described in an article in *Out*:

> The bitterest debate that took place at one of those meetings was
> the question of drag. In those days 'butch' lesbians rushed home

from work, thankfully shed their nylons and step-ins, changed into gents' natty suitings, plastered their perms with Brylcreem and appeared at meetings indistinguishable from slightly built men. As we were supposed to be an entirely female group this gave rise to ribald speculation among the barflies in the straight part of the pub, and great alarm among those of our number who would have had us all in twinsets and pearls.[13]

Letters of complaint were written in to *Arena Three*, asking that members attend meetings in conventional feminine attire and a debate was called to resolve the issue at the August meeting. A record number of seventy members and guests attended to hear the motion: 'That this house considers the wearing of male attire at MRG meetings is inappropriate.' Although a small majority rejected the motion, those hostile to butch lesbian identities had made it clear that these women were not welcome in the MRG community. Emily Hamer has argued that there was a class dimension to this hostility to butch lesbianism, suggesting that the 'butch' lesbian was perceived by middle-class readers to be presenting an explicitly sexualised lesbian identity to the public. She claims that, from the perspective of many *Arena Three* readers:

> 'Butch' working-class lesbians were blatantly sexual and dangerously stupid because they did not care what straight society thought of them. Straight-acting middle-class lesbians were 'decent people', i.e. not 'butch', not working-class and not dangerous. They could not afford to be recognised as lesbians and did not wish to be seen as sharing a common identity with 'butch dykes'.[14]

This concern that butch identities were too explicit and represented a threat to middle-class norms of respectability was also apparent in discussions of the lesbian bar culture. Few readers appeared to be aware of the existence of the bar scene, and references to it in *Arena Three* were overwhelmingly negative in the first years of publication, despite the fact that Cynthia Reid, Julie Switsur and other founders were regulars on the scene. There may have been a geographical dimension to the hostility, with readers from outside London and other large cities, who had limited access to lesbian bars, imagining the scene in negative terms. MS, from Gloucester, commented in a letter to the magazine in 1965:

I don't believe that the lesbians who gravitate to London's square
mile or two of vice are typical of the breed – they certainly aren't
in need of being rescued from loneliness. It seems to me that they
are already very well catered for compared with the rest of us who
are scattered throughout the country.[15]

By the following year, however, such views were less likely to be expressed
in the magazine and MRG began to hold its social meetings in the
Gateways.

Although few debates demonstrated the level of hostility and anger
roused in the drag dispute, the nature of lesbian identity and what
it meant to be a lesbian continued to be discussed in *Arena Three*
throughout its existence. Married lesbians and lesbian mothers
represented a significant minority of *Arena Three* readers, and the
dilemmas faced by women in this position were debated regularly
in the magazine. In an article on lesbian mothers in 1965, Janice O'Brien
examined the reasons which prompted lesbians to marry. Asking 'Why,
being as she is, does a lesbian have children, anyway?', she explained:

Many reasons, some of them common to both heterosexual and
homosexual women. Longing for a child can be a most intense
emotion – strong enough to lead into marriage those who might
otherwise remain outside it.

Some women have tried using marriage and motherhood
as a 'cure' – mostly, as far as I have observed, unsuccessfully.

Others have become aware of their lesbian tendencies fully only
after marriage and the birth of children. Somewhat different
is the case of the marriage where both partners are homosexual
or bisexual – presumably they will agree about some of the most
important aspects of life.[16]

Although the difficult decisions faced by married lesbians were
discussed sympathetically in the magazine, married lesbians nevertheless
represented a disadvantaged minority amongst readers. Prompted
by warnings from Antony Grey of the HLRS about the potential legal
implications of allowing married women to subscribe to the magazine,
the original founders had decided to require a husband's written consent
to married women's subscriptions. Inevitably, many women were not
in a position to obtain their husband's signature, and the magazine

received a number of letters from women who were prevented from subscribing. Mrs BB from Devon wrote, in 1964:

> You will understand why I haven't got my husband's signature. He is not the type to begin to understand my difficulties, though I've tried to tell him many times. He just won't accept. [I] am 42 years, and have gradually realised my position for 20 years. However I have plenty to occupy me so I do not dwell too much on my sexual unhappiness. All the same, a pen friend would be a Godsend and I truly mean that.[17]

Other women joined MRG together with their husbands, such as Mr and Mrs B from Northampton, who wrote in to the same issue in 1964:

> Are there any other young married couples among MRG members who'd like to correspond with us, perhaps meet and compare notes? We'll acknowledge all replies.

However, married couples who joined MRG were further marginalised within the group. Letters from men were rarely published in the letters' pages, and as a result of responses to a membership questionnaire in 1965, men were subsequently excluded from social meetings.

The balance between the magazine and social meetings remained a source of tension in MRG in the first few years and culminated in a split in the group in 1966. Although Esme Langley had been committed to the magazine from the outset and retained editorial control throughout *Arena Three*'s existence, a number of MRG members, including Cynthia Reid and Julie Switsur, were more interested in social meetings. Attempts to put MRG under collective control, with finances separate from Esme Langley's personal bank account, led to a dispute and a number of members left to form a separate social organisation, named Kenric. Sheila described how it happened:

> It was around Christmas, these two ladies in Upper Richmond Road had a mulled wine and mince pie evening. Doreen said, 'Why don't we form a breakaway group for social activities, as well as going to the main MRG meetings?' It was formed out of the 20, 25 people there. I was picked as Treasurer because I worked in a bank and looked honest.[18]

Kenric was established in a democratic format, with its own constitution. Primarily a social organisation, Kenric held meetings initially in members' homes, moving to the lesbian nightclub, the Gateways, in 1967. Jill Gardiner records that, early in 1967, the Gateways' proprietor, Gina, decided to close the club on a Monday night as custom was scarce. Kenric approached her, requesting that the club open for Kenric members on this night and Kenric meetings began to be held monthly and then fortnightly in the club. These meetings were usually social events, but Kenric occasionally held debates and other events in the club. In 1974, a discussion on the budget was held there and from May 1973 onwards, Kenric held monthly library meetings at Gateways. The MRG library had been transferred to Kenric in 1966, and Julie Switsur and Cynthia Reid's mothers, who had joined Kenric to give their support, attended the meetings with the boxes of books and organised the library.

The social aspect of Kenric was very popular with London lesbians. Julie Switsur described the first few years of Kenric's existence as 'very exciting' and the group had 396 members by 1969. Ruth Magnani remembered Kenric socials as an opportunity to dance and enjoy herself:

> Pat introduced me to Kenric because it had a lot of social things going on, and I'm a very social person – I love people and I love parties. I like getting out and about and enjoying myself. The biggest plus for me is that gay people within their own circle never seem to grow old. Now I like dancing and if I went to a heterosexual disco, everyone would say 'What's that silly old bag doing here? What does she think she's doing?' But as it is, I can go to a gay disco and dance the night away. No one thinks it's strange.[19]

However, while Kenric meetings were popular with members in the 1960s and 1970s, some of the regular clientele at the Gateways regarded them rather differently. Pip, a Gateways' regular in this period, recalled:

> We used to call the Kenric nights 'Grab a Granny'. These were the ladies that were in their late 30s or 40s or 50s and didn't join in the dancing so much or their dancing consisted of the hop from one foot to the other. They obviously all knew each other and chatted but they weren't the regulars.[20]

Sam also remembered the Kenric meetings as very sedate:

> I turned up at the Gates once on a Monday night and somehow
> I managed to slip in. That was another world, almost Radclyffe
> Hall type women. Women with short hair and suits and ties. Then
> very genteel, very feminine women, frocks, and cleavage some
> of them, kind of subdued cleavage, just slightly tantalising.
> I thought, This is an odd night, it's very sedate and there's no beer
> spilt anywhere. The jukebox was playing, but it was fairly subdued,
> romantic music. I don't think anyone was dancing – they were just
> talking. They were all in couples or small groups of couples.[21]

Kenric apparently held a reputation as middle class and inward-
looking amongst the lesbian community in the 1960s and 1970s.
Rene Sawyer commented that when she came across Kenric she found
it 'elitist and cliquey', 'snobby and frightened – closeted'. In her
experience the members 'didn't make any allowances for people
like myself who were not professional and didn't have a political
position … ordinary working people'.[22] Diana Chapman, a member
in the late 1960s, observed that the organisation was intentionally
inward-looking: it was 'just somewhere where people could go, meetings
in people's houses, there was no sort of proselytising about lesbianism'.[23]
Despite this, Kenric members were involved in a number of media
interviews and research projects in the later 1960s, contributing
alongside *Arena Three*. Cynthia Reid and Julie Switsur, in particular,
were interviewed several times, including an article in *The News of the
World*, in which they gave their real names and allowed their house
to be photographed.

While Kenric was sometimes accused of being primarily inward-
looking, the *Arena Three* community regarded one of its central aims
as the attempt to improve the public image of lesbianism and much of the
content of the magazine reflected this concern. The first issue of *Arena
Three* proclaimed the aims of MRG to be:

> [T]o conduct and to collaborate in research into the homosexual
> condition, especially as it concerns women; and to disseminate
> information and items of interest to universities, institutes, social
> and education workers, writers, poets, editors, employers and,

in short, all those genuinely in quest of enlightenment about what has been called 'the misty, unmapped world of feminine homosexuality'.[24]

Early issues of the magazine explored recent representations of lesbianism. In the first issue, an article entitled 'Scouting for – The Public Image' aimed to 'track down the public image of the woman homo-sexual'. The author, Hilary Benno (one of Esme Langley's pseudonyms), claimed: 'A BBC friend told me he'd wanted to do a documentary programme on Lesbianism some time back now. But it had been strangled at birth. High-level shush-shush policy, he said sadly.' Moving on to the field of law, the article referred to a defamation action concerning an accusation of lesbianism during the Second World War, in which Lord Asquith as judge declared that 'Nobody could doubt for a moment that "a Lesbian" was a creature of the "grossest unchastity", on a par, indeed, with the common prostitute. The mere allegation to only one other person was enough to damage a woman's prospects in the marriage market – and so act to her financial detriment.' Summing up psychiatric approaches to lesbians as 'cases of arrested development', the article then outlined a range of views from the 'man on the street':

> 'My idea of the typical Liz?' This was a tall gentleman in big, thoughtful spectacles who runs a worthy charitable organisation. 'Oh, er.. tweed suit, loud bossy voice, ready to mow you down, and all that, I suppose. Or is it? Lots of women carry on like that, and still they have little henpecked husbands and hordes of children tucked away at home.' He looked baffled. 'Lord, I don't know at all, really.'

While Hilary Benno's ultimate conclusion was that there were endless different images of lesbians, *Arena Three* focused primarily on the fields of psychiatry and the media, which had dominated debates about female homosexuality in the post-war period.

New medical and psychiatric works on lesbianism were extensively reviewed in the magazine and frequently subjected to cutting criticism. A review of American psychologist Daniel Cappon's *Toward an Under-standing of Homosexuality* claimed: 'The book is an epitome of all the

most grotesque clichés about homosexuality', while Anthony Storr's
Sexual Deviation was dismissed as:

> disappointingly stereotyped and facile. He seems to have nothing
> original or creative to offer on this subject; which is surprising
> in view of his background as a psychiatrist and a predominantly
> Jungian analyst.[25]

However, while classic psychological works such as these were almost
invariably criticised in *Arena Three*, works which adopted a statistical
or sociological approach to the issue received a more enthusiastic
reception. Alfred Kinsey's US statistical survey, *Sexual Behaviour in the
Human Female*, reviewed in *Arena Three* in July 1967, was praised
for dismissing Freud's theories on lesbianism, although Kinsey's own
conclusions were not completely endorsed. However, *Sexual Deviance*,
by American sociologists John Gagnon and William Simon, received
a glowing review in the magazine and was described as a 'uniquely
thoughtful book'.[26]

Minorities Research Group and *Arena Three* also engaged more
directly with the medical profession by taking part in a number
of research projects. The organisation represented the first openly lesbian
group to be formed in Britain and as such provided researchers with
unprecedented access to lesbian research subjects. Nine researchers
conducted projects with volunteers from MRG. These researchers
included D. Stanley-Jones, whose proposed research was into 'The
unmarried lesbian and maternal instinct'; Charlotte Wolff, researching
her book *Love between Women*; Mrs Morwenna Jones, conducting
research into the erotic imagination of lesbians on behalf of an unnamed
American psychologist; Mary Cecil, conducting a handwriting study;
and Marvin Siegelman, Associate Professor in Psychology at the City
University of New York, comparing the personality, attitude and
parental background of homosexuals and heterosexuals.

The attitude towards these researchers was mixed. While the founding
members remained committed to the idea of participating in scientific
research into lesbianism, some magazine subscribers were apparently
less enthusiastic. Cynthia Reid was prompted to write an article for the
magazine in 1965 outlining the arguments in favour of collaboration
with scientific research and attempting to reassure readers that potential
researchers were carefully vetted before being given access to members.

The editorial line on medical literature also became increasingly hostile in the late 1960s. Alison Oram has argued that:

> It is clear that the MRG expected 'unbiased' research to reflect their own views. They believed that the 'truth' of their own minds and bodies could reshape the scientific agenda, away from pathologising lesbianism and towards their concept of lesbian normality. Its largely middle-class and educated readers were possibly more inclined to believe in the ultimate neutrality of science, whose authority could be used to make their case to the general public.[27]

As a result, early researchers such as Eva Bene, who approached the MRG in 1965 for assistance in a study of the role of parent–child relations in the development of female homosexuality, received a warm welcome. Eva Bene even appears to have stayed at Esme Langley's house in the early stages of her research. However, as it became increasingly clear from the published results of these projects that MRG views on lesbianism were not necessarily going to be endorsed, discussion of medical research in *Arena Three* became increasingly critical. In October 1967, a survey of the current state of research into lesbianism concluded with the sarcastic editorial comment:

> On our own side of the field we have had a helpful suggestion, too. Why do we not set up a homosexual study group to do some serious research into the mentality of heterosexuals (including researchers into homosexuality)?[28]

A similar pattern of increasing hostility was apparent in *Arena Three*'s approach to the media. Media representations of lesbianism were clearly influential in shaping public attitudes to the issue, and, in the climate of increased debate surrounding the Wolfenden proposals, journalists were increasingly interested in discussing homosexuality. A number of journalists approached MRG requesting interviews, including Anne Sharpley of *The Evening Standard*, Ron Mount at *The News of the World* and Monica Furlong at *The Daily Mail*. By the mid-1960s, this interest had spread to regional newspapers and Barbara Buchanon's article on lesbianism, as part of her 'Taboo Subjects' series, appeared in *The Bristol Evening Post* on 2 December 1965. Women's magazines were increasingly open to discussing lesbianism in the late 1960s and features appeared in *Nova*, *She*, *Nineteen* and *Woman* between 1966 and 1969. Many of these articles followed MRG's lead and represented lesbians as different from other women only in their choice of sexual partner. In making a case for greater social tolerance, the journalists stressed the extreme isolation experienced by many lesbians, using headlines such as 'Easing the isolation and unhappiness of lesbianism' and 'Life for these women offers no more than utter, appalling oneliness'.

Minorities Research Group was also involved in a number of television programmes which tackled the issue of lesbianism in the late 1960s. In July 1964, *Arena Three* was approached by a television company, Associated Rediffusion, for assistance in producing a television programme on lesbianism. Bryan Magee, the journalist responsible for the project, had already aired a programme on male homosexuality as part of the *This Week* current affairs programme and hoped to make a second programme focusing on lesbianism. As part of his research, Magee was invited to attend one of MRG's monthly meetings, normally barred to men, and a number of MRG members appeared on the programme. MRG was apparently happy with the programme, although a subsequent article by Bryan Magee in *The New Statesmen* was received less positively. Two years later, in 1967, a second programme was made as part of the *Man Alive* series, again with collaboration from MRG. Although the programme included interviews with Cynthia Reid, Julie Switsur and Olive Ager, the write-up of the programme in *Arena Three* objected to

> a very long drawn out interview with Steve Rogers – a youthful 'Colonel Barker' whose over-riding compulsion is to pass as a male, even to the point of 'courting' and getting engaged to another girl and using an artificial penis. (And, for all that Mr. Wilcox says about 'hairsplitting', we still feel that to devote so much programme time, in a Lesbian sequence, to this rare and way-out case of transvestism (if not indeed of trans-sexuality) was unfortunate, and could only add to the confusion of the public that the programme was meant to enlighten.[29]

Such comments suggest that, while MRG welcomed increased discussion of lesbianism in the media, they were concerned that, as in the field of psychiatry, any representations of the subject should conform to their own notion of the lesbian 'public image'.

Despite the increased discussion of the subject in the press and
on television in the 1960s and the inevitable publicity which this gave
to the magazine, MRG faced considerable difficulties throughout the
period in placing advertisements. The magazine did not go on public sale
in newsagents and lesbian venues until 1969, operating until this point
on a private subscription basis only. As a result, MRG was dependent
on advertising as a means of reaching potential readers. The US
organisation, Daughters of Bilitis, was supportive from the outset and
advertised *Arena Three* in its magazine *The Ladder* and further adverts
were placed in *The Spectator*, *Private Eye* and *The New Statesmen*.
Adverts invited 'lonely lesbians' to read *Arena Three* or advised
readers that 'Women with homosexual problems read *Arena Three*'.
The wording of these adverts appears to have caused some confusion
among readers, however. A letter to *Arena Three* in 1971 complained:

> On press publicity – I knew about how I felt long before I saw your
> ad. in 'New Statesman', and could have done with meeting others
> like me. However, it was several years after this that I actually read
> a copy of A3, because the 'New Statesman' ad was worded:
> 'Women with homosexual problems read Arena Three'. I didn't
> have any problems and deduced from this wording that I was likely
> to be sat in front of a psychiatrist who'd say 'Don't be silly,
> of course you're not homosexual' and try to involve me
> in a heterosexual way of living.[30]

However, despite the rather pessimistic approach to lesbianism which
the wording of the advertisements implied, many newspapers refused
to carry advertisements which included the words 'homosexual' or
'lesbian'. In October 1967, an article in *Arena Three* noted that *The
Sunday Telegraph* had refused to publish MRG's advert, and in December
copies of protest letters sent by Esme Langley to the editors of *The
Observer* and *The Sunday Times* were reprinted in the magazine. The
editorial stance on this issue became increasingly militant in the late 960s,
and in 1970 a Press Freedom Group was formed. Under the leadership of
Jackie Forster, newly appointed Advertising Manager, a complaint
was made to the Press Council, but in April 1971, the Press Council
upheld the right of newspaper editors to refuse to carry advertisements.

Arena Three ceased publication around the time of this decision,
releasing its final issue in July 1971. Esme Langley was apparently ready

for a new challenge and had moved to Malawi to take up a new job. The magazine had already been suffering from financial difficulties and did not survive her departure. However, the Press Freedom Group, which had been meeting for a year, had given renewed vigour to the magazine enterprise and became a new focal point in the months after Esme's departure. Jackie Forster explained that they 'kept having the monthly meetings for a few months not knowing what to do', until 'all these women kept coming from Hull and Devon ... wanting to know what was going on and saying that the group had to start another magazine'.[31] It was agreed that twelve women, including Angie Chilton, Angie's lover, Caz, Roz Stott, Jenny Green and Helen Milton, should meet weekly to decide how the magazine would work and then report to the next monthly meeting. A document was drafted which agreed that a magazine was to be written 'about lesbians by lesbians', including photographs, cartoons, articles, news stories, fiction, poems, a list of places where lesbians could meet and small personal adverts. Jackie Forster recalled that the name 'Sappho' was agreed upon 'and they said that's great because she was a wife, a widow, a mother and she started this college on Lesbos where women learned, loved and lived together and we felt that covered the Lesbian scene as we knew it then.' The first issue was produced in April 1972 from the home of Jackie Forster and her partner, Babs Todd, in Connaught Square. The magazine advertised in *Time Out* and *Gay News* and was sold over the counter in the Gateways in the 1970s.[32]

In addition to the magazine, Sappho continued the *Arena Three* social events and meetings were held at the Euston Tavern, once a month. Speakers were invited every six weeks or so, and included Mary Stott, Women's Editor of *The Guardian*, and May Hobbs, a Communist. At meetings which did not have a speaker, small group discussions were held on a variety of topics. Jackie Forster recalls that in the first years of Sappho, 'we never had socials – Sappho was about getting things done.'

For many women in the 1970s and 1980s, Sappho meetings represented their first encounter with other lesbians and were remembered as an introduction to a lesbian community. Betty recalled:

> We read about Sappho in *Time Out* – we were a bit scared
> to go along, but we figured we ought to. We started attending
> there and we've really been linked with Sappho ever since. I helped

to run it for a year in 1984 and she [Betty's partner] took a turn after that. And then of course we really did meet other lesbians from all walks of life.

We were relieved and very excited, because we could actually be ourselves – particularly in circles where we were with other women. It was a great time. Tuesdays were not to be missed, because these were the only times, the only two or three hours, that you could really be yourself, and be affectionate with each other, demonstrably so. Nobody raised eyebrows, you didn't have to jump apart if somebody came in the door.[33]

Unlike previous lesbian organisations, Sappho was recalled as representing a diverse lesbian community. Jackie Forster remembered Sappho as a cross-class organisation, observing, 'And at one stage, in Sappho, when we moved to the Chepstow [public house] from the Euston [Tavern], an enormous number of black women would come along; working-class women; women who were out of prison, just out, and it didn't matter. It was being lesbian.' Nina Miller also recalled Sappho members as a diverse group, commenting:

I remember the first night I went there, I sat with my back to the wall and I looked around the room and I was absolutely amazed. I thought if you'd gone along Oxford Street and taken one woman in every ten, you'd have that range of women there. I'd got no idea so many different women were lesbians. And that was really nice.

Sappho magazine continued throughout the 1970s, enjoying a circulation of approximately 2,000 at its peak. However, the organisation encouraged lesbians to form local groups or start local newsletters, and as a result, circulation dropped to about 700 a month in 1980. Jackie Forster recalls that copies were being returned unsold and it was ultimately agreed to cease publication when they reached Volume 10, number 12, towards the end of 1981. The discos and meetings continued, however, into the 1990s and provided an introduction for many women into a number of new organisations which were founded in the 1970s and 1980s. Nina Miller remembered:

[Sappho] led on to other things, like getting in touch with Sequel and they had a monthly supper together in a public restaurant.

They arranged walks sometimes. I discovered there was a local
gay group in Essex called Octopus and the Quaker group called
the Friends Homosexual Fellowship – which was a mixed group.
So my social life widened out enormously after that.[34]

The social organisations of the 1960s and 1970s performed a vital
function in enabling isolated women to meet other lesbians and
in providing a forum for women to discuss what it meant to be a lesbian.
Many of these groups followed an overtly political agenda, seeking
to alter public opinion on lesbianism or to improve the social position
of lesbians. In this sense, these groups laid the groundwork for the new
campaigning organisations and political ideologies which emerged in the
1970s and 1980s.

Chapter 10

The Politics of Lesbianism, 1970–2000

By the end of the 1960s, lesbian social organisations such as Minorities Research Group and Kenric were being joined by emerging political movements campaigning for gay and women's rights. In the October 1969 issue of *Arena Three*, an article entitled 'News from the United States: The Birth of Gay Power' reported on riots, prompted by a police raid on the Stonewall Inn gay bar in New York, and announced the subsequent founding of the Gay Liberation Front (GLF).[1] Throughout 1970, the magazine offered regular updates on the development of this new political movement and in August 1970, at the height of the magazine's press freedom campaign, the editor observed, 'The GAY LIBERATION movement is going great guns in the States. It is high time we had a little more positive action over here.'[2] Others in Britain were thinking the same, and on Wednesday, 13 October 1970, two gay men, Bob Mellors and Aubrey Walter, called a meeting to discuss the news from America and the possibility of starting a London equivalent. The meeting was held in a basement classroom at the London School of Economics (LSE) and was attended by between nine and nineteen people, including one woman, Bev Jackson. Sociologist Mary McIntosh, who worked at the LSE at the time, and her lover, psychiatric social worker Elizabeth Wilson, joined soon afterward. Numbers were relatively small in the first few weeks, drawn largely from student activists and academics at the LSE, but Elizabeth recalled 'There weren't very many women, there was all this buzz.'[3] By November, the group had begun leafleting in Earls Court and elsewhere, in an attempt to attract a broader cross section of members, and numbers increased dramatically. Amongst those drawn in through this recruitment campaign were women from the lesbian bars, such as Carla Toney, who recalled:

Sometimes there were only a dozen (women), sometimes fifty – it grew fairly rapidly but there were very few at first. The belief that women would go off with men if offered that choice, that lesbians didn't exist – in the initial phase it was very important to identify as a lesbian or as gay, homosexual … I didn't know many women

there. I was at the Gateways with Rosie, and Beverley handed
us a leaflet, so we went together.[4]

Strongly influenced by the US gay movement and by the left-wing
revolutionary counterculture developing in Britain in this period, the
London Gay Liberation Front (GLF) represented a new approach
to lesbian and gay rights. Early meetings formulated a list of demands,
which proclaimed:

> THE GAY LIBERATION FRONT DEMANDS ...
> – that all discrimination against gay people, male and
>   female, by the law, by employers, and by society at large,
>   should end
> – that all people who feel attracted to a member of their
>   own sex be taught that such feelings are perfectly normal
> – that sex education in schools stop being exclusively
>   heterosexual
> – that psychiatrists stop treating homosexuality as though
>   it were a problem or sickness, thereby giving gay people
>   senseless guilt complexes
> – that gay people be as legally free to contact other
>   gay people through newspaper ads, on the
>   streets and by any other means they want, as are
>   heterosexuals, and that police harassment should cease
>   øright now
> – that employers should no longer be allowed to
>   discriminate against anyone on account of their sexual
>   preferences
> – that the age of consent for gay males be reduced to the
>   same as for straights
> – that gay people be free to hold hands and kiss in public,
>   as are heterosexuals
> GAY IS GOOD!
> ALL POWER TO OPPRESSED PEOPLE!
> COME OUT – JOIN GAY LIBERATION FRONT![5]

As the demands suggested, the GLF articulated a newly self-confident
gay political agenda, based on a positive attitude to homosexuality and
a belief in the importance of proudly proclaiming one's sexual identity,

or 'coming out'. This fundamental belief was apparent through the forms of protest carried out by the group, but was also integral to its internal rules and structures, as Angie Weir discovered:

> I remember the meeting at which I came out, which I think was the second meeting I attended. I was announcing a demonstration, some women's liberation one that we were doing ... I was about to sit down and [the chairperson] Warren said, 'We have a rule here and anyone who speaks has to declare whether they're straight or gay' ... and I thought, I can't walk away from this moment so I staggered out 'I think I'm gay' and sat down and collapsed. That's how I came out.[6]

However, the movement also went beyond a specific political agenda, developing a broader political philosophy which connected the GLF with other movements for social change. The set of principles agreed on 9 December 1970 outlined an ideology which sought to 'defend the immediate interests of gay people against discrimination and all forms of social oppression' but which understood that 'the roots of the oppressions that gay people suffer run deep in our society ... While existing social structures remain, social prejudice and overt repression can always emerge.'[7] The GLF therefore saw itself as part of a wider movement fighting all forms of social oppression and allied itself with women's liberation, black people and other minorities, the working class, the youth counterculture and people oppressed by imperialism.

The first GLF demonstration took place on 27 November 1970 at Highbury Fields. Billed as a protest against the arrest of a London man, Louis Eakes, during a police entrapment operation, the demonstration also aimed to make a wider protest against the policing of homosexuality. Protesters walked around the park at night and lit each other's cigarettes (the action which had led to Eakes' arrest), before kissing openly. Speeches were made and the protesters then retired to a nearby pub. Approximately fifty people attended, and the protest was watched both by the police and journalists. Symbolic protests and attempts to challenge conventional thinking about gender and sexuality were common aspects of GLF campaigning, which used street theatre, 'radical drag' and 'zaps' or protests targeted at specific institutions which were thought to be involved in the oppression of lesbians and gay men. The GLF also formed close links with other protest movements, taking part in a number of Women's Liberation actions, including the protest against the Miss World Competition in 1971.

Although many GLF members frequented gay bars, where the group leafleted in an attempt to attract new members, the GLF tended to be rather suspicious of the commercial bar scene, which they regarded as underground, apolitical and potentially exploitative. As a result, the movement was active in organising its own social events from the outset and held its first openly gay dance at the LSE on 4 December 1970. This was followed by a 'GLF People's Dance' at Kensington Town Hall on 22 December, which aimed to attract people from outside the movement. Tickets cost 6 shillings and the event was so well attended that after 750 people had been admitted, a further 500 had to be turned away due to lack of space. Although the dance itself was a success and was subsequently covered by the press in a good-humoured way, Angie Weir recalled one confrontation, which occurred before the dance:

> I went with my women's group and it was preceded by an incident in a pub in [Kensington] Church Street. In those days it was very unusual for a crowd of women in short hair and trousers to be together in any numbers and men would scream at you and pick fights and so on. That happened all the time, constantly. You went out with women who were harassed. These men started having a go at us and ended up pouring their beer all over us and the police were called and that's how it started. These incidents were absolutely commonplace, they seemed to happen all the time. You were attacked with impunity by men, by police, you could be arrested and tried and put in prison, it's hard to imagine that it would cause such a furore but I suppose it was radical for the time.[8]

Women were a constant, minority presence in the GLF from the first meeting. Mary McIntosh and Elizabeth Wilson were active members and the GLF Counter-Psychiatry Group met at their house. However, after the initial excitement of establishing a gay political group had worn off, a number of differences, including those of gender, began to emerge. Men represented a large majority in the meetings and frequently dominated both discussion and campaigning issues, leaving many women feeling that they did not have a voice. In December 1970, following a suggestion by Angie Weir, a separate women's group was formed, which met weekly on a Friday. By the spring of 1971, the group was beginning to receive a number of guest speakers, including Jill Johnston and Kate Millett from the United States. The women's group carried out their own protests, often with the assistance of men from the larger movement, including a demonstration at Gateways and the spray painting of graffiti outside institutions such as the Tavistock clinic and the Stock Exchange. In early summer 1971, the group produced a Women's Issue of the GLF newsletter, *Come Together*. However, while the women's group united to produce this issue, overcoming emerging differences over class, sexuality and politics, by the autumn of 1971, these tensions were becoming more pronounced. Many of the older women members, who had been involved from the outset, adopted a broadly socialist perspective and were committed to working jointly with the men for gay liberation. However, a new, younger group, centred on the women's commune at Faraday Road, increasingly articulated a radical feminist separatist politics, which advocated working independently of the men for women's liberation. At the main meeting on 9 February 1972, one of these women took the microphone and announced the women's decision to leave the group. Nettie Pollard recalled:

> That night I was there. I went with all the other women to a pub near All Saints Hall and the women got quite emotional and were saying things like, the men didn't care about them, all they cared about was cottaging and cruising. It was the radical feminist type women rather than the socialist feminist type women. It was Faraday Road and the women who hung about with them. I don't really remember specifically who it was but it was a general feeling … There were quite a lot of women there, about forty or fifty, but obviously they had come in strength in order to walk out. And then we went in and it was the ordinary part of the meeting, and then one of the women got up and said why the women were going to leave.[9]

The decision was supported by many of the men, some of whom were apparently happy to see the women leave, while others were reluctant but wished to support the women's decision. Not all the women left, however, and women remained a part of the organisation in London until it folded in 1974, while women worked alongside men in regional groups across the country throughout the 1970s.

For those women who left, the Women's Liberation Movement (WLM) represented the attractive alternative of working with other women to develop a feminist political agenda. By the end of 1969, growing discontent amongst women, voiced in community groups and in socialist and other revolutionary movements, was coalescing into a co-ordinated women's movement, and a national conference was being planned to link a range of different groups. The first national conference was held at Ruskin College, Oxford, in the autumn of 1969 and local groups were formed across the country in the early 1970s. The first four demands – equal pay, equal education and job opportunities, free 24-hour childcare, and free contraception and abortion on demand – adopted in 1970 reflected a desire to achieve social and economic equality for women. However, the WLM, like the GLF, was also committed to challenging the social attitudes which were thought to underpin the oppression of women. Although influenced by theories proposed in a number of key feminist texts, such as Kate Millett's *Sexual Politics* and Shulamith Firestone's *The Dialectic of Sex: The Case for Feminist Revolution*, the movement also placed considerable emphasis on the relationship between theory and individual practice. The slogan 'the personal is political' was central to WLM ideology, and local activism, particularly in the early 1970s, was focused around consciousness-raising groups, in which individual women shared their personal experiences and used them as a basis for developing a collective political agenda.[10]

Although lesbians were active in the WLM from the outset, the movement was not initially particularly welcoming of lesbians. Some feminists were concerned that accusations of lesbianism would be used by opponents to discredit the feminist cause, and Betty Friedan, author of the seminal feminist text *The Feminine Mystique* and president of the US National Organization for Women, had referred to lesbians within the movement in 1969 as the 'lavender menace'. Her views were apparently shared by some British feminists in the early years. When the London GLF Women's Group first formed, they wrote to the secretary of Women's Liberation, Maysel Brah, asking to join, and Angie Weir recalls that 'she wrote me back a letter saying that lesbians couldn't be part of women's liberation and returned my postal order'.[11] However, lesbians continued to work within the women's movement in the early

1970s and gradually pushed other feminists to recognise their concerns. At the second national conference of the WLM in Skegness, in the winter of 1970, lesbians from the GLF were instrumental in leading a challenge to a group of Maoist men and women who had sought to dominate the conference, and the lesbians apparently gained some standing amongst other women from the grass roots as a result. In 1974, at the national conference in Edinburgh, lesbians' concerns were added to the list of WLM demands, with the sixth demand reading 'The right to our own self-defined sexuality and to an end to discrimination against lesbians'. In the spring of the same year, the first lesbian conference was held in Canterbury.[12] Black lesbians were also struggling to gain acknowledgement and discussion of the specific issues raised by race in the feminist movement in the 1980s. However, the predominantly white, middle-class movement was slow to react and it was not until 1993 that the first book about black lesbians in Britain appeared.[13]

From the early 1970s onwards, some lesbians began to articulate a specific radical feminist agenda, centred on the concept of separatism. Janet Dixon, a separatist lesbian for five years in the early 1970s, defined the ideology behind separatism as:

> Separatism is shamelessly exclusive. The rules are simple: whatever your race or class, provided you are a woman, you are a potential separatist. Whatever your race or class, if you are a man you are irredeemably the enemy. The separatist position was clear. It was not that men held the power, but that men were the power. Something inherent in maleness necessitates its expression in systems of oppressive hierarchies. Competitiveness, aggression, brutality and maleness are all one in the same. That Y chromosome, that mutated afterthought, was the cause of it all.[14]

Radical feminists, many of whom – but not all – were separatists, emphasised the importance of women focusing their time and energy on other women. Their philosophy was important in shaping the development of women-only spaces, rape crisis centres and women's refuges. For those women who aimed at total separatism, the ideology required a complete removal of men and male culture from their lives. Janet Dixon explained:

> Pure separatism involves a woman taking steps to remove men from her life. She must live with women, be a mother only to girl

children. Male culture in all its manifestations is shunned.
She must abandon all relationships with men, lovers, fathers
and brothers. Sexually she is either celibate or lesbian. Politically
and socially, her contact is confined to women. The music she listens
to must be composed and played by women, the books
she reads must have a woman author. Her morality is not dictated
by patriarchal norms, but rather guided by the belief that women's
needs are her sole concern. To steal from men is not theft,
it is reclamation.[15]

Separatists were present in the women's movement throughout the early
1970s, attempting to argue their position with other women and seeing
the national conferences in particular as an opportunity to spread the
word to others. However, by 1974, tensions were beginning to increase
between the radical feminist separatists and socialist feminists, who
advocated political autonomy from men but not necessarily a withdrawal
from living with men. A number of arguments occurred over the nature
and organisation of one of the key London WLM groups, the London
Women's Liberation Workshop, and over the presence of men on the
International Women's Day marches. In the autumn of 1974, the
Workshop's newsletter began a serialisation of 'The CLIT statement',
an article outlining a radical feminist separatist agenda, which had first
appeared in the New York radical feminist publication *Off Our Backs*.
The statement claimed:

> straight women think, talk, cross their legs, dress, come on like
> male transvestite femme drag queens. Bisexuality maintains
> the patriarchy. Lesbianism understood is a revolt against the
> patriarchy ... Everybody knows from the first minute the
> Women's Liberation Movement hit that feminism means
> lesbianism.

Another instalment claimed: 'The danger of straight women is their
disguise, they look like women ... they are men in disguise.'[16] The
statement prompted a number of women to complain to the Newsletter
and the serialisation was apparently discontinued. A number of feminist
and other historians have argued that these divisions between radical
and socialist feminists prompted the decline of the WLM from the

mid-1970s onwards. However, Eve Setch has argued that ideological divisions and arguments over structure and organisation were not only commonplace in the WLM from the outset but integral to the feminist commitment to an inclusive political agenda and structure which enabled all women to voice their opinions. She also points to the continued existence of the movement and a wide range of feminist groups and campaigns into the late 1970s and beyond, as evidence that the WLM and feminism more broadly did not decline as a result of these tensions.[17]

In the late 1970s, a new strand of radical feminism, calling itself revolutionary feminism, emerged. One of the most vocal exponents, the Leeds Revolutionary Feminists, articulated a new and more radical critique of heterosexuality. In a 1979 pamphlet entitled 'Political Lesbianism: The Case Against Heterosexuality', they claimed that penetration of a woman's vagina by a man's penis is 'an act of great symbolic significance, by which the oppressor enters the body of the oppressed' and they argued that women who engaged in penetrative sex with men were 'collaborators with the enemy' and help to 'maintain the oppression of her sisters and hinder[…] our struggle'. Instead, they argued, all women should be 'political lesbians':

> Our definition of a political lesbian is a woman-identified woman who does not fuck men. It does not mean compulsory sexual activity with women.[18]

In 1980, Adrienne Rich developed this critique of heterosexuality and the notion of lesbianism as a political act further in her radical feminist classic, 'Compulsory Heterosexuality and Lesbian Existence'. She argued that in a patriarchal or male-dominated society, heterosexuality should be understood as a social institution (heteropatriarchy) which women are coerced into. However, rather than advocating political lesbianism for all women, she argued that women's sexuality, both heterosexual and lesbian, needed further analysis. She suggested that women should work together to achieve this and proposed the concept of a 'lesbian continuum', encompassing a broad range of relationships between women, from sexual ones to mother–daughter bonds and passionate friendships.[19]

The Politics of Sex

By the 1980s, debates within feminism and between lesbians were increasingly centring on the issue of sex. Lesbian feminists had begun to develop a politics of lesbian sexual practice in the late 1970s and 1980s, which emerged out of the notion of lesbianism as a political rejection of heteropatriarchy. While no clear or unified political view was ever espoused, a number of sexual practices came to be regarded as either acceptable or unacceptable. Monogamy was viewed by many lesbian feminists as a heteropatriarchal practice, designed to limit women's sexual and affectionate expression, and a number of lesbian feminists therefore experimented with non-monogamy in their relationships. The theory that sex between women was an extension of a broader feminist emotional and supportive commitment to all women meant that non-monogamy was not thought to pose a threat of jealousy, and this mutual trust was also to be supported by honest and open communication about sexual partners and sexual practices between all women. However, this ideal scenario was not always achievable. Penny Wallace recalled:

> My partner's non-monogamy led to problems, even though she was clear from the beginning that she wanted to be non-monogamous. Intellectually, I thought it was an interesting concept, but intellectual theory is different from being faced with reality. I discovered that non-monogamy is fine when you are doing it, but very different when your partner is doing it. I became jealous and though I tried to explore what I was jealous of, it made very little difference.[20]

'Fancying' women, on the other hand, could be regarded as sexually objectifying women as men were perceived to do and was therefore not appropriate. A similar attitude was taken towards pornography, which was the focus of a sustained feminist campaign in the 1980s. Penetrative sex, using a dildo or fingers, was also thought by some women to be replicating the power imbalances inherent in heterosexual relationships. Lesbian feminist sex was frequently imagined, instead, in terms of equality, with relationships between women being essentially caring and supportive.

By the 1980s, there was growing disillusionment within the lesbian community with a lesbian feminist viewpoint, which was thought to prioritise politics rather than sex in its approach to lesbianism. In 1982, American lesbian feminist Celia Kitzinger presented the lesbian feminist approach to sex in these terms:

> Lesbianism to a feminist is much more than just a question of sex. It's a question of lifestyle; it's a question of sexual politics. It's much wider than the sexual act.
>
> The important thing about being a lesbian is not the sexual act itself. It's the self-definition in that way as a woman-identified woman, and the commitment to women.[21]

Arguments such as this and the Leeds Revolutionary Feminists' claim that political lesbianism 'does not mean compulsory sexual activity with women' angered an increasing number of lesbians in the early 1980s for whom desire for women was central to lesbianism and who wanted to explore their sexuality in more detail. These debates, which have come to be labelled the 'sex wars', became increasingly heated in the 1980s and centred on sadomasochism (S/M) and a small number of other sexual practices. Debate was sparked by the 1982 publication, by a US S/M collective, of *Coming to Power: Writings and Graphics on Lesbian S/M*. The book provoked considerable controversy, prompting British lesbians to start looking for S/M lesbians in their own midst, and culminated in a number of confrontations in 1984 and 1985, over the right of S/M lesbians to share lesbian feminist and lesbian space. Lesbian feminists regarded S/M within heterosexual relationships as an extreme example of male dominance over women and were therefore shocked by its presence in lesbian sexuality. As the debates continued, lesbian feminists also began to make links between S/M and fascism and racism, based on the use of scenarios such as mistresses punishing slaves or Nazis punishing Jews in S/M sex play. S/M lesbians, on the other hand, stressed the consensual nature of S/M activity and the way in which it allowed women to explore and play out issues of domination and racism in a 'safe' environment, through fantasy. For other lesbians, who did not personally practice S/M sex, supporting S/M lesbians was important as a statement about the right to personal choice and an opposition to a perceived policing of lesbian sexuality by lesbian feminists.

In the late 1980s, the issue of dominance in lesbian relationships resurfaced with a debate about the apparent resurgence of butch/femme.

Feminists and gay liberationists in the early 1970s had developed
a powerful critique of the butch/femme culture in lesbian bars, arguing
that it replicated the power imbalance inherent in heterosexual
relationships. As a result, butch/femme culture in lesbian clubs such
as the Gateways had been gradually pushed out by a younger generation
of political lesbians. However, in the late 1980s, encouraged by the
publication of US lesbian Joan Nestle's celebration of butch/femme,
A Restricted Country (1988), the phenomenon resurfaced. Lesbian
feminists such as Sheila Jeffreys linked a depoliticised butch/femme with
the sexual dominance they opposed in S/M sexual practice, claiming:

> The 'male–female polarity' is a polarity of dominance and
> submission. That is why difference in this context cannot be benign.
> Under male supremacy it is the subordination of women and male
> power that are eroticised. Sexual attraction is constructed around
> 'difference', i.e., dominance and submission. Those lesbians
> who are revalidating butch and femme are not discovering that
> they are innately butch or femme, they are engaging in an erotic
> communication based on sadomasochism, the eroticising of power
> difference.[22]

The debates about S/M and butch/femme resulted in the declining
influence of a lesbian feminist perspective within the lesbian community
by the end of the 1980s and a greater openness in discussion about sexual
practices. In the late 1980s, Thrilling Bits, Britain's first mail-order sex
shop, began to market dildos and other sex toys for lesbians. In 1989,
Sheba Feminist Publishers published the first British collection of lesbian
erotica, Serious Pleasure, and the same year, a new lesbian sex magazine,
Quim, was launched. The growing commercialisation of lesbian sex
in the 1990s was also mirrored by an expansion in the lesbian and gay
commercial bar and club scene, catering to a broader range of lesbian
and gay identities.

Discussion about sex and sexual practices was also prompted, in the
1980s, by the emergence of the sexually transmitted disease, AIDS. The
first British case of AIDS appeared in 1982, when Terrence Higgins,
a bar manager at the gay nightclub, Heaven, died of the disease. The
news was reported five months later in the London newspaper, Capital
Gay, and a benefit was held at Heaven to raise money for research into
the disease. A charity, named the Terrence Higgins Trust, was established

to administer the money raised. Although the number of cases increased throughout the early 1980s, reaching 241 in October 1985, the Conservative government was slow to fund research into the disease or begin education campaigns to inform those at risk, regarding it as a 'gay disease'. Gay organisations were therefore at the forefront of the response to AIDS in the early 1980s. The London Lesbian and Gay Switchboard, established in 1974 to provide information and advice to the lesbian and gay community, played a key role in educating and counselling the community through the crisis. Lisa Power, who volunteered at the Switchboard during this period, recalled that the AIDS crisis transformed the nature of Switchboard work, leading to the introduction of safe-sex training and factual updates for volunteers and the provision of bereavement counselling training.[23] Many lesbians, some of whom had moved away from collective gay activism to work within a feminist arena in the late 1970s, worked with gay men in campaigning on the issue and supporting people who were HIV positive. Barbara Bell volunteered as a 'buddy' in Brighton, providing emotional and practical support to individual people with HIV and AIDS. She recalled:

I thought, now I've got to do something about these boys because we're not suffering – look at all these women laughing their heads off and look at you boys, you need help. What can I do? I'll do anything, scrub floors, make beds, go to the launderette, make food.[24]

Providing emotional support often required persistence when those she had befriended did not always want to see her, and she described her relationships with them as 'humbling'. Attending funerals became a common occurrence and Barbara remembered:

It was very depressing. In the beginning they were very serious affairs … the first funeral I went to broke my heart. I was sobbing and crying all over the place, couldn't help it. This young fella, he was only a kid of about nineteen … But as time went on there was a gradual change. You don't go to weep about a life that's gone, you go to rejoice about a life that's been. It's a thanksgiving that they've been here and given such love, or pleasure or joy.[25]

Lesbians were also affected by the political and social reaction to the disease, which grew out of a broader right-wing backlash against lesbians and gay men in the 1970s and 1980s. In the 1970s, figures such as Mrs Mary Whitehouse had spearheaded a public campaign to remove discussion of sex and sexuality from the media and to return Britain to the Christian moral order which was perceived to have existed before the sexual revolution of the 1960s. In the 1980s, these concerns were picked up by a Conservative government, under Margaret Thatcher, which promoted a New Right political agenda based on a return to traditional, family-centred sexual values. The conflict between these vocal, moralist agendas and the emerging movements for women's and gay liberation in the 1970s and 1980s meant that sexuality and lesbianism became topics of unprecedented public debate in these decades.

Lesbians and the Family

The role of lesbians both within the traditional nuclear family and in forging new concepts of 'family' emerged as a focus for political debate and controversy in the later decades of the twentieth century. Although many women had been lesbians and mothers before 1970, the issue of lesbian motherhood emerged into public debate in the 1970s and 1980s in a number of ways. Women who had had children in the context of a heterosexual marriage, before separating from their husbands and forming a lesbian relationship, began to find themselves losing their children in custody cases. Courts regarded lesbians, and particularly those who also expressed feminist views, as 'unfit mothers' and the feminist magazine, *Spare Rib*, reported in 1976 that to date, no British lesbians had won custody of their children in a court battle. In one early case, a woman who had feminist literature in her home was accused of creating 'an exotic atmosphere in which intellectual opinions expressing themselves as an eagerness for total feminine freedom, sexual and otherwise, will have a marked influence' on her daughters, causing them to grow up with 'little or no respect for the ordinary obligations of family life' and 'be exposed to propaganda about sexual morality which could expose them to quite extraordinary risks in adolescence.' Judges frequently expressed concern about the impact exposure to a mother's lesbian relationship might have on a child. In awarding a lesbian mother limited access to her son, one judge stipulated that he must be 'protected from the lesbian relationship' and that the two women must sleep apart and act as 'just friends' during the boy's visits.[26] In the mid-1970s, in response to a number of high-profile custody battles involving women who were active members of the feminist movement, lesbian mothers began to organise a collective political campaign on the issue. A campaigning group, called Action for Lesbian Parents, was formed in late 1975, providing support for lesbian mothers and information on how to fight custody cases and, in 1983, the Greater London Council funded a research project by the feminist legal group, Rights of Women, into lesbian custody cases.[27]

The issue of lesbian motherhood hit the news again in 1978 when a media controversy broke about lesbians' use of artificial insemination by donor. A female journalist from the London *Evening News* visited the offices of the lesbian organisation Sappho, with a female friend, posing as a prospective lesbian mother and asking for information about lesbian pregnancy methods. Sappho referred them to a local doctor who was helping lesbians to get pregnant by artificial insemination, and the journalist later asked to be put in touch with other lesbian mothers, which Sappho also did. The journalists obtained names and photographs of some of these women and reappeared at the Sappho offices, two days before the story was due to break, asking for photographs of the office to complete the story. Sappho attempted to obtain an injunction to prevent the story from appearing and was successful in limiting the publication of the lesbian mothers' personal details. Instead, the final article focused on the doctor, appearing on a double-page spread in the first week of January 1978, under the headline: 'Dr Strangelove: *The Evening News* today reveals the extraordinary and disturbing case of the London doctor who is helping lesbian couples to have babies.'[28] The story was then picked up by other newspapers, which began to explore the wider implications of lesbians as mothers and the issues of children being brought up in a fatherless home. In an article published on 7 January, *The Guardian* reported the views of a number of experts:

Dr Rhodes Boyson, MP for Brent North, called it an horrific practice … Dr Mia Kellmer Pringle, director of the National Children's Bureau, also said she was concerned. Children of lesbians, she said, would suffer from having no father, which could lead to a confusion of the children's sexual identity … Mr Ray

Booth, honorary secretary of the Royal College of Obstetricians and Gynaecologists, said, 'I personally find this extremely bizarre. If sex donors knew that their sperm was going to lesbians, one can't help wondering if they would think it was a good thing.'[29]

However, a number of newspapers then went on to argue that children were not actually harmed by being brought up by lesbians and *The Observer* featured the son of a lesbian couple who, *The Observer* claimed, appeared to be completely normal.

Visibility

The concept of visibility has been central to lesbian politics since the late 1960s. The Gay Liberation Front used the slogan: 'Come Out! Join the Gay Liberation Front' on much of its recruitment and advertising material and advocated individuals' openness about their sexual identity as a central ideological tenet. For the GLF, personal and collective visibility represented both a political statement about the validity of a lesbian and gay identity and a means of reaching out to other gay people and to the wider community. GLF used street theatre, 'radical drag' and public demonstrations of gay sexuality, such as holding hands and kissing in the street, as a means of challenging social and cultural assumptions about gender and sexual identity. On 1 July 1972, the GLF also organised the first Gay Pride parade, as a public demonstration of their central ideological tenet, 'Gay is good', and GLF lesbians participated, marching under a banner which read 'Gay Women's Liberation'.

Many of the GLF protests attracted considerable media attention, and throughout the 1970s and 1980s, lesbians continued to be the subject of sporadic but intense media interest. In 1976, media speculation about Labour MP Maureen Colquhoun prompted her to confirm that her 26-year marriage had ended and she was now living with her girlfriend Barbara Todd. Although the media did not explicitly name her as a lesbian at this stage, this was implied by reference to Barbara Todd as 'regional director of the magazine *Sappho*. The publication describes itself as "the only lesbian magazine in Europe" and its headings say "Gay women read *Sappho*." '[30] *The Daily Mail* published an image of the road sign on Maureen Colquhoun's street, with the result that she and her children and friends were harassed in the street and by telephone. The media coverage had a negative impact on Colquhoun's career, creating tensions within her local constituency party in Northampton. Accusing her of 'passing herself off as a married woman', the local party sought to sack her but was blocked by a more supportive Labour Party national executive, on technical grounds. By 1978, most of the press coverage of Maureen Colquhoun focused on any comments she had made about her own or other people's sexuality, and a number of journalists accused her of discussing sexuality endlessly and professed to be bored by the subject. *The Sun* dubbed her 'Maureen the Mouth' and claimed: 'Ordinary voters are not yet ready for an anything goes society. Wouldn't it be better if she simply shut up?'[31] Others questioned her use of the word 'gay', claiming that it was subverting the word's true meaning of 'happy'. Veronica Papworth in *The Daily Express* observed:

> 'I'm gay and I'm proud of it,' said that much publicised left-wing MP ... Far be it from me to comment on her private life – no matter how public she chooses to make it. All I question is 'gaiety' in this context. Good grief, I'm gay, I'm gay as a lark. But may I no longer say so? On the other hand, pictured all over the papers fiercely defending her sexuality, the lady in question exudes as little gaiety as Guy the Gorilla.[32]

The woman's magazine, *Woman's Own*, attempted to counter this negative publicity in a detailed interview with Maureen Colquhoun, which focused on the romantic aspect of her relationship with Barbara Todd, portraying her as a conventionally emotional woman whose love life was more important than her career.[33]

Lesbians and gay men again dominated the media in the late 1980s with the campaigns surrounding Clause 28 of the Local Government Bill. The clause was introduced to a government Bill by Private Amendment, by Conservative MP David Wiltshire and proposed to make it unlawful for local authorities to 'intentionally promote homosexuality' and for maintained schools to promote the acceptability of homosexuality as a 'pretended family relationship'. The clause has been seen as part of a broader attack on so-called loony left local authorities, which were accused by the Conservative government and some sections of the public

and media, of failing to cater to the needs of 'ordinary people' because
of an over-investment in services for minority groups. The amendment
was first debated in Parliament on 15 December 1987, at the Bill's second
reading, and immediately became the focus of opposition by lesbian
and gay activists. A broad coalition, called 'Stop the Clause', based
primarily in London and Manchester, but with other regional groups,
was formed by a number of lesbian and gay activists, but soon attracted
mass support from the wider gay community and from the public
at large. The campaign aimed to raise public awareness about the issue
and mobilise opposition, organising petitions, distributing leaflets and
stickers and selling badges. A number of more traditional lobbying
groups were also formed, such as the Arts Lobby, based at the Drill Hall
Arts Centre in London and headed by actors Ian McKellen and Michael
Cashman, who played a gay character in the television soap opera
EastEnders. The Arts Lobby enjoyed a high media profile and used
this to stress a respectable image of homosexuality. These campaigners
were also supported by a number of anonymous underground activists,
who used guerrilla tactics to draw attention to the issue. On 1 February
1988 a group of lesbians abseiled from the public gallery in the House
of Lords during the Lords' debate on the Bill. In other protests, lesbians
invaded the BBC newsroom during live transmission of the *Six O'Clock
News*, and chained themselves to railings outside Buckingham Palace.
The tactics, derived from Women's Liberation campaigns and those
used at the women's peace protest at Greenham Common, were based
on the concept of non-violent revolt, aimed at capturing the public's
imagination by juxtaposing lesbians (regarded by society as 'the
abnormal') with institutions which held huge symbolic power (and
which were involved in reinforcing society's ideas of 'the normal').
Although the campaign was unsuccessful in preventing the Bill from
passing into law in May 1988, the debate was important in promoting
public discussion of lesbian and gay issues.[34]

The type of high-profile media-oriented tactics used by lesbian
activists during the campaign against Clause 28 became an increasing
feature of 'queer' activism in the 1990s. Articulated by a number of new
activist groups, including ACTUP (AIDS Coalition to Unleash Power)
in New York and London, *Queer Nation* in New York and *OutRage!*
in London, queer activism aimed to develop a new, confrontational style
of lesbian and gay campaigning. Appropriating the insult 'queer', which
had been used to denigrate lesbians and gay men, the group sought

to 'affirm the right of lesbians and gay men to sexual freedom, choice and self-determination' and to promote the right of lesbians and gay men to be different. Aiming at challenging social attitudes towards lesbians and gay men, *OutRage!* organised a number of protests throughout the 1990s, including 'outing' celebrities and public figures, and were successful in attracting considerable media attention.[35] Although lesbians were involved in *OutRage!* and a focus group, named LABIA (Lesbians Answer Back In Anger), organised protests on a number of lesbian issues, the group was frequently criticised for being too male, white and middle class. In June 1993, a new group, the Lesbian Avengers, was founded by six lesbian activists, who wanted a direct action group which would fight specifically for lesbian issues and visibility. After meeting with some lesbian activists from the United States, who had already founded a group there, Lynne Sutcliffe and Roz Hopkins organised a public meeting, which was attended by seventy women. The Lesbian Avengers became involved in a number of high-profile protests, including a zap of Queen Victoria's statue at Buckingham Palace, to protest against her alleged role in promoting lesbian invisibility, and a protest against the funding of 'ex-gay' therapy groups by the Sainsbury trust, in which Lesbian Avengers chained themselves to the main staircase of the Sainsbury Wing in the National Gallery.[36]

In the 1980s and 1990s, as lesbian political and sexual identities proliferated, lesbians increasingly used personal style and fashion as a visual means of communicating their sexual identity both to each other and to the wider community. For S/M lesbians, fashion represented a means of both conveying an S/M identity to a wider lesbian community and making a distinction between different sexual roles within S/M. Therefore fashion for 'top' or 'butch' S/M lesbians revealed the body from the waist up, with women wearing vests, waistcoats without shirts, or no clothes at all on the upper body. 'Bottom' or 'femme' S/M lesbians wore skirts, dresses, lingerie and high heels, while both top and bottom fashion incorporated a use of leather, rubber and uniform styles. 'Roots' lesbians, or lesbians from non-white ethnic backgrounds, also used fashion as a means of communicating their ethnic identity, mixing styles drawn from their ethnic community with Western fashions. Hostility to fashion as time-consuming and damaging to health, epitomising women's oppression by men, had been central to feminist arguments about femininity from the late 1960s onwards. Inge Blackman and

Kathryn Perry argue that radical lesbian feminists continued to adopt a style that was intended to reveal the 'real' woman beneath the cultural construct of femininity, into the 1990s:

> With flat shoes, baggy trousers, unshaven legs and faces bare of make-up, their style combines practicality with a strong statement about not dressing for men.[37]

In contrast, 'lipstick lesbians', widely feted by the media in the 1990s, adopted mainstream hyper-feminine fashions in a playful way, aiming to subvert femininity by using it to attract women instead of men, or by undermining it visually by combining it with a 'masculine' fashion accessory.

In a phenomenon referred to as 'lesbian chic', lesbians became the focus of widespread media attention in the 1990s. The term 'lipstick lesbians' was coined in the United States by *Los Angeles Times* writer Lindsey Van Gelder, who used the term in 1991 to describe the clientele of West Hollywood lesbian bar, Girl Bar, and it was subsequently adopted by the British media.[38] In August 1993, the front cover of the US magazine *Vanity Fair* featured the cross-dressed lesbian singer k.d.lang being shaved by supermodel Cindy Crawford and in 1992, the box office hit *Basic Instinct* featured Sharon Stone as a beautiful lesbian seductress. Other celebrities flirted with the phenomenon, including the singer Madonna, who used lesbian imagery in performances and videos such as 'Justify My Love'. While 'lesbian chic' arguably spoke more to a heterosexual than a lesbian audience, lesbians also began to be targeted in specifically lesbian and gay television and film-making in the 1990s.[39] On Valentine's Day 1989, Channel Four was the first mainstream commercial television station in the world to commission and broadcast a lesbian and gay series, which it named *Out on Tuesday*. Later renamed *OUT*, the programme had gone into its fifth series in 1994, employing a primarily lesbian and gay staff to address a range of issues, from music and film to pets and politics, of concern to lesbians and gay men.[40] In September 1995, Channel Four extended its lesbian and gay broadcasting with a series of four programmes, called *Dyke TV*, shown on Saturday nights and including feature film premieres and documentaries. These magazine-style programmes were also joined by a number of lesbian dramas and, in 1990, the BBC adaptation of Jeannette Winterson's lesbian novel, *Oranges Are Not the Only Fruit*,

attracted over six million viewers per episode and won the British
Academy of Film and Television Arts award for 'Best Drama'.

By the end of the century, lesbian issues were beginning to acquire
greater visibility in the media and in public debate. The political activism
and ideologies of a range of political movements had begun to have
an impact, both on public attitudes and on the ways in which lesbians
perceived their own sexuality and sexual identity. A lesbian subculture,
which had begun to emerge in the early twentieth century, had developed,
and bars and nightclubs catering to lesbians and to a mixed lesbian and
gay clientele had proliferated in many British cities. These venues, and
a burgeoning literature produced by and targeted at lesbians, enabled
lesbians to make contact with each other and develop a collective identity
and sense of history.

List of Illustrations

1. Front and back view of a hermaphrodite. Wellcome Library, London.
2. Jacopo Amigoni, *Jupiter and Callisto*. AKG-Images.
3. Sailors drinking the health of Hannah Snell. Mary Evans Picture Library.
4. Irish adventuress and cross-dresser Mrs Christian Davies. Mary Evans Picture Library.
5. Lady Eleanor Butler and the Honourable Miss Sarah Ponsonby. Mary Evans Picture Library/Alamy.
6. 'Passionate female literary types'. Mary Evans Picture Library.
7. A 'New Woman' joins the men in the smoking compartment. Mary Evans Picture Library.
8. Maud Allan performing the 'Vision of Salomé'. Mary Evans Picture Library.
9. Edward Linley Sambourne, *Two Nude Models*. Linley Sambourne House, London, UK/Bridgeman Art Library.
10. *Punch* cartoon satirising women in uniform. Punch Cartoon Library.
11. Vita Sackville-West. Topfoto.
12. Lady Una Troubridge and Radclyffe Hall. Topfoto.
13. Union Hotel. A. Dawson/Manchester Archives and Local Studies.
14. Susannah York, Beryl Reid and Coral Browne in *The Killing of Sister George*. Everett Collection/Rex Features.
15. 'Bridegroom' Violet Ellen Katherine Jones and her 'bride' Joan Mary Lee. NMeM/Science and Society Picture Library.
16. Lesbian wedding, Clapham Common. Eve Arnold/Magnum Photos.
17. Cover of *Odd Girl Out*. Ann Bannon.
18. Anne Heywood and Sandy Dennis in *The Fox*. Bettmann/Corbis UK Ltd.
19. Cover of *Arena Three*. Glasgow Women's Library.
20. Jackie Forster. Popperfoto/Alamy.
21. Members of the Gay Liberation Front demonstrating outside Bow Street Magistrates' Court. PA Photos.
22. Lesbian and Gay Pride, London. Photofusion Picture Library.
23. Lesbian women at Birmingham Pride. Photofusion Picture Library.
24. Lesbian Avengers hijack a bus in Piccadilly Circus. David Hoffman Photo Library/Alamy.

Bibliography

Introduction

Abelove, Henry, Michele Aina Barale, and David M. Halperin (eds.). 1993. *The Lesbian and Gay Studies Reader*. London: Routledge.

Bell, David, and Gill Valentine (eds.). 1995. *Mapping Desires: Geographies of Sexualities*. London: Routledge.

Ingram, Gordon Brent, Anna-Marie Bouthillette, and Yolanda Retter (eds.). 1997. *Queers in Space: Communities; Public Places; Sites of Resistance*. Washington: Bay Press.

de Lauretis, Teresa. 1991. 'Queer Theory: Lesbian and Gay Sexualities: An Introduction'. *differences: A Journal of Feminist Cultural Studies* 3.2: iii–xviii.

Penn, Donna. 1995. 'Queer: Theorising Politics and History'. *Radical History Review* 62: 24–42.

Sinfield, Alan. 1994. *The Wilde Century: Effeminacy, Oscar Wilde and the Queer Moment*. London: Cassell.

Traub, Valerie. 1999. 'The Rewards of Lesbian History'. *Feminist Studies* 25.2: 363–394.

Valentine, Gill (ed.). 2000. *From Nowhere to Everywhere: Lesbian Geographies*. New York: Harrington Park Press.

Vicinus, Martha. 1994. 'Lesbian History: All Theory and No Facts or All Facts and No Theory?'. *Radical History Review* 60: 57–75.

Wiesen Cook, Blanche. 1979. 'The Historical Denial of Lesbianism'. *Radical History Review* 20: 60–65.

Wiesen Cook, Blanche. 1979. 'Women Alone Stir My Imagination: Lesbianism and the Cultural Tradition'. *Signs* 4.4: 718–739.

Wilton, Tamsin. 1995. *Lesbian Studies: Setting an Agenda*. London: Routledge.

Chapter 1: Invisibility or Cultural Renaissance? Same-Sex Desire, 1500–1800

Faderman, Lillian. 1985. *Surpassing the Love of Men: Romantic Friendship and Love Between Women from the Renaissance to the Present*. London: The Women's Press Ltd.

Faderman, Lillian (ed.). 1994. *Chloe Plus Olivia: An Anthology of Lesbian Literature from the Seventeenth Century to the Present*. London: Penguin.

Hunt, Margaret. 1999. 'The Sapphic Strain: English Lesbians in the Long Eighteenth Century'. In *Singlewomen in the European Past, 1250–1800*. Edited by Judith M. Bennett and Amy M. Froide, Philadelphia: University of Pennsylvania Press, 270–296.

Lanser, Susan S. 1998–1999. 'Befriending the Body: Female Intimacies as Class Acts'. *Eighteenth-Century Studies* 32.2: 179–198.

Park, Katharine. 1997. 'The Rediscovery of the Clitoris: French Medicine and the Tribade, 1570–1620'. Pp.171–193 in *The Body in Parts: Fantasies of Corporeality in Early Modern Europe*. Edited by David Hillman and Carla Mazzio. New York and London: Routledge.

Norton, Rictor. 1992. *Mother Clap's Molly House*. London: GMP Publishers Ltd.

O'Driscoll, Sally. 1996. 'Outlaw Readings: Beyond Queer Theory'. *Signs* 22.1: 30–51.

Traub, Valerie. 2002. *The Renaissance of Lesbianism in Early Modern England*. Cambridge: Cambridge University Press.

Chapter 2: Cross-Dressing and Female Husbands, 1600–1800

Castle, Terry. 1982. 'Matters Not Fit to be Mentioned: Fielding's *The Female Husband*'. *ELH* 49.3: 602–622.

Donoghue, Emma. 1993. *Passions Between Women: British Lesbian Culture 1668–1801*. London: Scarlet Press.

Garber, Marjorie. 1992. *Vested Interests: Cross-Dressing and Cultural Anxiety*. London: Routledge.

Wheelwright, Julie. 1989. *Amazons and Military Maids: Women Who Dressed as Men in the Pursuit of Life, Liberty and Happiness*. London: Pandora.

Chapter 3: Romantic Friendship, 1700–1900

Binhammer, Katherine. 2003. 'The "Singular Propensity" of Sensibility's Extremities: Female Same-Sex Desire and the Eroticization of Pain in Late-Eighteenth-Century British Culture'. *GLQ* 9.4: 471–498.

Castle, Terry. 1993. *The Apparitional Lesbian: Female Homosexuality and Modern Culture*. New York: Columbia University.

Clark, Anna. 1996. 'Anne Lister's Construction of Lesbian Identity'. *Journal of the History of Sexuality* 7.1: 23–50.

Dollimore, Jonathan. 1991. *Sexual Dissidence: Augustine to Wilde, Freud to Foucault*. Oxford: Clarendon Press.

Lesbian History Group (ed.). 1989. *Not a Passing Phase: Reclaiming Lesbians in History 1840–1985*. London: The Women's Press.

Liddington, Jill (ed.). 1999. *Female Fortune: Land, Gender and Authority*. London: Rivers Oram Press.

Marcus, Sharon. 2007. *Between Women: Friendship, Desire, and Marriage in Victorian England*. Princeton and Woodstock: Princeton University Press.

Mavor, Elizabeth. 1971. *The Ladies of Llangollen: A Study in Romantic Friendship*. London: Penguin.

Stanley, Liz. 1992. 'Romantic Friendship? Some Issues in Researching Lesbian History and Biography'. *Women's History Review* 1.2: 193–216.

Whitbread, Helena. 1988. *I Know My Own Heart: The Diaries of Anne Lister, 1791–1840*. London: Virago Press.

Whitbread, Helena. 1992. *No Priest but Love: The Journals of Anne Lister from 1824–1826*. Otley: Smith Settle.

Chapter 4: 'New Women', 1850–1900

Edwards, Elizabeth. 1995. 'Homoerotic Friendship and College Principals, 1880–1960'. *Women's History Review* 4.2: 149–163.

Faderman, Lillian. 1983. *Scotch Verdict: Pirie and Woods v. Dame Cumming Gordon*. New York: William Morrow.

Hall, Lesley. 2000. *Sex, Gender and Social Change in Britain Since 1880*. Basingstoke: Macmillan.

Ledger, Sally. 1997. *The New Woman: Fiction and Feminism at the fin de siecle*. Manchester: Manchester University Press.

Lewis, Jane. 1984. *Women in England: Sexual Divisions and Social Change, 1870–1950*. London: Wheatsheaf.

Newton, Esther. 1984. 'The Mythic Mannish Lesbian: Radclyffe Hall and the New Woman'. *Signs* 9.4: 557–575.

Pugh, Martin. 1992. *Women and the Women's Movement in Britain 1914–1959*. Basingstoke: Macmillan.

Purvis, June (ed.). 1995. *Women's History: Britain, 1850–1945*. London: UCL Press.

Richardson, Angelique, and Chris Willis (eds.). 2001. *The New Woman in Fiction and Fact*. Basingstoke: Palgrave.

Vicinus, Martha. 1985. *Independent Women: Work and Community for Single Women: 1850–1920*. London: Virago.

Vicinus, Martha. 2004. *Intimate Friends: Women Who Loved Women, 1778–1928*. London and Chicago: Chicago University Press.

Weeks, Jeffrey. 1977. *Coming Out: Homosexual Politics in Britain from the Nineteenth Century to the Present*. London: Quartet Books.

Weeks, Jeffrey. 1981. *Sex, Politics and Society: The Regulation of Sexuality Since 1800*. London: Longman.

Chapter 5: Sexology and the Science of Sex, 1880s–1920s

Bland, Lucy, and Laura Doan (eds.). 1998. *Sexology in Culture: Labelling Bodies and Desires*. Cambridge: Polity Press.

Bland, Lucy, and Laura Doan (eds.). 1998. *Sexology Uncensored: The Documents of Sexual Science*. Cambridge: Polity Press.

Bristow, Joseph. 1997. *Sexuality*. London: Routledge.

Chauncey, George. 1989. 'From Sexual Inversion to Homosexuality: The Changing Medical Conceptualization of Female "Deviance" '. In *Passion and Power: Sexuality in History*. Edited by Kathy Peiss and Christina Simmons. Philadelphia, PA: Temple University Press, 87–117.

Hall, Lesley. 1995. ' "Disinterested Enthusiasm for Sexual Misconduct": The British Society for the Study of Sex Psychology, 1913–47'. *Journal of Contemporary History* 30: 665–686.

Mort, Frank. 2000. *Dangerous Sexualities: Medico-Moral politics in England Since 1830*, 2nd edition. London: Routledge.

Oosterhuis, Harry. 2000. *Stepchildren of Nature: Krafft-Ebing, Psychiatry and the Making of Sexual Identity*. Chicago: University of Chicago Press.

Porter, Roy, and Lesley Hall. 1995. *The Facts of Life: The Creation of Sexual Knowledge in Britain, 1650–1950*. New Haven, CT: Yale University Press.

Teich, Mikulas, and Roy Porter (eds.). 1994. *Sexual Knowledge, Sexual Science: A History of Attitudes to Sexuality*. Cambridge: Cambridge University Press.

Chapter 6: Sapphism and the First World War, 1914–1918

Bland, Lucy. 1998. 'Trial by Sexology?: Maud Allen, Salome and the "Cult of the Clitoris" Case'. Pp.183–198 in *Sexology in Culture: Labelling Bodies and Desires*. Edited by Lucy Bland and Laura Doan. Cambridge: Polity Press.

Doan, Laura. 2006. 'Topsy-Turvydom: Gender Inversion, Sapphism and the Great War'. *GLQ* 12.4: 517–542.

Humphries, Steve. 1991. *A Secret World of Sex. Forbidden Fruit: The British Experience 1900–1950*. London: Sidgewick and Jackson.

Chapter 7: Identity Crisis? The Emergence of the Modern Lesbian, 1918–1939

Baker, Michael. 1985. *Our Three Selves: A Life of Radclyffe Hall*. New York: Morrow.

Bullough, Vern, and Bonnie Bullough. 1977. 'Lesbianism in the 1920s and 1930s: A Newfound Study'. *Signs* 2.4: 895–904.

Castle, Terry. 1996. *Noel Coward and Radclyffe Hall: Kindred Spirits*. New York: Columbia University Press.

Cline, Sally. 1997. *Radclyffe Hall: A Woman Called John*. London: John Murray.

Doan, Laura. 2001. *Fashioning Sapphism: The Origins of a Modern English Lesbian Culture*. New York: Columbia University Press.

Doan, Laura, and Jay Prosser. 2002. *Palatable Poison: Critical Perspectives on* The Well of Loneliness. New York: Columbia University Press.

Doan, Laura, and Jane Garrity. 2006. *Sapphic Modernities: Sexuality, Women and National Culture*. New York: Palgrave.

Gilmore, Leigh. 1994. 'Obscenity, Modernity, Identity: Legalizing "The Well of Loneliness" and "Nightwood" '. *Journal of the History of Sexuality* 4.4: 603–624.

Griffin, Gabriele. 1994. *Heavenly Love? Lesbian Images in Twentieth-Century Women's Writing*. Manchester: Manchester University Press.

Jeffreys, Sheila. 1985. *The Spinster and Her Enemies: Feminism and Sexuality, 1880–1930*. London: Pandora.

Oram, Alison. 1989. "Embittered, Sexless or Homosexual": Attacks on spinster teachers 1918–1939. Pp.99–118 in *Not a Passing Phase: Reclaiming Lesbians in History 1840–1985*. Edited by Lesbian History Group. London: The Women's Press.

Rolley, Katrina. 1990. 'The Dress of Radclyffe Hall and Una Troubridge'. *Feminist Review* 35: 54–76.

Ruehl, Sonja. 1982. 'Inverts and Experts: Radclyffe Hall and the Lesbian Identity'. Pp.15–36 in *Feminism, Culture and Politics*. Edited by Rosalind Brunt and Caroline Rowan. London: Lawrence Wishart.

Rule, Jane. 1976. *Lesbian Images*. London: Peter Davies.

Souhami, Diana. 1999. *The Trials of Radclyffe Hall*. London: Virago.

Vernon, James. 2000. ' "For Some Queer Reason": The Trials and Tribulations of Colonel Barker's Masquerade in Interwar Britain'. *Signs* 26.1: 37–62.

Chapter 8: Lesbian Bars, 1920s–1970s

Bell, Barbara. 1999. *Just Take Your Frock Off: A Lesbian Life*. Brighton: Ourstory Books.

Brighton Ourstory Project (ed.). 1992. *Daring Hearts: Lesbian and Gay Lives of 50s and 60s Brighton*. Brighton: QueenSpark Books.

Davis, Madeline, and Elizabeth Lapovsky Kennedy. 1993. *Boots of Leather, Slippers of Gold: A History of a Lesbian Community*. London: Routledge.

Gardiner, Jill. 2003. *From the Closet to the Screen: Women at the Gateways Club, 1945–85*. London: Pandora.

Jennings, Rebecca. 2007. *Tomboys and Bachelor Girls: A Lesbian History of Post-War Britain, 1945–71*. Manchester: Manchester University Press.

Jivani, Alkarim. 1997. *It's Not Unusual: A History of Lesbian and Gay Britain in the Twentieth Century*. London: Michael O'Mara Books Ltd.

Neild, Suzanne, and Rosalind Pearson (eds.). 1992. *Women Like Us*. London: The Women's Press.

Nestle, Joan (ed.). 1992. *The Persistent Desire: A Femme-Butch Reader*. Boston: Alyson Publications Inc.

Nestle, Joan. 1996. *A Restricted Country: Documents of Desire and Resistance*. London: Pandora.

Stewart-Pack, Angela, and Jules Cassidy. 1977. *We're Here: Conversations with Lesbian Women*. London: Quartet.

Summerfield, Penny. 1998. *Reconstructing Women's Wartime Lives: Discourse and Subjectivity in Oral Histories of the Second World War*. Manchester: Manchester University Press.

Chapter 9: Lesbian Social Organisations, 1960s–1970s

Collis, Rose. 1997. *A Trouser-Wearing Character: The Life and Times of Nancy Spain*. London: Cassell.

Faderman, Lillian. 1992. *Odd Girls and Twilight Lovers: A History of Lesbian Life in Twentieth-Century America*. London: Penguin.

Lewis, Jane. 1992. *Women in Britain Since 1945*. Oxford: Blackwell.

Oram, Alison, and Annmarie Turnbull. 2001. *The Lesbian History Sourcebook*. London: Routledge.

Oram, Alison. Forthcoming. 'Little by Little?: Arena Three and Lesbian Politics in the 1960s'. In *The Permissive Society and Its Enemies: Sixties British Culture*. Edited by Marcus Collins. London: Rivers Oram Press.

Rupp, Leila J. 1991. ' "Imagine My Surprise": Women's Relationships in Mid 20th Century America'. Pp.395–410 in *Hidden from History: Reclaiming the Gay and Lesbian Past*. Edited by Martin Duberman, Martha Vicinus, and George Chauncey. London: Penguin.

Smith, Patricia Juliana (ed.). 1999. *The Queer Sixties*. London: Routledge.

Zimet, Jaye. 1999. *Strange Sisters: The Art of Lesbian Pulp Fiction 1949–69*. London: Penguin.

Chapter 10: The Politics of Lesbianism, 1970–2000

Ainley, Rosa. 1995. *What Is She Like? Lesbian Identities from the 1950s to the 1990s*. London: Cassell.

Bourne, Stephen. 1996. *Brief Encounters: Lesbians and Gays in British Cinema 1930–1971*. London: Cassell.

Campbell, Beatrix. 1980. 'A Feminist Sexual Politics: Now You See It, Now You Don't'. *Feminist Review* 5: 1–18.

Cant, Bob, and Susan Hemmings (eds.). 1988. *Radical Records: Thirty Years of Lesbian and Gay History*. London: Routledge.

Cohen, Derek, and Richard Dyer. 1980. 'The Politics of Gay Culture'. Pp.172–186 in *Homosexuality: Power and Politics*. Edited by Gay Left Collective. London: Allison and Busby.

Faderman, Lillian. 1992. 'The Return of Butch and Femme: A Phenomenon in Lesbian Sexuality of the 1980s and 1990s'. *Journal of the History of Sexuality* 2.4: 578–596.

Gay Left Collective (ed.). 1980. *Homosexuality: Power and Politics*. London: Allison & Busby.

Green, Sarah. 1997. *Urban Amazons: Lesbian Feminism and Beyond in the Gender, Sexuality and Identity Battles of London*. Basingstoke: Macmillan.

Hallett, Nicky. 1999. *Lesbian Lives: Identity and Auto/Biography in the Twentieth Century*. London: Pluto Press.

Hamer, Diane, and Belinda Budge (eds.). 1994. *The Good, the Bad and the Gorgeous: Popular Culture's Romance with Lesbianism*. London: Pandora.

Hamer, Emily. 1996. *Britannia's Glory: A History of Twentieth-Century Lesbians*. London: Cassell.

Healey, Emma. 1996. *Lesbian Sex Wars*. London: Virago.

Howes, Keith. 1993. *Broadcasting it: An Encyclopaedia of Homosexuality in Film, Radio and TV in the UK, 1923–1993*. London: Cassell.

Inness, Sherrie. 1997. *The Lesbian Menace: Ideology, Identity and the Representation of Lesbian Life*. Amherst: University of Massachusetts Press.

Jeffreys, Sheila. 1990. *Anticlimax*. London: Women's Press.

Jeffreys, Sheila. 1994. *The Lesbian Heresy: A Feminist Perspective on the Lesbian Sexual Revolution*. London: Woman's Press.

Jeffreys, Sheila. 1994. 'The Queer Disappearance of Lesbian Sexuality in the Academy'. *Women's Studies International Forum* 17.5: 459–472.

Lucas, Ian. 1998. *OutRage! An Oral History*. London: Cassell.

Mason-John, Valerie, and Ann Khambatta. 1993. *Lesbians Talk: Making Black Waves*. London: Scarlet Press.

Miller, Neil. 1995. *Out of the Past*. London: Vintage.

Munt, Sally R. 1997. *Butch - Femme: Theorizing Lesbian Genders*. London: Cassell.

Munt, Sally R. 1998. *Heroic Desire: Lesbian Identity and Cultural Space*. London: Cassell.

Plummer, Ken (ed.). 1992. *Modern Homosexualities: Fragments of Lesbian and Gay Experience*. London: Routledge.

Porter, Kevin, and Jeffrey Weeks (eds.). 1980. *Between the Acts: Lives of Homosexual Men 1885–1967*. London: Routledge.

Power, Lisa. 1995. *No Bath but Plenty of Bubbles: An Oral History of the Gay Liberation Front*. London: Cassell.

Rich, Adrienne. 1981. *Compulsory Heterosexuality and Lesbian Existence*. London: Onlywomen Press.

Sinfield, Alan. 1999. *Out on Stage: Lesbian and Gay Theatre in the Twentieth Century*. London: Yale University Press.

Smith, Patricia Juliana. 1997. *Lesbian Panic: Homoeroticism in Modern British Women's Fiction*. New York: Columbia University Press.

Stein, Arlene. 1992. 'Sisters and Queers: The Decentring of Lesbian Feminism'. *Socialist Review* 22.1: 33–55.

Stein, Arlene. 1995. 'All Dressed Up but No Place to Go? Style Wars and the New Lesbianism'. Pp.476–483 in *Out in Culture: Gay, Lesbian and Queer Essays on Popular Culture*. Edited by Corey K. Creekmur and Alexander Doty. London: Cassell.

Williams, Carmen, Gail Lewis, Shaila Shah and Pratibha Parmar. 1984. 'Becoming Visible – Black Lesbian Discussions'. *Feminist Review* 17: 53–72.

Notes

Introduction

1. Sarah Churchill, Duchess of Marlborough (assisted by N. Hooke), *An Account of the Conduct of the Dowager Duchess of Marlborough, from Her First Coming to Court, to the Year 1710* (London: George Hawkins, 1742), 56–57, 76, 131, 137–139, 141, 148, 161, 211, as cited in Emma Donoghue, *Passions between Women: British Lesbian Culture 1668–1801* (London: Scarlet Press, 1993), 160.

2. Arthur Maynwaring (attrib.), 'A New Ballad to the Tune of Fair Rosamond' [1708], in *Poems on Affairs of State: Augustan Satirical Verse, 1660–1717*, vol. VII, ed. Frank H. Ellis (New Haven, CT: Yale University Press, 1975), 309, as cited in Donoghue, *Passions between Women*, 162.

3. Quoted in Edward Gregg, *Queen Anne* (London: Ark Paperbacks, 1984), 275–276, as cited in Donoghue, *Passions between Women*, 162.

4. Blanche Wiesen Cook, 'The Historical Denial of Lesbianism', *Radical History Review*, 20 (1979), 60–65.

5. M. Duberman, M. Vicinus, and G. Chauncey, eds., *Hidden from History: Reclaiming the Gay and Lesbian Past* (New York: Penguin, 1989); Lesbian History Group, ed., *Not a Passing Phase: Reclaiming Lesbians in History 1840–1985* (London: The Women's Press, 1989).

6. Lesbian History Group, *Not a Passing Phase*, 1–2.

7. Rictor Norton, *The Myth of the Modern Homosexual* (London: Cassell, 1997).

8. Michel Foucault, *The History of Sexuality*, Volume 1: *An Introduction* (Harmondsworth: Penguin, 1978).

9. In the same period, a feminist critique of heterosexuality was developed in the work of theorists such as Adrienne Rich, who argued that an assumption of heterosexuality was fundamental to cultural constructions of femininity. Adrienne Rich, 'Compulsory Heterosexuality and Lesbian Existence', *Signs*, 5 (Summer 1980), 631–660.

10. Martha Vicinus, 'Sexuality and Power: A Review of Current Work in the History of Sexuality', *Feminist Studies*, 8:1 (1982), 133–156; Martha Vicinus, ' "They Wonder to Which Sex I Belong": Women's Relationships in Mid Twentieth Century America', *Feminist Studies*, 18:3 (1992), 467–497.

11. Cook, 'The Historical Denial of Lesbianism', 64.

12. Rich, 'Compulsory Heterosexuality'.

13. Madeline Davis and Elizabeth Lapovsky Kennedy, *Boots of Leather, Slippers of Gold: A History of a Lesbian Community* (London: Routledge, 1993).

14. A. Berube and J. Escoffier, 'Queer/Nation', *OUT/LOOK*, 11 (Winter 1991), 12.

15. Judith Butler, *Bodies that Matter: On the Discursive Limits of 'Sex'* (London: Routledge, 1993).

16. Donna Penn, 'Queer: Theorizing Politics and History', *Radical History Review*, 62 (1995), 36.

Chapter 1: Invisibility or Cultural Renaissance? Same-Sex Desire, 1500–1800

1. Elspeth King, *The Hidden History of Glasgow's Women* (Edinburgh: Mainstream Publishing Co., 1993), 31.

2. Valerie Traub, *The Renaissance of Lesbianism in Early Modern England* (Cambridge: CUP, 2002).

3. Juan Luis Vives, *A Very Fruitful and Pleasant Booked Called the Instruction of a Christian Woman* (1523), trans. Richard Hyrde (London: c.1529), as cited in Traub, *The Renaissance of Lesbianism*, 51.

4. Nicholas Fontanus, *The Womans Doctour, or, An Exact and Distinct Explanation of All Such Diseases as Are Peculiar to that Sex* (London: John Blague and Samuel Howes, 1652), 6, as cited in Traub, *The Renaissance of Lesbianism*, 84.

5. Seigneur de Brantome [Pierre De Bourdeille], *Lives of Fair and Gallant Ladies* (1665), trans. Alfred Richard Allinson (New York: Liveright Publishing Corp., 1933), 128. See Lillian Faderman, *Surpassing the Love of Men: Romantic Friendship and Love between Women from the Renaissance to the Present* (London: The Women's Press, 1985), 23–24, and Traub, *The Renaissance of Lesbianism*, 54–55.

6. Brantome, *Lives of Fair and Gallant Ladies*, 135.

7. Ibid., 131.

8. Margaret Hunt, 'The Sapphic Strain: English Lesbians in the Long Eighteenth Century', in *Singlewomen in the European Past, 1250–1800*, eds. Judith M. Bennett and Amy M. Froide (Philadelphia: University of Pennsylvania Press, 1999), 281.

9. Traub, *The Renaissance of Lesbianism*, 53.

10. Edmund Spenser, *The Faerie Queene (1590–1609)*, ed. Thomas P. Roche, Jr. (New Haven and London: Yale University Press, 1987), 568–569 (Book 4, Canto 1, Stanzas 15–16), as cited in Traub, *The Renaissance of Lesbianism*, 58.

11. Sir Philip Sidney, *The Countess of Pembroke's Arcadia*, ed. Maurice Evans (Harmondsworth: Penguin, 1977), 245.

12. Richard Brome, *The Antipodes* (London: 1640), 1.3.

13. John Cleland, *Fanny Hill: or, Memoirs of a Woman of Pleasure* (London: Penguin, 1985 [1789]), 48–9.

14. Traub, *The Renaissance of Lesbianism*, 174.

15. William Shakespeare, *A Midsummer Night's Dream*, 3.2.203–214.

16. Ibid., 3.2.215.

17. Ibid., 2.1.124.

18. Robert Withers, 'The Grand Signiors Serraglio', in *Purchase His Pilgrimes*, vol. II, ed. Samuel Purchase (London: 1625), 1586–1587, as cited in Traub, *The Renaissance of Lesbianism*, 199.

19. Ibid., 1590.

20. Jean-Baptiste Tavernier, *Nouvelle relation de l'interieur du serrail du Grand Seigneur* (Paris: 1675), trans. as 'A New Relation of the Present Grand Seignor's Seraglio', in *The Six Voyages of John Baptista Tavernier, Baron of Aubonne; Through Turky, into Persia and the East-Indies, for the Space of Forty Years* (London: 1678), 88, as cited in Traub, *The Renaissance of Lesbianism*, 199.

21. Nicholas de Nicholay, *The Navigations, Peregrinations, and Voyages, Made into Turkie* (Paris: 1567), trans. T. Washington (London: 1585), 60, as cited in Traub, *The Renaissance of Lesbianism*, 200.

22. For example, A. G. Busbequius, *Travels into Turkey* (J. Robinson & W. Payne, 1744), 146–7. See Emma Donoghue, *Passions between Women: British Lesbian Culture 1668–1801* (London: Scarlet Press, 1993), 63–64.

23. Susan S. Lanser, 'Befriending the Body: Female Intimacies as Class Acts', *Eighteenth-Century Studies*, 32:2 (1998–1999), 186.

24. Frances Frazier Senescu, ed., *James Shirley's 'The Bird in a Cage': A Critical Edition* (New York and London: Garland, 1980), sig H2v, 32–35, as cited in Traub, *The Renaissance of Lesbianism*, 176.

25. Margaret Cavendish, Duchess of Newcastle, *The Convent of Pleasure*, in *Playes, Never Before Printed* (London: 1668). See Traub, *The Renaissance of Lesbianism*, 177–179.

26. John Bale, *The Actes of the Englishe Votaryes, Comprehending their Unchast Practyses and Examples of All Ages* (London: 1546), as cited in Traub, *The Renaissance of Lesbianism*, 63.

27. Denis Diderot, *La Religieuse* [1796], trans. as *The Nun* (Dublin: G. Smith, 1797).

28. Donoghue, *Passions between Women*, 191.

29. Henry Fielding, *The Female Husband and Other Writings*, ed. Claude E. Jones (Liverpool: Liverpool University Press, 1960 [1746]), English Reprints Series 17. See Terry Castle, 'Matters Not Fit to be Mentioned: Fielding's *The Female Husband*', *ELH*, 49:3 (Autumn 1982), 602–622, and Donoghue, *Passions between Women*, 73–80.

30. Donoghue, *Passions between Women*, 35.

31. *Ovid's Metamorphoses in Latin and English*, trans. Garth et al. (New York: Garland, 1976 [1717, 1732]).

32. Giles Jacob, *A Treatise of Hermaphrodites* (published with John Henry Meibomius, *A Treatise of the Use of Flogging at Venereal Affairs*) (London: E. Curll, 1718). See Donoghue, *Passions between Women*, 45–48.

33. Anon., *Aristotle's Book of Problems*, 30th ed. (New York: Garland, 1986 [1776]), 72.

34. Nicholas Venette, *Tableau de l'amour conjugal*, trans. as *The Mysteries of Conjugal Love Reveal'd*, 2nd ed. (1707), 453–467.

35. David Halperin, 'Homosexuality', in *Oxford Classical Dictionary*, 3rd ed., eds. Simon Hornblower and Antony Spawforth (Oxford: OUP, 1996), 722–723.

36. Realdo Colombo, *De re anatomica* (Venice: 1559), as cited in Katharine Park, 'The Rediscovery of the Clitoris: French Medicine and the Tribade, 1570–1620', in *The Body in Parts: Fantasies of Corporeality in Early Modern Europe*, eds. David Hillman and Carla Mazzio (New York and London: Routledge, 1997), 176–177.

37. Helkiah Crooke, *Microcosmographia: A Description of the Body of Man* (London: 1615), 238.

38. Thomas Bartholin, *Bartholinus Anatomy* (London: John Streater, 1668), 77, as cited in Traub, *The Renaissance of Lesbianism*, 208–209.

39. Anon., *The Supplement to the Onania* (New York: Garland, 1986 [after 1725?]), 152–153.

40. Robert James, *A Medicinal Dictionary*, vol. III (T. Osborne, 1745), entry for *Tribades*, as cited in Donoghue, *Passions between Women*, 50.

41. Jane Barker, 'The Unaccountable Wife', in *A Patch-Work Screen for the Ladies* (London: E. Curll & T. Payne, 1723), 97–105.

42. Anthony Hamilton, *Memoirs of the Life of Count de Grammont*, trans. Boyer (London: J. Round, W. Taylor, J. Brown, W. Lewis, J. Graves, 1714), 234–235.

43. *A Sapphick Epistle, from Jack Cavendish to the Honourable and Most Beautiful Mrs D_* (London: c.1781), as cited in Rictor Norton, *Mother Clap's Molly House* (London: GMP Publishers Ltd, 1992), 235.

44. *The Whig Club, or a Sketch of Modern Patriotism*, as cited in Norton, *Mother Clap's Molly House*, 235.

45. 'The Spirit of the Ring: Containing Secret Anecdotes of Many Illustrious Personages of This and the Neighbouring Kingdoms', *Bon Ton Magazine*, September 1795–February 1796, October 1795, 280.

46. Katherine Binhammer, 'The "Singular Propensity" of Sensibility's Extremities: Female Same-Sex Desire and the Eroticization of Pain in Late-Eighteenth-Century British Culture', *GLQ*, 9:4 (2003), 471–498.

47. 'Female Flagellists: A Club, in Jermyn Street', *Bon Ton Magazine*, December 1792, 379, as cited in Binhammer, 'The "Singular Propensity" of Sensibility's Extremities', 480.

48. Ibid., 379–380.

49. Ibid., 379.

Chapter 2: Cross-Dressing and Female Husbands, 1600–1800

1. *Freethinker* 108 (1719), as cited in Emma Donoghue, *Passions between Women: British Lesbian Culture 1668–1801* (London: Scarlet Press, 1993), 90.

2. Katrina Straub, 'The Guilty Pleasures of Female Theatrical Cross-Dressing and the Autobiography of Charlotte Charke', in *Body Guards: The Cultural Politics of Gender Ambiguity*, eds. Julia Epstein and Kristina Straub (London: Routledge, 1991), 142–166.

3. Benjamin Victor, *The History of the Theatres of London and Dublin from the Year 1730 to the Present Time*, vol. II (London: T. Davies, R. Griffits, T. Becket, and P. A. de Hond, G. Woodfall, J. Coote, G. Kearsley, 1761), 4–5, as cited in Straub, 'The Guilty Pleasures', 144.

4. Jacqueline Pearson, *The Prostituted Muse: Images of Women and Women Dramatists 1642–1737* (Hemel Hempstead: Harvester Wheatsheaf, 1988), 40, 109, as cited in Donoghue, *Passions between Women*, 89.

5. William Shakespeare, *Twelfth Night*, 1.5.263–271.

6. Ibid., 2.2.34, 3.4.302–303, as cited in Valerie Traub, *The Renaissance of Lesbianism in Early Modern England* (Cambridge: CUP, 2002), 56.

7. Eliza Haywood, *La Belle Assemblee: Being a Curious Collection of Some Very Remarkable Incidents Which Happen'd to Persons of the First Quality in France*, 7th ed. 4 vols., trans. Madame de Gomez (London: D. Browne: 1754), 2:87, as cited in Sally O'Driscoll, 'Outlaw Readings: Beyond Queer Theory', *Signs*, 22:1 (1996), 38.

8. Ibid., 2:81.

9. Rictor Norton, *Mother Clap's Molly House* (London: GMP Publishers Ltd, 1992), 236.

10. Lillian Faderman, *Surpassing the Love of Men: Romantic Friendship and Love between Women from the Renaissance to the Present* (London: The Women's Press, 1985), 61.

11. Anon., *The Life and Adventures of Mrs Christian Davies, the British Amazon*, 2nd ed., part I (Richard Montagu, 1741), 27–28, 32, as cited in Donoghue, *Passions between Women*, 94–95.

12. Anon., *The Female Soldier or the Surprising Life and Adventures of Hannah Snell* [1750], intro. Dianne Dugaw (Los Angeles: William Andrews Clark Memorial Library, 1989), Augustan Reprint 257, as cited in Donoghue, *Passions between Women*, 91–94.

13. Ibid., 6–10, 20, 24–25, 28.

14. Julie Wheelwright, *Amazons and Military Maids: Women Who Dressed as Men in the Pursuit of Life, Liberty and Happiness* (London: Pandora, 1989), 59–60.

15. Peter Anthony Motteux, ed., *Gentleman's Journal* (April 1692), 22–23.

16. Cited in Patricia Crawford and Laura Gowing, *Women's Worlds in Seventeenth-Century England: A Sourcebook* (New York and London: Routledge, 2000), 151.

17. Donoghue, *Passions between Women*, 91.

18. Giovanni Bianchi, *The True History and Adventures of Catherine Vizzani*, trans. John Cleland (W. Reeve & C. Sympson, 1755), 3–4.

19. Donoghue, *Passions between Women*, 80.

20. Bianchi, *The True History*, 3–4.

21. Ibid., 13–14.

22. Ibid., 35.

23. Rudolph M. Dekker and Lotte C. van de Pol, *The Tradition of Female Transvestism in Early Modern Europe* (London: Macmillan, 1989), 55, 57.

24. Faderman, *Surpassing the Love of Men*, 54.

25. Mary Turner, 'Two Entries from the Marriage Register of Taxal, Cheshire', *Local Population Studies*, 21 (Autumn 1978), 64.

26. Donoghue, *Passions between Women*, 65.

27. Ibid., 62.

28. Martha Vicinus, *Intimate Friends: Women Who Loved Women, 1778–1928* (London and Chicago: Chicago University Press, 2004), 22–25.

29. John Southerden Burn, *The Fleet Registers* (London: Rivingtons and others, 1833), 49, 50, 61, as cited in Donoghue, *Passions between Women*, 66.

30. *Gentleman's Magazine*, July 1766. See Donoghue, *Passions between Women*, 70.

31. Cited in Sheridan Baker, 'Henry Fielding's "The Female Husband": Fact and Fiction', *PMLA*, 74 (1959), 222.

32. See Terry Castle, 'Matters Not Fit to be Mentioned: Fielding's *The Female Husband*', *ELH*, 49:3 (Autumn 1982), 602–622.

33. Cited in Baker, 'Henry Fielding's "The Female Husband"', 221.

34. Henry Fielding, *The Female Husband and Other Writings*, ed. Claude E. Jones (Liverpool: Liverpool University Press, 1960 [1746]), English Reprints Series 17.

35. Castle, 'Matters Not Fit to be Mentioned'.

36. Donoghue, *Passions between Women*, 73.

37. Anthony a Wood, *The Life and Times of Anthony a Wood* (London: Wishart, 1932), entry for 10 July 1694, as cited in Donoghue, *Passions between Women*, 64.

38. Donoghue, *Passions between Women*, 69.

39. *Gentleman's Magazine*, 5 July 1777; *Annual Register*, 1777, 91–92; Andrew Knapp and William Baldwin, *The Newgate Calendar*, vol. III (London: Nuttall, Fisher and Dixon, 1810), 395, as cited in Donoghue, *Passions between Women*, 68–69.

40. Traub, *The Renaissance of Lesbianism*, 50.

41. *London Chronicle*, 24 March 1760, vol. VII, 291.

42. Ibid., 5–8 April 1760, vol. VII, 338.

43. Baker, 'Henry Fielding's "The Female Husband"', 220.

44. Donoghue, *Passions between Women*, 79.

45. *London Chronicle*, 2 February 1760, vol. VII, 117.

46. Donoghue, *Passions between Women*, 62–63.

47. Vicinus, *Intimate Friends*, 24–25.

Chapter 3: Romantic Friendship, 1700–1900

1. Elizabeth Mavor, *The Ladies of Llangollen: A Study in Romantic Friendship* (London: Penguin, 1971).

2. Carroll Smith-Rosenberg, 'The Female World of Love and Friendship', in *Disorderly Conduct: Visions of Gender in Victorian America*, ed. Smith-Rosenberg (New York: Knopf, 1985), 53–76; Lillian Faderman, *Scotch Verdict: Pirie and Woods v. Dame Cumming Gordon* (New York: William Morrow, 1983).

3. Susan S. Lanser, 'Befriending the Body: Female Intimacies as Class Acts', *Eighteenth-Century Studies*, 32:2 (1998–1999), 179–198.

4. Emma Donoghue, *Passions between Women: British Lesbian Culture 1668–1801* (London: Scarlet Press, 1993), 113.

5. Lanser, 'Befriending the Body', 183.

6. Valerie Traub, *The Renaissance of Lesbianism in Early Modern England* (Cambridge: CUP, 2002), 72.

7. William Rounseville Alger, *The Friendships of Women*, 10th ed. (Boston: Roberts Brothers, 1882), 4, as cited in Martha Vicinus, *Intimate Friends: Women Who Loved Women, 1778–1928* (London: University of Chicago Press, 2004), xviii.

8. Helena Whitbread, *I Know My Own Heart: The Diaries of Anne Lister, 1791–1840* (London: Virago Press, 1988); Helena Whitbread, *No Priest but Love: The Journals of Anne Lister from 1824–1826* (Otley: Smith Settle, 1992).

9. Terry Castle, *The Apparitional Lesbian: Female Homosexuality and Modern Culture* (New York: Columbia University Press, 1993), 96.

10. Whitbread, *I Know My Own Heart*, 105.

11. Ibid., 99.

12. Castle, *The Apparitional Lesbian*; Anna Clark, 'Anne Lister's Construction of Lesbian Identity', *Journal of the History of Sexuality*, 7:1 (1996), 23–50; Jill Liddington, *Female Fortune: Land, Gender and Authority* (London: Rivers Oram Press, 1998).

13. Vicinus, *Intimate Friends*, xvi–xx.

14. Samuel Richardson, *Sir Charles Grandison* (London: 1753–1754), as cited in Donoghue, *Passions between Women*, 105.

15. Katherine Binhammer, 'The "Singular Propensity" of Sensibility's Extremities: Female Same-Sex Desire and the Eroticization of Pain in Late-Eighteenth-Century British Culture', *GLQ*, 9:4 (2003), 483–485.

16. Liz Stanley, 'Romantic Friendship? Some Issues in Researching Lesbian History and Biography', *Women's History Review*, 1:2 (1992), 197.

17. Whitbread, *I Know My Own Heart*, 210.

18. Cited in Castle, *The Apparitional Lesbian*, 96.

19. Whitbread, *I Know My Own Heart*, 48–49.

20. Castle, *The Apparitional Lesbian*, 100–102.

21. Donoghue, *Passions between Women*, 107.

22. William Wordsworth, 'To the Lady E.B. and the Hon. Miss P., Composed in the Grounds of Plass Newydd, near Llangollen, 1824', in *The Poetical Works of William Wordsworth*, 3:43, as cited in Castle, *The Apparitional Lesbian*, 94.

23. Lanser, 'Befriending the Body', 187.

24. Whitbread, *I Know My Own Heart*, as cited in Lanser, 'Befriending the Body', 190.

25. Lanser, 'Befriending the Body', 190.

26. Donoghue, *Passions between Women*, 112.

27. Cited in Traub, *The Renaissance of Lesbianism*, 72.

28. Donald F. Bond, ed., *The Spectator*, vol. I (Oxford: Clarendon Press, 1965), 462–463, as cited in Traub, *The Renaissance of Lesbianism*, 72–74.

29. Donoghue, *Passions between Women*, 122–130.

30. Anna Seward, *The Poetical Works*, vol. III, ed. Walter Scott (Edinburgh: John Ballantyne & others, 1810), 131, as cited in Donoghue, *Passions between Women*, 120.

31. Donoghue, *Passions between Women*, 130–139.

32. Charlotte Brontë to Ellen Nussey, in T. J. Wise and J. A. Symington, *The Brontes: Their Lives, Friendships and Correspondence*, vol. I (Oxford: Shakespeare Head, 1932), 146, as cited in Elaine Miller, 'Through All Changes and Through All Chances: The Relationship of Ellen Nussey and Charlotte Bronte', in *Not a Passing Phase: Reclaiming Lesbians in History 1840–1985*, ed. Lesbian History Group (London: The Women's Press, 1989), 36.

33. Charlotte Brontë to Ellen Nussey, 26 July 1839, in Wise and Symington, *The Brontes*, vol. I, 182–183, 188–190, as cited in Miller, 'Through All Changes', 37–38.

34. Donoghue, *Passions between Women*, 129.

35. Charlotte Brontë to Ellen Nussey, in Wise and Symington, *The Brontes*, vol. I, 173–175, as cited in Miller, 'Through All Changes', 37. Martha Vicinus discusses a number of American women, including Charlotte Cushman and Emma Crow, who did use marriage to male relations as a means of overcoming practical obstacles to the women's relationship; see Vicinus, *Intimate Friends*, 38–46.

36. Charlotte Brontë to George Smith, 25 April 1854, in Wise and Symington, *The Brontes*, vol. IV, 118–119, as cited in Miller, 'Through All Changes', 48.

37. Whitbread, *I Know My Own Heart*, 145.

38. Castle, *The Apparitional Lesbian*, 101–105; Clark, 'Anne Lister's Construction of Lesbian Identity'.

39. Mavor, *The Ladies of Llangollen*, 97–98.

40. Binhammer, 'The "Singular Propensity" of Sensibility's Extremes', 489.

Chapter 4: 'New Women', 1850–1900

1. Sarah Grand, 'The New Woman and the Old', in *Lady's Realm* (1898), 466, as cited in Angelique Richardson and Chris Willis, eds., *The New Woman in Fiction and Fact* (Basingstoke: Palgrave, 2001), 13.

2. M. Eastwood, 'The New Woman in Fiction and in Fact', *Humanitarian*, 5 (1894), 375–379, as cited in Richardson and Willis, *The New Woman*, 10–11.

3. Jeffrey Weeks, *Sex, Politics and Society: The Regulation of Sexuality Since 1800* (London: Longman, 1981), 21.

4. Weeks, *Sex, Politics and Society*, 24–32.

5. John Ruskin, 'Of Queens' Gardens', in *Sesame and Lilies* (1865).

6. Ibid.

7. Unlike earlier patterns of property inheritance, based on primogeniture and entailing, which only required that the first son be legitimate, new middle-class forms of property distribution, which divided inheritance equally between all offspring, required that all children from a marriage be legitimate. It was therefore essential that women maintained chastity before marriage and fidelity during it. See Weeks, *Sex, Politics and Society*, 29–30.

8. *The Industrial and Social Position of Women in the Middle and Lower Ranks* (London: 1857), 21–22, as cited in Lillian Faderman, *Surpassing the Love of Men: Romantic Friendship and Love between Women from the Renaissance to the Present* (London: The Women's Press, 1985), 181.

9. Richardson and Willis, *The New Woman*, 6–7.

10. Faderman, *Surpassing the Love of Men*, 184.

11. Patricia Hollis, *Women in Public: The Women's Movement, 1850–1900* (London: George Allen & Unwin, 1981 [1979]), 45, 53.

12. Sandra Stanley Holton, 'Women and the Vote', in *Women's History. Britain 1850–1945*, ed. June Purvis (London: UCL Press, 1995), 277–306.

13. Martha Vicinus, *Independent Women: Work and Community for Single Women 1850–1920* (London: Virago, 1985), 261.

14. Naomi Jacob, *Me: A Chronicle About Other People* (London: Hutchinson, 1933), 60, as cited in Emily Hamer, *Britannia's Glory: A History of Twentieth-Century Lesbians* (London: Cassell, 1996), 21.

15. Hamer, *Britannia's Glory*, 23, 30–32.

16. Vicinus, *Independent Women*, 157.

17. Louisa M. Hubbard, 'Statistics of Women's Work', in *Women's Mission: A Series of Congress Papers on the Philanthropic Work of Women by Eminent Writers*, ed. Baroness Burdett-Coutts (London: Sampson Low, Marston, 1893), 364, as cited in Vicinus, *Independent Women*, 212.

18. E. O. Somerville and Martin Ross, *Irish Memories* (New York: Longmans, Green and Co., 1917), 326, as cited in Faderman, *Surpassing the Love of Men*, 206.

19. Vicinus, *Independent Women*, 216, 221.

20. Deborah Epstein Nord, '"Neither Pairs Nor Odd": Female Community in Late Nineteenth-Century London', *Signs*, 15:4 (1990), 736.

21. Somerville and Ross, *Irish Memories*, 125, as cited in Faderman, *Surpassing the Love of Men*, 208.

22. Michael Field, *Underneath the Bow*, 3rd ed. (Portland, ME: Thomas B. Mosher, 1898 [1893]), 50, as cited in Faderman, *Surpassing the Love of Men*, 209.

23. Faderman, *Surpassing the Love of Men*, 208–213.

24. Constance Maynard, unpublished autobiography, section 54 (1891), 286–287, Westfield College Archives, as cited in Vicinus, *Independent Women*, 160.

25. Vicinus, *Independent Women*, 158–161.

26. Bertha Vyver, *Memoirs of Marie Corelli* (London: Alston Rivers, 1930), 97, as cited in Faderman, *Surpassing the Love of Men*, 214.

27. Betty Askwith, *Two Victorian Families* (London: Chatto & Windus, 1971), 192, as cited in Faderman, *Surpassing the Love of Men*, 208.

28. Geraldine Cummins, *Dr E O Somerville: A Biography* (London: Andrew Dakers Ltd, 1952), 104, as cited in Faderman, *Surpassing the Love of Men*, 208.

29. Esther Newton, 'The mythic mannish lesbian: Radclyffe Hall and the new woman', *Signs*, 9:4 (1984), 564.

30. Jeffrey Weeks, *Coming Out: Homosexual Politics in Britain from the Nineteenth Century to the Present* (London: Quartet Books, 1977), 97.

31. Marie Corelli, *The Sorrows of Satan* (Oxford: Oxford University Press, 1996 [1895]), 178, as cited in Richardson and Willis, *The New Woman*, 20.

32. Richardson and Willis, *The New Woman*, 24–25.

33. Sally Ledger, *The New Woman: Fiction and Feminism at the fin de siecle* (Manchester: Manchester University Press, 1997), 124–125.

34. Edith Arnold, *Platonics: A Study* (Bristol: Thoemmes Press, 1995 [1894]), 25–26, as cited in Ledger, *The New Woman*, 125.

35. Ibid., 23, 26.

36. Thomas Hardy, *Desperate Remedies* (London: Macmillan, 1986 [1871]), 64, as cited in Ledger, *The New Woman*, 127.

37. Elizabeth Wetherell, *The Wide, Wide World* (London and Edinburgh: Nelson and Sons, 1852), as cited in Ledger, *The New Woman*, 127.

38. George Meredith, *Diana of the Crossways* (London: Virago, 1980 [1885]), 41, 132, as cited in Ledger, *The New Woman*, 135.

39. Meredith, *Diana of the Crossways*, 72–73, as cited in Ledger, *The New Woman*, 136.

40. Ibid., 75.

41. Faderman, *Surpassing the Love of Men*, part 3, chap. 3; Leila J. Rupp, 'Sexuality and Politics in the Early Twentieth Century: The Case of the International Women's Movement', *Feminist Studies*, 23:3 (1997), 577–605; Hamer, *Britannia's Glory*, 66–92.

42. *Punch*, 27 April 1895, 203, as cited in Lyn Pykett, *The 'Improper' Feminine: The Women's Sensation Novel and New Woman Writing* (London: Routledge, 1992), 138.

43. *Punch's Almanack for 1897*, as cited in Richardson and Willis, *The New Woman*, 23.

44. H. M. Stutfield, 'Tommyrotics', *Blackwood's*, 157 (1895), 836, as cited in Pykett, *The 'Improper' Feminine*, 141.

Chapter 5: Sexology and the Science of Sex, 1880s–1920s

1. See Frank Mort, *Dangerous Sexualities: Medico-Moral Politics in England Since 1830*, 2nd ed. (London: Routledge, 2000), 51–52.

2. Michel Foucault, *The History of Sexuality, Volume 1: An Introduction* (Harmondsworth: Penguin, 1978), 43.

3. Jeffrey Weeks, *Sex, Politics and Society: The Regulation of Sexuality Since 1800* (London: Longman, 1981), 146.

4. Patrick Geddes and J. Arthur Thompson, *The Evolution of Sex* (London: Walter Scott, 1889).

5. William Acton, *The Functions and Disorders of the Reproductive Organs, in Childhood, Youth, Adult Age, and Advanced Life, Considered in their Physiological, Social and Moral Relations* (London: John Churchill, 1857).

6. Havelock Ellis, as cited in Jeffrey Weeks, *Coming Out: Homosexual Politics in Britain from the Nineteenth Century to the Present* (London: Quartet Books, 1977), 92.

7. George Chauncey, 'From Sexual Inversion to Homosexuality: The Changing Medical Conceptualization of Female "Deviance"', in *Passion and Power: Sexuality in History*, eds. Kathy Peiss and Christina Simmons (Philadelphia, PA: Temple University Press, 1989), 89.

8. Richard von Krafft-Ebing, *Psychopathia Sexualis: With Especial Reference to the Antipathic Sexual Instinct. A Medico-Forensic Study*, 12th ed., trans. F. A. Davis (Philadelphia, PA: 1903 [1886]), 395–399.

9. Sigmund Freud, *Three Essays on the Theory of Sexuality*, trans. James Strachey et al. (New York: Basic Books Inc., 1962).

10. Havelock Ellis, 'Sexual Inversion', in *Studies in the Psychology of Sex*, 3rd rev. ed., vol. 2 (Philadelphia, PA: 1915), 250.

11. Chauncey, 'From Sexual Inversion', 92–94.

12. Havelock Ellis, 'Sexual Inversion in Women', *Alienist and Neurologist*, 34 (1913), 147–148, as cited in Chauncey, 'From Sexual Inversion', 95.

13. Robert Latou Dickinson and Lura Beam, *The Single Woman: A Medical Study in Sex Education* (London: Williams and Norgate Ltd., 1934), 212.

14. Krafft-Ebing, *Psychopathia Sexualis*, 294–296.

15. Chauncey, 'From Sexual Inversion', 99–101.

16. Laura Doan and Chris Waters, 'Introduction: Homosexualities', in *Sexology Uncensored*, eds. Lucy Bland and Laura Doan (Cambridge: Polity Press, 1998), 42.

17. Karl Heinrich Ulrichs, *The Riddle of 'Man-Manly' Love: The Pioneering Work on Male Homosexuality*, 2 vols., trans. Michael A. Lombardi-Nash (Buffalo, NY: Prometheus Books, 1994 [1864–1880]), 35.

18. Ulrichs, *The Riddle of 'Man-Manly' Love*, 81. Joseph Bristow offers a detailed discussion of Ulrichs' arguments in his *Sexuality* (London: Routledge, 1997).

19. Doan and Waters, 'Introduction: Homosexualities', 42; Edward Carpenter, *The Intermediate Sex: A Study in Some Transitional Types of Men and Women* (London: Allen & Unwin, 1916 [1908]).

20. Ellis, *Studies in the Psychology of Sex*.

21. Stella Browne, 'Studies in Feminine Inversion', *Journal of Sexology and Psychoanalysis*, Vol. 1 (1923), 51–58.

22. Sigmund Freud, *The Standard Edition of the Complete Psychological Works of Sigmund Freud*, vol. XIX, trans. James Strachey (London: Hogarth Press, 1961).

23. Sigmund Freud, 'The Psychogenesis of a Case of Homosexuality in a Woman', in *Case Histories II*, vol. IX, ed. Angela Richards (Harmondsworth: Penguin, 1979).

24. Chris Waters, 'Havelock Ellis, Sigmund Freud and the State: Discourses of Homosexual Identity in Interwar England', in *Sexology in Culture: Labelling Bodies and Desires*, eds. Lucy Bland and Laura Doan (Cambridge: Polity Press, 1998), 165.

25. Sheila Jeffreys, *The Spinster and Her Enemies: Feminism and Sexuality 1880–1930* (London: Pandora, 1985), 105.

26. Lillian Faderman, *Surpassing the Love of Men: Romantic Friendship and Love between Women from the Renaissance to the Present* (London: The Women's Press, 1985), 252.

27. Edward Carpenter, *Love's Coming of Age* (London: Allen & Unwin, 1913 [1896]), 66.

28. Chauncey, 'From Sexual Inversion', 104.

29. Iwan Bloch, *Sexual Life in Our Time* (London: Heinemann, 1909), as cited in Jeffreys, *The Spinster and Her Enemies*, 108.

30. Ellis, 'Sexual Inversion', 262.

31. Emily Hamer, *Britannia's Glory: A History of Twentieth-Century Lesbians* (London: Cassell, 1996), 11.

32. Havelock Ellis, *Studies in the Psychology of Sex, Complete in Two Volumes* (New York: Random, 1942 [1902]), xxii, as cited in Doan, 'Acts of Female Indecency: Sexology's intervention in legislating lesbianism', *Sexology in Culture: Labelling Bodies and Desires*, eds. Lucy Bland and Laura Doan (Cambridge: Polity Press, 1998), 199–213.

33. 'Editorial on the Publication of Havelock Ellis's *Sexual Inversion*', *The Lancet*, 19 November 1896, 1344–1345, as cited in Bland and Doan, eds., *Sexology Uncensored*, 51–52.

34. Faderman, *Surpassing the Love of Men*, 244, 454 n. 19.

35. Liz Stanley, 'Romantic Friendship? Some Issues in Researching Lesbian History and Biography', *Women's History Review*, 1:2 (1992), 193–216.

36. Edward Carpenter Archive letters, 358.15, 358.16.

37. Stanley, 'Romantic Friendship?', 206–208.

38. Edward Carpenter Archive letters, 386.218, 386.262, 386.355, 386.409.

39. Lesley A. Hall, '"Disinterested Enthusiasm for Sexual Misconduct": The British Society for the Study of Sex Psychology, 1913–47', *Journal of Contemporary History*, 30 (1995), 666.

40. Alison Oram, '"Sex is an Accident": Feminism, Science and the Radical Sexual Theory of Urania, 1915–40', in Bland and Doan, eds., *Sexology in Culture*, 214–230.

41. *Urania*, 75 and 76 (May–August 1929), as cited in Oram, 'Sex is an Accident', 225.

42. Oram, 'Sex is an Accident', 218.

43. Ibid., 219.

Chapter 6: Sapphism and the First World War, 1914–1918

1. Susan R. Grayzel, *Women and the First World War* (London: Longman, 2002), 12.

2. Tony Howarth, ed., *Joe Soap's Army Song Book* (London: IWM Great War Series, 1976), 2, as cited in Nicoletta F. Gullace, 'White Feathers and Wounded Men: Female Patriotism and the Memory of the Great War', *Journal of British Studies*, 36 (1997), 193.

3. 'To the Young Women of London', Imperial War Museum 4903, reproduced in Maurice Rickards, *Posters of the First World War* (London: Evelyn, Adams, & Mackay, 1968), 23.

4. 'Women's War: White Feathers for "Slackers"', *Daily Mail*, 31 August 1914, 3, as cited in Gullace, 'White Feathers and Wounded Men', 178.

5. Major Leonard Darwin, 'On the Meaning of Honour', a lecture delivered to the Women's League of Honour, 1915, IWM, WW, BO6/3/2/8, 6, as cited in Gullace, 'White Feathers and Wounded Men', 186.

6. Edith Sellers, 'Boy and Girl War-Products: Their Reconstruction', *The Nineteenth Century and After*, 84 (October 1918), 704, as cited in Angela Woollacott, '"Khaki Fever" and Its Control: Gender, Class, Age and Sexual Morality on the British Homefront in the First World War', *Journal of Contemporary History*, 29 (1994), 330–331.

7. 'Problems of the Day: The Need for Policewomen', *The Englishwoman*, 32 (November 1916), 107, as cited in Woollacott, '"Khaki Fever" and Its Control', 331.

8. For example, in Rose Allatini, *Despised and Rejected* (London: C. W. Daniel, 1918).

9. *Imperialist*, 26 January 1918, as cited in Lucy Bland, 'Trial by Sexology? Maud Allan, Salome and the "Cult of the Clitoris" Case', in *Sexology in Culture: Labelling Bodies and Desires*, eds. Lucy Bland and Laura Doan (Cambridge: Polity Press, 1998), 184.

10. *Vigilante*, 16 February 1918, 183, as cited in Bland, 'Trial by Sexology?', 183.

11. Quoted in *Pall Mall Gazette*, 11 March 1908, as cited in Bland, 'Trial by Sexology?', 185.

12. *Vigilante*, 6 April 1918, as cited in Bland, 'Trial by Sexology?', 186.

13. Artemis Cooper, ed., *A Durable Fire: The Letters of Duff and Diana Cooper, 1913–1950* (London: Collins, 1983), as cited in Bland, 'Trial by Sexology?', 187.

14. 31 May 1918 and 5 June 1918, in Cooper, ed., *A Durable Fire*, 66, 70, as cited in Bland, 'Trial by Sexology?', 194–195.

15. Philippa Levine, '"Walking the Streets in a Way No Decent Woman Should": Women Police in World War One', *Journal of Modern History*, 66:1 (1994), 34–78.

16. Grayzel, *Women and the First World War*, 39.

17. Ibid., 37–38.

18. Imperial War Museum, London, Women's Work Manuscript Collection, 42.4/2, as cited in Levine, 'Walking the Streets', 46.

19. Joan Lock, *The British Policewoman: Her Story* (London: Robert Hale, 1979), 20 and Mary Sophia Allen, *The Pioneer Policewoman* (London: Chatto & Windus, 1925), 17, as cited in Emily Hamer, *Britannia's Glory: A History of Twentieth-Century Lesbians* (London: Cassell, 1996), 43.

20. Hamer, *Britannia's Glory*, 48.

21. Ibid., 55.

22. Ibid., 56.

23. Ibid., 57.

24. *Daily Express*, 10 June 1918, 2, as cited in Laura Doan, *Fashioning Sapphism: The Origins of a Modern English Lesbian Culture* (New York: Columbia University Press, 2001), 64.

25. Angela Woollacott, 'Dressed to Kill: Clothes, Cultural Meaning, and World War I Women Munitions Workers', in *Gender and Material Culture*, vol. 2, *Representations of Gender from Prehistory to the Present*, eds. Moira Donald and Linda Hurcombe (London: Macmillan, 2000), as cited in Doan, *Fashioning Sapphism*, 64–65.

26. Mary Allen, *The Pioneer Policewoman*, ed. and arranged Julie Helen Heyneman (London: Chatto & Windus, 1925), 84–85, as cited in Doan, *Fashioning Sapphism*, 73–74.

27. Naomi Jacob, *Me in War-Time* (London: Hutchinson, 1940), 208 and Marchioness of Londonderry, *Retrospect* (London: Frederick Muller, 1938), 127–128, as cited in Doan, *Fashioning Sappism*, 65.

28. Mary Agnes Hamilton, 'Changes in Social Life', in *Our Freedom and Its Results*, ed. Ray Strachey (London: Hogarth Press, 1936), 250, as cited in Doan, *Fashioning Sapphism*, 65.

29. Hamer, *Britannia's Glory*, 46.

30. August Forel, *The Sexual Question: A Scientific, Psychological, Hygienic, and Sociological Study for the Cultured Classes* (New York: Rebman Company, 1908 [1906]), 254, as cited in Doan, *Fashioning Sapphism*, 76.

31. Radclyffe Hall, *The Well of Loneliness* (New York: Anchor Books, 1990 [1928]), 271.

32. Naomi Jacob, *Me – and the Swans* (London: William Kimber, 1963), 157–158.

33. Lock, *The British Policewoman*, 128, as cited in Doan, *Fashioning Sapphism*, 75.

34. Michael Baker, *Our Three Selves: The Life of Radclyffe Hall* (New York: Morrow, 1985), 267, as cited in Doan, *Fashioning Sapphism*, 77.

35. Laura Doan, 'Topsy-Turvydom: Gender Inversion, Sapphism and the Great War', *GLQ*, 12:4 (2006), 517–542.

36. Gladys de Havilland, *The Women's Motor Manual* (London: Temple, 1918), 72, as cited in Doan, 'Topsy-Turvydom', 527.

37. David Mitchell, *Women on the Warpath: The Story of the Women of the First World War* (London: Jonathan Cape, 1965), 129, as cited in Doan, 'Topsy-Turvydom', 528.

38. Doan, 'Topsy-Turvydom', 534.

39. 'The New Woman: An Historical Note', *Times*, 6 January 1916, as cited in Doan, 'Topsy-Turvydom', 519.

40. F. Tennyson Jesse, 'A Night with a Convoy: An Eyewitness's Account of the Work of the Voluntary Aid Detachment in France', *Vogue*, 51:11 (1918), 70, as cited in Doan, 'Topsy-Turvydom', 529.

41. Pat Beauchamp [P. B. Waddell, later Washington], *FANY Goes to War* (London: John Murray, 1919), 16, as cited in Doan, 'Topsy-Turvydom', 531.

Chapter 7: Identity Crisis? The Emergence of the Modern Lesbian, 1918–1939

1. Hansard Parliamentary Debates: Official Report, House of Commons, 5th series, vol. 145 (hereafter 145 H.C.Deb. 5s), 1799.

2. Sheila Jeffreys, *The Spinster and Her Enemies: Feminism and Sexuality, 1880–1930* (London: Pandora, 1985), 113–115.

3. Hansard Parliamentary Debates: Official Report, House of Lords, 5th series, vol. 46 (hereafter 46 H.L.Deb. 5s), 566–567.

4. 145 H.C.Deb. 5s, 1803.

5. Ibid., 1800; 46 H.L.Deb. 5s, 567–568.

6. 145 H.C.Deb. 5s, 1800. A wife's sexual affair with another woman was not recognised as 'adultery' under English law and could therefore not be cited by the husband as grounds for divorce. However, in a very small number of cases during the twentieth century, husbands successfully cited lesbian affairs as examples of marital 'cruelty'.

7. 145 H.C.Deb. 5s, 1804.

8. Ibid., 1799.

9. Ibid., 1803.

10. 46 H.L.Deb. 5s, 573.

11. 145 H.C.Deb. 5s, 1803.

12. Ibid., 1803.

13. 46 H.L.Deb. 5s, 569–570.

14. Ibid., 572.

15. Ibid., 574.

16. Ibid., 573.

17. 145 H.C.Deb. 5s, 1804–1805.

18. James Douglas, *Sunday Express*, 19 August 1928, 10.

19. Catharine R. Stimpson, '"Zero Degree Deviancy": The Lesbian Novel in English', in *Classics in Lesbian Studies*, ed. E. D. Rothblum (New York: The Haworth Press Inc, 1997), 177–194.

20. *The Times*, 17 November 1928, 5.

21. Michael Baker, *Our Three Selves: The Life of Radclyffe Hall* (New York: Morrow, 1985).

22. Havelock Ellis, as quoted in Baker, *Our Three Selves*, 205.

23. Radclyffe Hall, *The Well of Loneliness* (London: Virago, 1982 [1928]), 9.

24. Ibid., 56.

25. Laura Doan, *Fashioning Sapphism: The Origins of a Modern English Lesbian Culture* (New York: Columbia University Press, 2001), 144–163; Jane Rule, *Lesbian Images* (London: Peter Davies, 1976), 53.

26. Lillian Faderman, *Surpassing the Love of Men: Romantic Friendship and Love between Women from the Renaissance to the Present* (London: The Women's Press, 1985), 317.

27. Esther Newton, 'The Mythic Mannish Lesbian: Radclyffe Hall and the New Woman', *Signs*, 9:4 (1984), 572–573.

28. Hall, *The Well of Loneliness*, 59.

29. Jay Prosser, '"Some Primitive Thing Conceived in a Turbulent Age of Transition": The Transsexual Emerging from *The Well*', in *Palatable Poison: Critical Perspectives on The Well of Loneliness*, eds. Laura Doan and Jay Prosser (New York: Columbia University Press, 2002), 129–144.

30. Ibid., 318.

31. Ibid., 304.

32. Ibid., 318.

33. Emily Hamer, *Britannia's Glory: A History of Twentieth-Century Lesbians* (London: Cassell, 1996), 102.

34. *Birmingham Post*, 11 April 1927, 13, cited in Doan, *Fashioning Sapphism*, 111.

35. Doan, *Fashioning Sapphism*, 110–125.

36. *Sunday Express*, 19 August 1928, 10.

37. *Daily Herald*, 21 August 1928, 1.

38. *Arena Three*, 4:10 (October 1967), 10.

39. Ibid., p.11.

40. National Sound Archive, Hall Carpenter Collection (C456), F2095–F2096, Rosanna Hibbert.

41. Mary Renault, *The Friendly Young Ladies* (London: Virago, 1984), 281, as cited in Hamer, *Britannia's Glory*, 104.

42. For example, Lillian Faderman, *Surpassing the Love of Men: Romantic Friendship and Love between Women from the Renaissance to the Present* (London: The Women's Press, 1985), part 3.

43. Shari Benstock, *Women of the Left Bank: Paris, 1900–1940* (London: Virago, 1987).

44. Nigel Nicolson, as quoted in Neil Miller, *Out of the Past* (London: Vintage, 1995), 176.

45. Quentin Bell, as quoted in Blanche Wiesen Cook, '"Women Alone Stir My Imagination": Lesbianism and the Cultural Tradition', *Signs*, 4:4 (1979), 726.

46. Nigel Nicolson, ed., *A Change of Perspective: The Letters of Virginia Woolf, Vol. 3: 1923–1928* (London: Hogarth Press, 1977), 31 January 1928, 453.

47. Ibid., 5 December 1927, 443.

48. Ibid., 6 March 1928, 469.

49. Ibid., 9 October 1927, 426–427.

50. Virginia Woolf, *Orlando: A Biography*, ed. Rachel Bowlby (Oxford: Oxford University Press, 1992 [1928]), 132.

51. Ibid., 133.

52. Ibid., 147.

53. Ibid., 154–155.

54. Tom Harrison, *Britain Revisited* (London: Gollancz, 1961), 148, as cited in James Vernon, 'For Some Queer Reason: The Trials and Tribulations of Colonel Barker's Masquerade in Interwar Britain', *Signs*, 26:1 (2000), 52.

55. Vernon, 'For Some Queer Reason'.

56. Mass Observation, 'Moral Law', nd, Mass Observation Archive, University of Sussex, Brighton. Worktown Collection, box 60/c, 20–21, as cited in Vernon, 'For Some Queer Reason', 53–54.

Chapter 8: Lesbian Bars, 1920s–1970s

1. Barbara Bell, *Just Take Your Frock Off: A Lesbian Life* (Brighton: Ourstory Books, 1999), 45.

2. Ibid., 45.

3. Ibid., 45–46.

4. Lovat Dickson, *Radclyffe Hall at the Well of Loneliness: A Sapphic Chronicle* (London: Collins, 1975), 103.

5. Emily Hamer, *Britannia's Glory: A History of Twentieth-Century Lesbians* (London: Cassell, 1996), 131.

6. Bell, *Just Take Your Frock Off*, 71.

7. Alison Oram and Annmarie Turnbull, *The Lesbian History Sourcebook* (London: Routledge, 2001), 208–209.

8. Bell, *Just Take Your Frock Off*, 65–66.

9. Ellen, as cited in Suzanne Neild and Rosalind Pearson, eds., *Women Like Us* (London: The Women's Press, 1992), 45.

10. Pat James, as cited in Neild and Pearson, eds., *Women Like Us*, 58–59.

11. Ibid., 58–59.

12. Jill Gardiner, *From the Closet to the Screen: Women at the Gateways Club, 1945–85* (London: Pandora, 2003), 8, 13–15.

13. National Sound Archive, Hall Carpenter Collection (hereafter NSA, HCC) (C456), F2483–F2487, Sandy Martin; London Metropolitan Archive (hereafter LMA), PS/KEN/F/10, Register of Licences for the licensing district of Kensington and Chelsea.

14. NSA, HCC (C456), F2483–F2487, Sandy Martin; LMA, PC/ENT/2/12, list of applications for licenses from 1 January 1936, London County Council Entertainments Committee.

15. Alkarim Jivani, *It's Not Unusual: A History of Lesbian and Gay Britain in the Twentieth Century* (London: Michael O'Mara Books Ltd, 1997), 132.

16. Ibid., 133.

17. Brighton Ourstory Project, ed., *Daring Hearts: Lesbian and Gay Lives of 50s and 60s Brighton* (Brighton: QueenSpark Books, 1992), 13.

18. Ibid., 75.

19. James and Sheila, as cited in Brighton Ourstory Project, ed., *Daring Hearts*, 70.

20. Brighton Ourstory Project, ed., *Daring Hearts*, 62.

21. Ibid., 79.

22. Ibid.

23. Ibid., 75.

24. Madeline Davis and Elizabeth Lapovsky Kennedy, *Boots of Leather, Slippers of Gold: A History of a Lesbian Community* (London: Routledge, 1993); Janet Kahn and Patricia A. Gozemba, 'In and Around the Lighthouse: Working-Class Lesbian Bar Culture in the 1950s and 1960s', in *Gendered Domains: Rethinking Public and Private in Women's History*, eds. Dorothy O. Helly and Susan M. Reverby (London: Cornell University Press, 1992), 90–106; Lillian Faderman, *Odd Girls and Twilight Lovers: A History of Lesbian Life in Twentieth-Century America* (London: Penguin, 1992); Tamar Rothenberg, '"And She Told Two Friends ...", Lesbians Creating Urban Space', in *Mapping Desires: Geographies of Sexualities*, eds. David Bell and Gill Valentine (London: Routledge, 1995), 165–181; Rochella Thorpe, '"A House Where Queers Go": African-American Lesbian Nightlife in Detroit, 1940-1975', in *Inventing Lesbian Cultures in America*, ed. Ellen Lewin (Boston: Beacon Press, 1996), 40–61; Maxine Wolfe, '"Invisible Women in Invisible Places": Lesbians, Lesbian Bars, and the Social Production of People/Environment Relationships', *Architecture and Behaviour*, 8:2 (1992), 137–158.

25. Katie Gilmartin, '"We Weren't Bar People": Middle-Class Lesbian Identities and Cultural Spaces', *GLQ*, 3:1 (1996), 23.

26. The most extensive body of documentary material on the butch/femme culture and identities in the United States is that of Joan Nestle. Joan Nestle, ed., *The Persistent Desire: A Femme–Butch Reader* (Boston: Alyson Publications Inc., 1992); Joan Nestle, *A Restricted Country: Documents of Desire and Resistance* (New York: Firebrand Books, 1987). See also Leslie Feinberg, *Stone Butch Blues* (New York: Firebrand Books, 1993).

27. NSA, HCC (C456), F1328–F1330, Rene Sawyer.

28. Jivani, *It's Not Unusual*, 135.

29. Pat James, as cited in Neild and Pearson, eds., *Women Like Us*, 59–60.

30. Sheila Jeffreys, 'Butch and Femme: Now and Then', in *Not a Passing Phase: Reclaiming Lesbians in History 1840–1985*, ed. Lesbian History Group (London: The Women's Press, 1989), 158–187, offers a forceful illustration of lesbian feminist critiques of butch/femme. Recent contributions to the debate include Susan Ardill and Sue O'Sullivan, 'Butch/Femme Obsessions', *Feminist Review*, 34 (1990), 79–85; Faderman, *Odd Girls and Twilight Lovers*; Lillian Faderman, 'The Return of Butch and Femme: A Phenomenon in Lesbian Sexuality of the 1980s and 1990s', *Journal of the History*

of Sexuality, 2:4 (1992), 578–596; and Sally R. Munt, *Butch-Femme: Theorizing Lesbian Genders* (London: Cassell, 1997).

31. Joan Nestle, 'Butch-Femme Relationships: Sexual Courage in the 1950s', in Nestle, *A Restricted Country*, 97.

32. Davis and Kennedy, *Boots of Leather, Slippers of Gold*, 1–2.

33. Ibid., 29.

34. Feinberg, *Stone Butch Blues*.

35. Davis and Kennedy, *Boots of Leather, Slippers of Gold*, 42.

36. Claire Andrews, as cited in Jivani, *It's Not Unusual*, 137. Jennifer Hilton, *The Gentle Arm of the Law. Life as a Policewoman* (Reading: Educational Explorers, 1967), 60–61, offers an account of a club raid from the perspective of a policewoman.

37. Jivani, *It's Not Unusual*, 137.

38. Ibid., 138.

39. Brighton Ourstory Project, ed., *Daring Hearts*, 20.

40. Ibid., 72.

41. NSA, HCC (C456), F2109, Cynthia Reid.

42. Brighton Ourstory Project, ed., *Daring Hearts*, 79.

43. Gardiner, *From the Closet to the Screen*, 185.

Chapter 9: Lesbian Social Organisations, 1960s–1970s

1. Albertine Winner, 'Homosexuality in Women', *Medical Press and Circular*, 3 September 1947, 219.

2. Ibid.

3. George W. Henry, *Sex Variants: A Study of Homosexual Patterns* (London: Cassell, 1950 [1941]).

4. Eustace Chesser's main arguments relating to lesbianism were presented in *Sexual Behaviour: Normal and Abnormal* (London: Medical Publications Ltd, 1949); *Live and Let Live: The Moral of the Wolfenden Report* (London: Heinemann, 1958); *Women: A Popular Edition of the Chesser Report* (London: Jarrolds Publishers Ltd, 1958); *Odd Man Out: Homosexuality in Men and Women* (London: Victor Gollancz Ltd, 1959); *The Human Aspects of Sexual Deviation* (London: Jarrolds Publishers Ltd, 1971).

5. Leila J. Rupp, *A Desired Past* (Chicago: University of Chicago Press, 1999), 162.

6. Ibid.

7. London School of Economics, Hall Carpenter Archive/Albany Trust/14/80, letter from Esme Langley to 'The Secretary, Homosexual Law Reform Society', 10 May 1963.

8. Tony Geraghty, 'Letters to the Editor', *New Statesman*, 2 April 1965, 530. The article to which he referred was Ron Mount, *News of the World*, 13 December 1964.

9. Ceri Ager, as cited in Suzanne Neild and Rosalind Pearson, eds., *Women Like Us* (London: The Women's Press, 1992), 39–40.

10 .National Sound Archive, Hall Carpenter Collection (hereafter NSA, HCC) (C456), F2088, Diana Chapman.

11. Barbara Bell, *Just Take Your Frock Off: A Lesbian Life* (Brighton: Ourstory Books, 1999), 145.

12. Ibid., 146–148.

13. NSA, HCC (C456), F2088, Diana Chapman.

14. Emily Hamer, *Britannia's Glory: A History of Twentieth-Century Lesbians* (London: Cassell, 1996), 174.

15. *Arena Three*, 2:10 (October 1965), 13.

16. Ibid., 2:11 (November 1965), 2–4.

17. Ibid., 1:11 (November 1964), 12.

18. Sheila, as cited in Jill Gardiner, *From the Closet to the Screen: Women at the Gateways Club, 1945–1985* (London: Pandora, 2003), 122.

19. Ruth Magnani, as cited in Nield and Pearson, eds., *Women Like Us*, 86.

20. Gardiner, *From the Closet to the Screen*, 186.

21. Ibid., 187.

22. NSA, HCC (C456), F1328–F1330, Rene Sawyer.

23. Ibid., F2088, Diana Chapman.

24. *Arena Three*, 1:1 (January 1964), 2.

25. Ibid., 2:3 (March 1965), 6; Anthony Storr, *Sexual Deviation* (Harmondsworth: Penguin, 1964). Other books in the series examined alcoholism, depression and suicide, the violent criminal, and 'the meaning of madness'; *Arena Three*, 1:5 (May 1964), 9.

26. *Arena Three*, 4:8 (August 1967), 7.

27. Alison Oram, 'Little by Little?: Arena Three and Lesbian Politics in the 1960s', in *The Permissive Society and Its Enemies: Sixties British Culture*, ed. Marcus Collins (London: Rivers Oram Press, forthcoming).

28. 'Us and the Social Scene', *Arena Three*, 4:10 (October 1967), 2.

29. *Arena Three*, 4:7 (July 1967), 2–3.

30. Ibid., 8:1 (January 1971), 8.

31. NSA, HCC (C456), F1607–F1612, Jackie Forster.

32. Gardiner, *From the Closet to the Screen*, 185.

33. Betty, as cited in Nield and Pearson, eds., *Women Like Us*, 107–108.

34. Nina Miller, as cited in Nield and Pearson, eds., *Women Like Us*, 122–123.

Chapter 10: The Politics of Lesbianism, 1970–2000

1. *Arena Three*, 6:10/11 (October/November 1969), 6–7.

2. Ibid., 7:7 (August 1970), 6.

3. Lisa Power, *No Bath but Plenty of Bubbles: An Oral History of the Gay Liberation Front 1970–73* (London: Cassell, 1995), 23.

4. Ibid., 27.

5. Ibid., 23–24.

6. Ibid., 40.

7. Ibid., 36.

8. Ibid., 34–35.

9. Ibid., 238–239.

10. Anna Coote and Beatrix Campbell, *Sweet Freedom: The Struggle for Women's Liberation* (London: Pan Books Ltd, 1982); Eve Setch, 'The Face of Metropolitan Feminism: The London Women's Liberation Workshop, 1969–79', *Twentieth Century British History*, 13:2 (2002), 171–190.

11. Power, *No Bath but Plenty of Bubbles*, 117.

12. Sue Allen and Lynne Harne, 'Lesbian Mothers – the Fight for Child Custody', in *Radical Records: Thirty Years of Lesbian and Gay History*, eds. Bob Cant and Susan Hemmings (London: Routledge, 1988), 186.

13. Valerie Mason-John and Ann Khambatta, *Lesbians Talk: Making Black Waves* (London: Scarlet Press, 1993). See also Carmen Williams, Gail Lewis, Shaila Shah and Pratibha Parmar, 'Becoming Visible – Black Lesbian Discussions', *Feminist Review*, 17 (1984), 53–72, and Gerry Ahrens, Ahmed Farooqui, and Amitha Patel, 'Irrespective of Race, Sex and Sexuality', in *Radical Records: Thirty Years of Lesbian and Gay History*, eds. Bob Cant and Susan Hemmings (London: Routledge, 1988), 128–141.

14. Janet Dixon, 'Separatism: A Look Back at Anger', in Cant and Hemmings, eds., *Radical Records*, 70.

15. Ibid., 75–76.

16. Beatrix Campbell, 'A Feminist Sexual Politics: Now You See It, Now You Don't', *Feminist Review*, 5 (1980), 14–15.

17. Setch, 'The Face of Metropolitan Feminism'.

18. Leeds Revolutionary Feminist Group, 'Political Lesbianism: The Case Against Heterosexuality', first printed in *Wires* 81, reprinted in Coote and Campbell, *Sweet Freedom*, 225–227.

19. Adrienne Rich, 'Compulsory Heterosexuality and Lesbian Existence', *Signs*, 5 (Summer 1980), 631–660.

20. Emma Healey, *Lesbian Sex Wars* (London: Virago, 1996), 71.

21. Celia Kitzinger, *Case Studies from the Social Construction of Lesbianism* (London: Sage, 1987), 115, as cited in Healey, *Lesbian Sex Wars*, 84.

22. Sheila Jeffreys, '*Butch and Femme: Now and Then*', Gossip, 5 (1987), 84.

23. Lisa Power, 'Voices in My Ear', in *Radical Records: Thirty Years of Lesbian and Gay History*, eds. Bob Cant and Susan Hemmings (London: Routledge, 1988), 142–154.

24. Alkarim Jivani, *It's Not Unusual: A History of Lesbian and Gay Britain in the Twentieth Century* (London: Michael O'Mara Books Ltd, 1997), 190.

25. Ibid., 192.

26. Eleanor Stephens, 'Out of the Closet into the Courts', in *Spare Rib Reader*, ed. Marsha Rowe (Harmondsworth: Penguin Books, 1982), 91–98.

27. Allen and Harne, 'Lesbian Mothers – the Fight for Child Custody'.

28. Susan Hemmings, 'Horrific Practices: How Lesbians were Presented in the Newspapers of 1978', in Gay Left Collective, ed., *Homosexuality: Power and Politics* (London: Allison & Busby, 1980), 162.

29. Ibid., 164–165.

30. *Daily Express*, 24 April 1976, as cited in Hemmings, 'Horrific Practices', 158–159.

31. Hemmings, 'Horrific Practices', 160.

32. Ibid., 160.

33. Ibid., 161.

34. Vicki Carter, 'Abseil Makes the Heart Grow Fonder: Lesbian and Gay Campaigning Tactics and Section 28', in *Modern Homosexualities: Fragments of Lesbian and Gay Experience*, ed. Ken Plummer (London: Routledge, 1992), 217–226.

35. Ian Lucas, *OutRage! An Oral History* (London: Cassell, 1998).

36. Ibid., 180–181, 205–206.

37. Inge Blackman and Kathryn Perry, 'Skirting the Issue: Lesbian Fashion for the 1990s', *Feminist Review*, 34 (Spring 1990), 68.

38. Guinevere Turner, 'Lipstick Los Angeles: The L Word and Go Fish! Writer and Actor Takes a Stab at Defining a Lesbian Category in this City of Gorgeous Hollywood Women', *The Advocate*, 26 October 2004.

39. Diane Hamer and Belinda Budge, eds., *The Good, the Bad and the Gorgeous: Popular Culture's Romance with Lesbianism* (London: Pandora, 1994), 1–14.

40. Diane Hamer with Penny Ashbrook, '*OUT*: Reflections on British Television's First Lesbian and Gay Magazine Series', Hamer and Budge, eds., *The Good, the Bad and the Gorgeous*, 166–171.

Index